HIDDEN TRANSCRIPTS AND
THE ARTS OF RESISTANCE

Society of Biblical Literature

Semeia Studies

Gale A. Yee, General Editor

Number 48

HIDDEN TRANSCRIPTS AND
THE ARTS OF RESISTANCE
Applying the Work of James C. Scott
to Jesus and Paul

HIDDEN TRANSCRIPTS AND THE ARTS OF RESISTANCE

Applying the Work of James C. Scott
to Jesus and Paul

Edited by
Richard A. Horsley

Society of Biblical Literature
Atlanta

HIDDEN TRANSCRIPTS AND THE ARTS OF RESISTANCE

Library of Congress Cataloging-in-Publication Data

Hidden transcripts and the arts of resistance : applying the work of James C. Scott to Jesus and Paul / edited by Richard A. Horsley
     p. cm. — (Semeia studies ; no. 48)
    Includes bibliographical references.
    ISBN 1-58983-134-9 (paper binding : alk. paper)
    1. Jesus Christ—Political and social views. 2. Bible. N.T. Mark—Social scientific criticism. 3. Bible. N.T. Epistles of Paul—Social scientific criticism. 4. Opposition (Political science) in the Bible. 5. Scott, James C. I. Horsley, Richard A. II. Series: Semeia studies ; no. 48.
    BS2417.P6H53 2004
    225.6—dc22
                                       2004025190

CONTENTS

ABBREVIATIONS

AB	Anchor Bible
ABD	*Anchor Bible Dictionary*. Edited by D. N. Freedman. 6 vols. New York: Doubleday, 1992.
AJP	*American Journal of Philology*
AThR	*Anglican Theological Review*
BibInt	*Biblical Interpretation*
BibOr	Biblica et orientalia
CBQ	*Catholic Biblical Quarterly*
FCNTECW	Feminist Companion to the New Testament and Early Christian Writings
JAAR	*Journal of the American Academy of Religion*
JAC	*Jahrbuch für Antike und Christentum*
JBL	*Journal of Biblical Literature*
JRH	*Journal of Religious History*
JSJ	*Journal for the Study of Judaism in the Persian, Hellenistic, and Roman Periods*
JSNT	*Journal for the Study of the New Testament*
JSNTSup	Journal for the Study of the New Testament Supplement Series
JSOTSup	Journal for the Study of the Old Testament Supplement Series
JTSA	*Journal of Theology for Southern Africa*
LCL	Loeb Classical Library
NICNT	New International Commentary on the New Testament
NTS	*New Testament Studies*
SBLSP	Society of Biblical Literature Seminar Papers
SNTSMS	Society for New Testament Studies Monograph Series
TynBul	*Tyndale Bulletin*

Introduction
Jesus, Paul, and the "Arts of Resistance": Leaves from the Notebook of James C. Scott

Richard A. Horsley

James C. Scott offers a rich range of knowledge and theory that helps biblical studies broaden and deepen approaches to texts in contexts. Biblical studies, understandably for a field devoted to illumination of the Jewish and Christian scriptures, focuses heavily on the religious and cultural dimension to the neglect of other aspects of life that are also abundantly evident in biblical texts. As the product mainly of Protestant theology and North Atlantic societies that operate with a separation between church and state, biblical studies focuses on "the things of God," as opposed to "the things of Caesar." Trained as a political scientist, Scott is an expert in "the things of Caesar." Yet Scott insists throughout his scholarship that politics cannot be understood apart from culture and religion. His work can help biblical scholars understand the relation between often separated dimensions of texts and history.

Biblical studies, devoted to understanding the sacred writings central to the canon of established Western culture as well as of churches and synagogues, writings that played an instrumental role in Western European colonial rule of other peoples of the world, has tended to ignore power relations in texts and history. Yet all civilizations, including Western civilization in which the Bible has been instrumental, have been based on the domination and exploitation of the vast majority of people by an elite ruling class. Scott is unusual among political scientists not only in acknowledging the power relations that constitute civilizations but also in repeatedly coming up with sophisticated original ways of understanding relations of domination and resistance that can be helpful to biblical scholars, who are only recently discovering such issues.

Biblical studies, because of the Herculean tasks involved in learning ancient languages and sophisticated methods of criticisms, tends to be focused intensively but narrowly on the particular languages and cultures of ancient Israel and early Jewish and Christian groups in the ancient eastern Mediterranean world. In his rich and varied scholarly work James

Scott has drawn upon a broad knowledge of a wide range of peoples and periods (medieval European, modern English and Russian, modern Chinese and Indian, modern American, as well as contemporary Southeast Asian) and several academic disciplines (social and political history, sociology, and especially anthropology, as well as political science). His work can therefore be highly instructive to biblical scholars who are struggling to become more comparative and interdisciplinary.

Biblical scholars have assumed responsibility, in the academic division of labor, for significant ancient texts and their historical contexts in periods and places for which only limited and fragmentary evidence are available. It is impossible, of course, for them to observe and interrogate the people who produced the texts they study. Scott, by contrast, has done fieldwork in Malasian villages during which he had sustained opportunities to observe the concrete situations and circumstances in which people subject to domination and exploitative political-economic relations live and work. This gives his observations on and theorizing about subjugated peoples a down-to-earth sense lacking in many studies, and one that seems particularly appropriate to certain biblical materials that deal with similar situations and lore of common peoples' life.

It should not be surprising, therefore, that in the last decade or so several biblical scholars have found Scott's work stimulating and have used it to advantage, especially in examining domination and resistance. Clearly one of the principal reasons that Scott's analysis and theory are attractive to biblical scholars is its usefulness in aiding their own interest in liberative readings of the biblical text, in contrast with readings that authorize cultural and political forms of domination. The anthropological distinction between the "great tradition" and the "little tradition" was a key concept in the delineation of Judean and Galilean popular movements in late second temple times, and Scott's illuminating cross-cultural discussion of its importance in peasant movements in "Protest and Profanation: Agrarian Revolt and the Little Tradition," (1977) has played an important role in subsequent studies of Jesus and Gospel materials (Crossan 1991; 1998; Horsley with Hanson 1985; Horsley 1987; 1989; 2002; Horsley and Draper 1999). Similarly his books on peasant revolt and hidden forms of resistance, *The Moral Economy of the Peasant* (1976) and *Weapons of the Weak* (1985), began to inform treatments of Jesus and Jesus movements (Crossan 1998; Horsley 1987; Horsley and Draper 1999; Herzog 2000). The book that has proven stimulating to New Testament scholars on a wider range of issues is the more recent and theoretically oriented *Domination and the Arts of Resistance* (1990). This book was one of the principal reference points of the essays in "Rhetorics of Resistance," *Semeia* 79. It also plays a significant role in Gerald West's reflections on reading the Bible with ordinary readers in *The Academy of the Poor*. And this is the work of Scott that the essays in this volume will draw upon primarily in exploring key issues in the interpretation of Jesus and of Paul.

This project found its origin in an invitation to James C. Scott by Douglas Oakman, Chair of the "Social Scientific Criticism of the New Testament" Section to attend the 2001 SBL Annual Meeting. Three sessions were organized (one of which was not scheduled) in which Scott agreed to respond to papers that used his work in interpretation, respectively, of the historical Jesus, of Paul's letters (a session of the Paul and Politics Group), and of Q (a session of the Q Section). The papers of the latter session will appear in a separate issue of *Semeia Studies*. The papers drawing upon Scott in analysis of Jesus and Paul, revised and updated, with subsequent responses, form the contents of this issue.

Since none of the individual papers devoted to particular issues can offer an overview of Scott's overall presentation in *Domination and the Arts of Resistance*, I will presume to offer at least a sketch of how the book may be suggestive and stimulating for explorations of both Jesus and Paul, as well as for the politics of their interpretation.

A MORE COMPREHENSIVE APPROACH TO DOMINATION

In dealing with patterns of domination and subordination that have structured many historical and contemporary societies, Scott not only insists that religion and culture operate in close interrelationship with politics and economics, but presents subtle and sophisticated ways of dealing with that interrelationship. In many academic fields, particularly the "humanities," an understandable reaction against a reductionist focus on the cultural dimension, to the exclusion of the political and economic, led to what may have been an overemphasis on the material and social-structural dimensions. While holding the material dimension of domination and subjugation in focus, Scott shows how domination operates in the interrelated area of human feelings and passions through cultural forms of interaction in ways that make material domination possible and effective. Not only can Scott help biblical studies avoid reductionism, but he demonstrates how to enrich investigations of the domination and resistance evident in or just under the surface of many biblical texts. Scott's analysis focuses on heavily dominated peoples, such as African-American slaves and European serfs, and draws on many studies of peasant movements. It is not difficult to sort out the observations and generalizations applicable to the Palestinian peasantry among whom Jesus operated from those more specific to master-slave and patron-client relations in the cities where Paul carried out his mission.

Scott devised the concept of *public transcript* to deal with the most obvious aspects of domination. This is "a shorthand way of describing the open interaction between subordinates and those who dominate" (1990:2). "Given the usual power of dominant elites to compel perform-ances from others, however, the public transcript is "highly partisan," controlled by the powerful. "It is designed to be impressive, to affirm and naturalize the power of dominant elites, and to conceal or euphemize the dirty linen of their rule" (18). The public transcript consists of mecha-nisms of "public mastery and subordination (for example, rituals of hierarchy, deference, speech, punishment, and humiliation)" and "ideo-logical justification for inequalities (for example, the public religious and political world view of the dominant elite)" in order to manage the "material appropriation (for example, of labor, grain, taxes)," which is "largely the purpose of domination." Whereas materialist analysis "privileges the appropriation of surplus value as the social site of exploitation and resistance, our analysis here privileges the social expe-rience of indignities, control, submission, humiliation, forced deference, and punishment" (111).

Insofar as "appropriation is, after all, largely the purpose of domina-tion" (111), "these forms of domination are institutionalized means of extracting labor, goods, and services from a subject population. They embody formal assumptions about superiority and inferiority, often in elab-orate ideological form, and a fair degree of ritual and 'etiquette' regulates public conduct within them. In principle at least, status in these systems of domination is ascribed by birth, mobility is virtually nil, and subordinate groups are granted few if any political or civil rights" (21). These general-izations apply to both the Herodian and high priestly rulers who controlled Palestine for the Romans and the magnates who dominated the Greek cities of the East where Paul worked. The arbitrary personal rule that operated through mechanisms such as sexual violation and other personal terror were characteristic of master-slave relations in the Greco-Roman world but less so of the Jerusalem temple-state or Herodian rule.

Scott's analysis of rituals of "public mastery" and "ideological justi-fication for inequalities" suggest ways of interpreting the Jerusalem temple and high priestly practices that differ dramatically from standard presentations of "Judaism" (e.g., Sanders), yet that would provide illu-minating complements to recent analysis of the increasing conflict between the high priesthood and the Judean and Galilean people in the first century C.E. (Goodman; Horsley 1986). The rituals and ideology of the Jerusalem Temple and high priesthood, suggests Scott's analysis, would have been an elaborate "respectable performance," for the benefit both of the Judean people and of the priestly aristocracy, although in almost opposite ways.

To the extent that the high priestly performance was aimed at the people its purpose was "not to gain the agreement of subordinates but rather to awe and intimidate them into a durable and expedient compliance" (1990:67). The ideology of the temple and high priesthood, both being institutions of venerable antiquity, aimed to symbolize that these institutions ruled on behalf of the people, ensuring God's favor and blessings. By performing rituals and symbolic ideology as grand ceremony in the awesomely constructed sacred space at the center and height of the capital city, ceremony that only they were qualified to conduct, the priestly aristocracy (in collaboration with Herodian and Roman rulers) controlled public discourse (50–54). Anything else was defined as dangerous riot by the urban rabble or pilgrim mob (as Josephus' accounts repeatedly illustrate).

Much of the public performance by the elite, however, in this case the priestly aristocracy in the temple, is done for its own consumption, according to Scott. Rituals performed in such an awesome setting exclusively by those set apart by hereditary rank and special codes of purity were performed to bolster the priestly aristocracy's own self-image as powerful and justified in their positions of dominance. They served to create the appearance of unity among themselves and of consent among the ordinary Jerusalemites who served the hierocratic apparatus and its operation in one capacity or another, as well as among the Judean peasants who supported the whole with their tithes and offerings (1990:45–55). Sacrifices and service at the altar and in the holy of holies vividly illustrate Scott's comment that at points "the show is all actors and no audience" (59). The priests were literally "consumers of their own performance," including, at the material as well as symbolic level, the choicest portions of the animals sacrificed on the altar (49). The purpose of all the ceremony, suggests Scott, would have been primarily for the priestly aristocracy "to buck up their courage, improve their cohesion, display their power, and convince themselves anew of their high moral purpose," or in this case their divinely instituted role in channeling blessings to the people and land (67). The paean of praise lavished on the Oniad High Priest Simon II and his Aaronid brothers in Sirach 50 suggests that such performances were convincing to circles of scribes/sages who assisted the high priests in running the temple-state. From Josephus' accounts, however, it is clear that by mid-first century neither the Jerusalem mob nor the Judean and Galilean peasantry were effectively impressed and intimidated. And the distinctive literature produced by the Qumran community indicates that dissident Judean scribal-priestly circles were so severely alienated from the incumbent high priesthood that they remained in their wilderness exile for several generations.

Scott's generalizations illuminate even more how the Romans, along with the allied elites in control of Greek cities and provinces of the East, produced "performances of mastery and command" (1990:3–4, 11). New

Testament studies, like the classics scholarship on which it depends, has been somewhat slow to realize the degree to which the Roman imperial order, particularly in the Greek cities, was maintained not by occupying troops and extensive bureaucracy but through the symbolic arrangement of public space, the presence of images, and the performance of rituals. Scott's insight that "a good part of the maintenance work consists of the symbolization of domination by demonstrations and enactments of power" further illuminates the groundbreaking research and interpretive work of classical historians such as Simon Price and Paul Zanker (selections in Horsley 1997). They and others have made clear that imperial power relations were constituted by the rich array of imperial temples, shrines, and statues of the emperor placed in civic centers along with festivals and games conducted in honor of the emperor. As Price says, the presence of the emperor pervaded public space. Symbol and ceremony dramatized what the imperial ideology articulated, that the imperial order was imposed for the benefit of the subjects (Scott 1990:18). Caesar, the Lord and Savior of the world, had brought Salvation, Peace and Security, and was therefore appropriately being given divine honors for his beneficence. Most of this elaborate array of public ceremony, parade, and display were performed primarily for public consumption. The urban magnates who sponsored the city-wide imperial festivals, in which even the destitute could consume meat once a year, also held the offices of imperial priests and displayed publicly their own honorific titles in which they were closely associated with the emperor and imperial power. The elaborate architectural apparatus, ceremony, and festival sponsored and celebrated in honor of the emperor by the urban elite created "an effective façade of cohesion [augmenting] the apparent power of elites, thereby presumably affecting the calculations that subordinates might make about the risks of noncompliance or defiance" (56). As Scott emphasizes, even if such rituals and symbols of power do not gain the consent of the subordinated people, they are an impressive "means of demonstrating that, like it or not, a given system of domination is stable, effective, and here to stay" (66).

Scott includes yet another sort of ritual performance of domination (-and-subordination) that pertains directly and centrally to both the historical Jesus and the mission of Paul and others, an action whose ceremonial dimension is not usually noted in New Testament studies. In the already "civilized" areas of the empire such as the Greek cities, ceremony and festival generally sufficed to maintain order and elicit obedience from the laboring populace—or at least from the freeborn population. Slavery, of course, was enforced by forms of personal abuse such as beating and sexual violation. In the more recently subjugated areas like Palestine, the Romans simply terrorized the conquered people with slaughter and enslavement. Then subordination and especially rebellion were handled with further terror, only ritualized, in public execution by torturous crucifixion (Mattern). As Paul reminds the Galatians, Christ "was publicly exhibited as crucified" (Gal 3:1). The public defiance involved in "the traditional crime of lese-majeste ... requires a public reply" (57). The Roman reply to rebels and slaves was the public ritual of crucifixion, in which the rebel was beaten and publicly displayed being tortured to death on a cross in order further to intimidate the rest of the populace.

MOTIVES OF RESISTANCE AND REVOLT

Wherever there is domination by the powerful, however, there is almost invariably resistance by the subordinated. Scott's analysis of resistance is not only innovative and insightful, but opens to view aspects of resistance that previously went unnoticed in academic investigation. In many academic fields it is common to think of social-political order and disorder in terms of simple alternatives. Either people accept and acquiesce in the established order or they protest and rebel. In the absence of rebellion, people are assumed to have been relatively content (the "happy slave"). This is the way that New Testament scholarship has tended to treat the life and times of Jesus and Paul. While it is sometimes recognized that Judeans and Galileans repeatedly mounted movements of active resistance and wider revolts against Roman rule, Jesus is portrayed as a politically quiescent religious teacher. And while Paul is often seen as expecting some sort of transformation at the imminent parousia of the Lord, he is consistently portrayed as a social conservative.

Scott discerns that discontent and resistance are far more prevalent, widespread, and complex in their motives and methods than these simple alternatives allow. Subordinated people, says Scott, have developed a whole range of different forms of resistance that should be discerned as part and parcel of more complex political processes, forms of resistance in which the rare outbursts of rebellion and revolution are rooted and nurtured. It is in this connection that his work has the greatest potential for our understanding of Jesus and Paul, with wide-ranging implications from what our texts represent to how we use them as historical evidence. To state the possibilities bluntly: Just because Jesus does not lead an armed assault on the temple and the Roman garrison in Jerusalem does not mean that he was not engaged in a message and program of revolutionary change. And just because Paul did not organize attacks on Roman officials or the Roman slave system does not mean that he was a "social conservative" with regard to the Roman imperial order.

Most significantly, perhaps, Scott can help biblical scholars expand the spectrum of social reality that they deal with. To derive meaning from texts, biblical studies focuses heavily on cognitive and symbolic dimensions of words and stories. Dissatisfied with confinement to the cultural plane, some biblical scholars have recently dealt also with the material interests of biblical stories and the characters in them. Scott reminds us that what mediates between meaning and material circumstances are human feelings and desires. The political scientist reminds biblical scholars that people have a desire for dignity, yet are deprived of it by the circumstances of their lives. As noted just above, domination and control, and their purpose, appropriation, "unavoidably entails systematic social relations of subordination that impose indignities of one kind or another on the weak" (111). And it is these indignities of submission, humiliation, forced deference, and punishment that generate the anger, indignation, and frustration that fuels resistance with passion, energy, and cunning.

Reminded of the importance of dignity by Scott, biblical scholars can immediately discern frustration and anger in text after text. The deep resentment of early Israelite peasants erupts in the mocking of Sisera's fatal submission to the cunning of Yael and of his aristocratic mother's soliloquy from her palace, in the Song of Deborah (Judges 5). Jesus gives voice to Galilean peasants' sense of humiliation in many passages of Mark and Q, and the utter indignity as well as painful suffering of the cross is explicit in Paul's letters. Domination evokes resentment and resentment evokes resistance. Awareness of these dynamics should enable New Testament scholars to appreciate more fully the deep motives underlying the Jesus movement(s) in Palestine and the wider mission to other subject peoples of the Roman Empire led by Paul and others.

Seldom, however, does popular resentment fuel resistance that escalates into peasant revolts or popular movements with cadres of prophets, envoys, and community organizers. In an earlier path-breaking work (e.g., *Weapons of the Weak*) that led toward the insights of *Domination*, Scott opened to others' eyes the remarkable range of "hidden forms of resistance" as far more prevalent, more widespread, and more effective over the long haul than revolt, given the repressive power of the dominant. In effect, he "discovered" the fuller range of subversive popular politics that standard political science and other fields had been unaware of. In *Domination and the Arts of Resistance,* then, Scott offered a critical theory of that previously unnoticed fuller range of political life involved in domination and resistance that results from the interaction between the "public transcript" controlled by the dominant and the "hidden transcript" of subordinated people that is cultivated off-stage, beyond the control of the dominant. It is this hidden transcript, he suggests, that provides the seedbed of more extensive and organized popular resistance — such as the widespread Judean and Galilean revolts in 4 B.C.E. and 66–70 C.E., the popular prophetic movements in mid-first century Judea and Samaria, the Jesus movement(s) in Galilee and beyond, and the expanding mission catalyzed by Paul and other Diaspora Jews such as Prisca and Aquila in cities of the eastern Roman Empire.

VARIETIES OF POPULAR POLITICS (ROOTED IN THE HIDDEN TRANSCRIPT)

If the public transcript involves performance by the dominant elite, then it requires performance by the subjugated even more. What appears to be acceptance of the dominant order may be only a mask of acquiescence. Neither the slave nor the serf nor the sharecropper dare "speak truth to power." Living constantly under the repressive power and sometimes the regular surveillance of the dominant, the subordinate learn to wear masks of obedience. Unable to say what they are really thinking or to act on their feelings, they learn rather to act the part they are given in life while on the public stage.

When they are "offstage," however, the subordinate do say what they think and vent their feelings to each other. "The practices of domination and exploitation typically generate the insults and slights to human dignity that in turn foster a hidden transcript of indignation" (Scott 1990:7). Slaves or serfs or other peasants, "subject to the same terms of subordination, have a shared interest in jointly creating a discourse of dignity, of negation, and of justice" (114). In addition to its continuing cultivation as a shared *discourse,* Scott understands the hidden transcript to encompass a whole range of *practices* such as, among peasantries, poaching, pilfering, and clandestine tax-evasion (14). But it definitely has an ideological dimension. "Inasmuch as the major historical forms of domination have presented themselves in the form of a metaphysics, a religion, a worldview, they have provoked the development of more or less equally elaborate replies in the hidden transcript" (115). Since subordinate groups "confront elaborate ideologies that justify inequality, bondage, monarchy, caste, and so on ... resistance to ideological domination requires a counter-ideology—a negation—that will effectively provide a general normative form to the host of resistant practices invented in self-defense by any subordinate group" (118).

Perhaps one of the most important potential gains in recognizing the reality of the hidden transcript (for New Testament studies and other academic fields) is Scott's enlargement of the field of vision to include the emotional-cultural dimension of subordinated people's lives. "While the extraction of labor or grain from a subordinate population has something of a generic quality to it, the shape of personal domination is likely to be far more culturally specific and particular" (1990:112). "We know relatively little about a Malay villager if we know only that he is poor and landless. We know far more about the cultural meaning of his poverty once we know that he is particularly in despair because he cannot afford to feed guests on the feast of Ramadan, ... that he cannot bury his parents properly.... To know the cultural meaning of his poverty in this way is to learn the shape of his indignity and hence, to gauge the content of his anger.... It is these experienced indignities that form the bridge between his condition and his consciousness" (113). Awareness of such indignities enables the interpreter to understand what motivates a popular movement and to explain and interpret its origins and politics.

In explaining how a hidden transcript develops and works, Scott makes two interrelated moves that have great potential importance for New Testament studies, a field dominated by methodological individualism. He points out that the articulation of anger requires language (an unarticulated feeling of anger is strictly hypothetical!) and that resistance is social (the individual resisting subject is "an abstract fiction"). The articulation of indignation and indigenous discourse of dignity require social space for their cultivation. The expression of anger in language, moreover, "will necessarily impose a disciplined form to it." As "raw" anger becomes "cooked' indignation, the most resonant expressions rise to the sub-cultural surface. If a particular expression of indignation and dignity "is to become the social property of a whole category of subordinates it must carry effective meaning for them and reflect the cultural meanings and distribution of power among them." Furthermore—in contrast to much previous treatment of both Jesus' sayings and Paul' letters—"the hidden transcript has no reality as pure thought; it exists only to the extent it is practiced, articulated, enacted, and disseminated" (1990:118–19).

Two requirements are thus necessary for the cultivation of a hidden transcript. One is a "social space insulated from control, surveillance, and repression from above" (1990:120–23). It is especially difficult for slaves to create and defend such sequestered spaces. Many peasantries already have relatively autonomous social spaces in their village communities with which the dominant do not interfere except to collect taxes or to further humiliate and subordinate those who fail to pay up. Elites of course may deploy loyal retainers to keep the sites of the hidden transcript under surveillance, and subordinate groups may have to defend their sites which are often won only through resistant struggles (124–133). The second, particularly if subject people's indignity is to be transformed from "raw" to "cooked," is the role of active human agents who cultivate and disseminate the discourse (123–24). Such carriers of the hidden transcript are often people who have become displaced and marginalized, which has perhaps made them unusually sensitive to fluctuations in the fortunes of the subordinated and less vulnerable to the power that the dominant still wield over ordinary peasants or slaves.

If the hidden transcript is to give birth to a movement beyond local venting of indignation, moreover, a third component emerges in the discipline and infrapolitics that develops between leaders and participants. The sequestered sites in which the hidden transcript becomes more "cooked" are little centers of localized power in their own right; they "serve to discipline as well as to formulate patterns of resistance." Thus "the hidden transcript is a social product and hence a result of power relations among subordinates" as they struggle to win and defend a relative autonomy "in the teeth of power" (118–19).

The political dynamics of the conflictual relations between the dominant and the subordinated then develop in the interaction between the public and hidden transcripts. Here, finally, is the "pay-off," as Scott's reflections enable us to discern that the dynamics of political conflict are far more complex than "social stability," on the one hand, and violent "rebellion," on the other. Scott delineates "at least four varieties of political discourse among subordinate groups" (18–19). First, "the safest and most public form ... is that which takes as its basis the flattering self-image of the elites. Owing to the rhetorical concessions that this self-image contains, it offers a surprisingly large arena for political conflict" that exploits the elite's ideological justification that they rule for the benefit of the people in certain ways. A second mode of popular political discourse is the hidden transcript itself. This, moreover, is the nurturing matrix of bolder forms of resistance. Third, in the area between the first two, "is a politics of disguise and anonymity that takes place in public view but is designed to have a double meaning or to shield the identity of the actors." "Finally, the most explosive realm of politics is the rupture of the political *cordon sanitaire* between the hidden and the public transcript." Some brave subordinate who "can't take it anymore," "speaks truth to power." Such "moments of challenge and open defiance typically provoke either a swift stroke of repression or, if unanswered, often lead to further words and acts of daring." In an unusually favorable conjunction of circumstances they may also lead to a wider popular movement, even one that might pursue a revolutionary vision of ending domination and establishing a just social order. Scott thus opens up for New Testament interpreters a whole range of popular political dynamics that often lie hidden (underneath or "between the lines" of our sources) between passive acquiescence and active revolt.

IMPLICATIONS FOR NEW TESTAMENT STUDIES

Scott's "exposé" of the deeper dimensions of the politics of domination and resistance has some serious implications for New Testament studies as a field, as well as for the texts and history we interpret. For some of the subordinated peoples Scott examines, the Bible provided much of the central content of the "official transcript" of Western culture that legitimated various forms of domination, for example of medieval European peasants and African American slaves. Indeed, insofar as the Bible was integral to Western European colonization of much of the rest of the world and biblical studies, like other academic fields, developed during the heyday of Western imperialism, the assumptions, concepts, perspectives, and approaches of the field may well be implicated as part of the grand "official transcript" of academic and wider public interaction.

Yet subordinate peoples also found in biblical traditions materials they could use in resistance. Medieval English peasants asked, "When Adam delved and Eve span, who was then the gentleman?" Africans enslaved in the United States identified with Israel's slavery in and liberation from Egypt. German peasants' sense of "God's Justice" was informed by stories they had heard of Jesus' declarations about the "kingdom of God." And it was not lost on women listening to bible lessons that some of the leaders of the ostensibly "Pauline" communities were women, such as Prisca and Phoebe. Thus perhaps the first implication of Scott's work is the question whether the books, stories, laws, songs, and speeches in the Bible provide and can be appropriated as something more than simply part of the "official transcript" of Western culture. The contributors to this volume conclude that it does, despite the ambivalence of some biblical material and the clear subordinationist message of much biblical material. Whatever they became in established Christianity, some materials in the New Testament were, in their historical origins, representatives of "hidden transcripts," the politics of disguise, and even more public forms of resistance by subordinated people.

The obvious starting point for examination of those materials would then appear to be a reconsideration of how we evaluate the sources and their relation to historical events, processes, and movements. Since only a tiny elite in antiquity could write, most extant written sources not only represent the interests of the dominant, but are representations of the public transcript. Yet, as Scott points out, "the public transcript is not the whole story" (1990:3). In fact, it may even be positively misleading (2). Not surprisingly, taken by itself, the public transcript provides "convincing evidence for the hegemony of dominant values [and] discourse. Any analysis based exclusively on the public transcript is likely to conclude that subordinate groups endorse the terms of their subordination" (4). Behavior that results from inequalities of power is taken as evidence of ideological hegemony in the sense of active consent (66). In the most perverse cases, academic generalizations even come to resemble the racist or sexist or classist views of dominant groups who assume that the deferential behavior of slaves or women or peasants or colonized people is normal and natural, an inborn characteristic of a whole category of people (28, 35–36).

Thus standard works in the New Testament field, based squarely on extant sources from the public transcript, present generalizations about standard beliefs and practices of "Judaism" shared by "all Jews" or the "ordinary people" (e.g., Sanders); about Galileans as loyal to Temple and Torah (e.g., Freyne 1980); or about the common views of "Hellenism" (e.g., Hengel). Completely missing from studies based primarily on sources from the public transcript is any sense of the effect of domination on the views of both the dominant and (especially) the subjugated, who comprised the vast majority in Palestine and the cities of the Roman Empire and certainly those involved in both Jesus' movement and Paul's mission. Scholarship that fails to distinguish public and hidden transcripts in the context of domination and resistance in effect perpetuates the pretense of unanimity in the past and how that pretense may contribute to the perpetuation of domination in the present.

New Testament scholars can broaden their historical competence and balance their treatment by borrowing a few leaves from Scott's notebook. The first step would be to discern whether their sources provide a record of the public transcript (nearly all public inscriptions, coins, and most extant documents) or a record of the hidden transcript of the subordinated (e.g., Mark or Paul's letters?) or a record of the hidden transcript of the dominant (e.g., Josephus's *Life*?). Key would be a comparison between the public transcript and the hidden transcripts—or in the absence of the latter, a critical suspicion about the former—in order to discern the effects of domination on popular views and actions and the rich variety of modes of popular political resistance delineated in Scott's four types (15, etc.). And a little subtlety and sophistication with regard to language and gestures in grasping the difference between appearance and reality would help. "What we confront in the public transcript is a strange kind of ideological debate about justice and dignity in which one party has a severe speech impediment induced by power relations. If we wish to hear this side of the dialogue we shall have to learn its dialect and codes. Above all, recovering this discourse requires an appreciation of the arts of political disguise" (138).

THE EARLIEST GOSPELS AND PAUL'S LETTERS AS "WELL-COOKED" HIDDEN TRANSCRIPTS

Investigations into most places and periods are handicapped by the unavailability of sources for the hidden transcript of the subjugated. Peasants, serfs, slaves, and untouchables generally did not write. They left no records other than what archaeologists might dig up. Of course sources from the literate elite do complain bitterly when lesser mortals dare to disrupt the public order. One of the most instructive aspects of Scott's work is how he is able to utilize extremely limited sources for or from a variety of subordinated groups, such as novels and slave narratives, in order to overhear the off-stage discourse. In contrast to most other academic fields, New Testament studies is in an enviable position with regard to sources for the hidden transcript. At least some materials in some books in the New Testament are evidently records of the hidden transcript of Jesus movement(s). According to scholarly consensus, the Gospel of Mark and the speeches of Jesus paralleled in Matthew and Luke ("Q") arose from and addressed communities of Jesus-followers who were opposed to and opposed by the rulers. The later literate leadership and literary products of what had become "early Christianity," such as Luke (Luke-Acts) and those who claimed to be writing in Paul's name (the Pastoral Epistles) still address communities of subordinate people, although they have clearly acquiesced in various ways to the dominant order. But the earliest documents later included in the New Testament clearly represent movements of resistance and the hidden transcript of those movements.

Mark and Q, at least, from the Synoptic Gospel tradition (and perhaps other Gospel materials), can be seen to stem from and represent the hidden transcript of (what started as) peasant movements. Once we recognize the predominantly oral communication environment in antiquity it is evident that the Gospel of Mark, even if it existed in writing, was performed or read aloud in communities of ordinary people. Similarly Q (which was not a collection of sayings but a sequence of discourses on issues of importance to a movement), even if it existed in written form, was performed aloud, apparently in Galilean or nearby village communities. Mark and Q were not addressed to outsiders, certainly not the Herodian or high-priestly rulers in Palestine, and none figured in open discourse on the public stage of Tiberias or Jerusalem, even though Mark portrays events in which Jesus publicly confronted the rulers in Jerusalem.

In contrast to the Synoptic Gospel tradition embodied in Q and Mark, which took shape in repeated performances among popular communities, Paul's letters provide only one side of ongoing dialogues between one leader and the communities of ordinary people that he and others helped catalyze. Read aloud in community gatherings, they address particular circumstances and issues in particular assemblies. As with Mark and Q, Paul's "texts" were certainly not addressed to outsiders, certainly not the magnates and officials who controlled the Roman imperial order in Greek cities. None figured in open discourse on the public stage of a Thessalonica or a Corinth. In fact, Paul makes it abundantly clear (in

1 Thess 1–2; 5; 1 Cor 5–6, and Phil 1–3, at least) that he and his assemblies stood guardedly apart from the Roman imperial order. Indeed, they were even under attack, himself at points "under arrest," by the officials that enforced that order. Yet Paul was one of those marginal figures with self-proclaimed previous association with the "authorities" who had joined a popular movement and may not fully share the viewpoint of his addressees. In any case, as one side of ongoing conversations, Paul's letters provide at least windows onto (Paul's construction of) the "hidden transcript" that was developing among the ordinary residents of Philippi, Thessalonica, and Corinth who formed the "assemblies" he addressed.

Much scholarly investigation of the "Synoptic Gospel tradition" since the early days of *Formgeschichte* has paid little attention to social context. In his own monumental analysis, *Die Geschichte der synoptische Tradition,* Rudolf Bultmann emphasized the importance of the social context that another key formulator of "form criticism," Martin Dibelius, was exploring more fully. Bultmann's and Dibelius' successors, however, failed to follow through with more precise investigations of the "folklore" that helped inspire form criticism in the first place. Neither the developers of form criticism nor their successors who study Gospel materials, however, have paid much attention to the fundamental social forms that provided the social context in which Jesus-sayings originated and developed (i.e., households and village communities). The limitations of these investigations, of course, are rooted in certain theological assumptions, notably that many of those Jesus sayings were divine revelations through "early Christian prophets," making social context seem less relevant, and that not Jesus but the disciples/apostles founded the "churches," making the social forms involved in Jesus' mission virtually irrelevant to the investigation.

Scott's analysis of comparative material can help New Testament scholars appreciate the importance of the fundamental social form (the village community) that provided the sequestered sites of Jesus' mission and of the early development of the Synoptic Gospel tradition. Recent work on Mark and Q finds internal indications that these texts emerge from and address the concerns and situations of Galilean and other village communities. They repeatedly portray Jesus as active in villages of Galilee and nearby territories, hostile to the ruling cities and rulers, and drawing upon and adapting Israelite tradition in a version that Scott and others would call the "little tradition" of the peasantry (e.g., Scott 1977; Herzog; Horsley and Draper; Horsley 2001; Kloppenborg 2000). Jesus and his movement worked on the basis of an already-existing Galilean Israelite hidden transcript and creatively developed it, for example, in new exodus and new Elijah miracles (Mark 5–8), covenantal teaching (Mark 10; Q/Luke 6:20–49), and prophetic pronouncements against the

Jerusalem rulers (Q/Luke 13:34–35; Mark 11–12). It seems fairly clear therefore that, in Scott's terms (120), the hidden transcript in Mark and Q was voiced in the sequestered sites of village communities beyond the effective control of the rulers and their representatives and among communities composed of people who shared similar experiences of domination. One might even conclude that Jesus himself was a socially marginal figure insofar as his family must have lost its family inheritance at some point and had to make a living as artisans.

The communities that Paul and others catalyzed in Greek cities were engaged in building new sequestered sites, adapting for the purpose private urban houses far away from the public stage of the agorai and other civic spaces (that were permeated with the presence of Caesar). The picture of Paul and others preaching in civic spaces or in Jewish synagogues (assemblies) comes from the book of Acts and not from Paul's letters themselves. At points those communities came under attack by outsiders and/or public officials, so presumably they were concerned to guard the security of their household assemblies (1 Thess 1–2, 5; 1 Cor 5–6; Scott: 120–23). Although Paul and his colleagues also presupposed and worked on the basis of the Israelite popular tradition, they were, in effect, in each mission site new communities developing relatively new hidden transcripts. Although the Pauline community confidants were less homogeneous than in village communities, they apparently shared more or less similar experiences of domination insofar as none of them were from the urban elite of Thessalonica, Philippi, or Corinth. Paul and the co-workers in the mission in Greek cities such as Prisca and Aquila were also marginal figures insofar as they were mainly Diaspora Jews who became in effect "downwardly mobile" when they joined the movement (Scott 1990:120–24).

Both Paul's letters and the earliest Gospel documents, however, were highly unusual (records of) hidden transcripts. Most of the contents of Q and much of Mark seem parallel to the hidden transcripts cultivated by other peoples in secure off-stage locations. These components of the Synoptic Gospel tradition build upon and further develop Israelite popular traditions of a Moses- or Elijah-like prophet renewing covenantal teaching, wilderness feedings, and healings of a people suffering under oppressive, unjust rulers. Understanding the Q speeches of Jesus as parts of a popular hidden transcript enables us to move well beyond abstract categorization of Jesus sayings, say, as "sapiential" and into deeper appreciation of how they resonated with Galileans' emotional-cultural sense of dignity and indignation. "Blessed are the poor..., but woe to the rich..." restores a sense of dignity. "Love your enemies, do good, and lend" appeals to and revitalizes the traditional "moral economy" of the Galilean Israelite "little tradition" that the peasants were having difficulty maintaining because of the escalated economic pressures on household subsistence. Both Mark and Q also at points address problems of surveillance and repression and the people's resistance. Mark's extensive representation of the Pharisees' close surveillance on Jesus' and his disciples' every move is highly schematic (and surely questionable historically). Mark and Q both include repeated references to persecution of members of their respective movements and/or their prophetic predecessors. And both include an episode in which Jesus admonishes his followers to boldly confess their solidarity with the movement if/when they were apprehended and brought to trial (Mark 8:34–9:1; Q/Luke 12:2–12).

Similarly familiar from the hidden transcripts of other peoples are anticipations of political-economic reversal and divine condemnation of the dominant oppressors: the prayer for the kingdom, the beatitudes on the poor and woes on the rich, the baptism of fire, the promise of the kingdom coming with power in judgment on their persecutors, and the demonic (Roman) "Legion" being driven back into the Sea and destroyed (Q/Luke 11:2–4; Q/Luke 6:20–26; Q/Luke 3:7–9, 16–17; Mark 8:34–9:1; Mark 5:1–20, respectively; Scott 1990:199).

Yet other Q and Markan materials portray Jesus as having moved into what Scott calls "the arts of political disguise" and anonymity. At certain points in the Q speeches, Jesus pronounces prophetic condemnation of the Jerusalem ruling families in sufficiently ambiguous language that modern scholars who do not share the cultural knowledge of the Judean and Galilean peasants' Israelite "little tradition" (hidden transcript) tend not to "get it" (Q/Luke 13:28–29, where the "sons of the kingdom" who presume on their lineage from "Abraham" think they are secure in God's promise, as suggested already in John's speech in Q/Luke 3:7–9, 16–17!). Mark is full of Jesus' politics of ambiguity, anonymity, and disguise. Jesus chooses the anonymity of a large festival crowd for the semi-anonymous demonstration of his "entry" into Jerusalem as a popular messiah riding on a donkey (peasant mode of transportation; Mark 11:2–11; cf. Zech 9:9). And in that connection he chooses the occasion of the Passover festival, when the elite not only allowed but sponsored (in an attempt to control) the people's celebration of Israel's liberation from oppressive foreign rule, as the occasion for mounting his prophetic condemnation of the temple and confrontation with the Jerusalem rulers. He articulates his condemnation of the high priestly rulers in the ambiguous language of the parable of the tenants (that resonates with Isaiah's prophetic "love-song" of the vineyard that indicted the Jerusalem rulers of old; 12:1–9; Isa 5:1–13). He couches his declaration that the people did not owe Caesar a thing in a classic ambiguity that enabled him to wriggle out of the trap set by the Pharisees and

Herodians even though anyone familiar with Israelite covenantal tradition understood his meaning (12:13–17).

In Q and especially in Mark, however, Jesus even goes beyond the politics of disguise and boldly declares the hidden transcript of the Galilean (and Judean) villagers against the rulers on the public stage. Jesus' pronouncement of a prophetic lament over the Jerusalem ruling house as already condemned to destruction by God in Q/Luke 13:34–35 is hardly ambiguous, since the traditional Israelite form was as familiar to the elite as it was deeply resonant with peasants rooted in Israelite prophetic traditions. Similarly, Jesus' woes against the Pharisees and scribes in Q/Luke 11:39–52 are public condemnations addressed (ostensibly) directly to the representatives of the Jerusalem rulers. Even bolder is Jesus' action in Mark 11–12. Although he appears almost like the standard "trickster" figure in his cunning counters to the Pharisees' challenges earlier in Mark's story, his obstructive demonstration against the temple constituted an unmistakable prophetic condemnation of the whole system of domination at the center of the public stage in Jerusalem, the temple courtyard. Despite the disguised message of the parable of the tenants and his declaration about the tribute to Caesar, moreover, everyone knew full well that this was a public condemnation of the temple-state and its incumbents. And in Mark explicitly and Q implicitly (insofar as he is the successor of all the prophets that the Jerusalem rulers killed), Jesus' "challenge and open defiance" provokes "a swift stroke of repression" in the arrest, trial, and crucifixion of the leader who boldly "spoke truth to power."

Mark and Q are thus no longer just hidden transcripts proper, according to Scott's definition. They incorporate all four varieties of political discourse used in popular resistance, not just the hidden transcript itself. Or better, the new hidden transcripts that developed into the sequence of speeches in Q and the Gospel of Mark, performed in secure sites of communities of Jesus movements, included portrayals of Jesus engaged in all of those forms of resistance, including boldly speaking truth to power in public space. Those portrayals, moreover, are not purely the inventions of those communities. Jesus had apparently taken prophetic actions and delivered prophetic pronouncements. That is the most likely reason why he was apprehended and executed— by crucifixion, as a rebel against the Roman imperial order. And those bold prophetic actions and declarations, because they resonated among the people, were remembered and (re-) performed. He was apparently one of those rare cases among popular leaders whose irrevocable declaration of the hidden transcript in condemnation of the dominant order constituted a "political breakthrough" that escalated into a broader movement.

The "texts" Mark and Q are thus hidden transcripts that are the result of open political resistance that is highly unusual in peasant politics. Yet they are nevertheless still hidden transcripts in the sense that they are still cultivated and performed off-stage, still communication among peasants (or communities of urban poor) in sequestered sites in village synagogues (= assemblies). The new hidden transcript of the Jesus movement(s), however, now includes and cultivates those bolder forms of popular political resistance, and shifts the balance of power insofar as Jesus' breakthrough encourages participants in these movements to stand in solidarity against the dominant order that stands condemned under the rule of God proclaimed by Jesus. Scott, taking a leaf from the notebook of Levi-Strauss, speaks of a developed hidden transcript as "cooked," as opposed to "raw." Mark and Q are very well-cooked hidden transcripts that portray to their hearers a prophet who was spearheading bold, determined, and persistent popular resistance against their domination by Romans and their client rulers.

That bold declaration, furthermore, despite of or even because of "a swift stroke of repression" and continuing persecution, led to the formation of an even wider multiform movement of resistance to Roman imperial rule and renewal and formation of alternative local communities well beyond the area of Jesus' own mission. What makes Paul's letters unusual as records of a hidden transcript is that they enable us to see it in the process of formation. The hidden transcripts that are developing are not Paul's letters themselves, but the evolving discourses of the communities that he and his co-workers such as Timothy, Prisca, and Phoebe catalyzed among various subjugated peoples in different cities. Paul's letters are a window onto that process, a special window since he purports to be the founder and the principal and authoritative agent of creation and dissemination.

In this connection, investigators of the "Pauline" branch of the movement(s) have an unusual opportunity to explore particular aspects of how the hidden transcript of a resistance movement develops. One is the discourse itself. Paul may have taught his own "gospel." But the different peoples among whom he taught and organized were from various cultural backgrounds themselves and took the gospel in their own directions. It was, after all, an "international" movement, and Paul as a matter of principle did not require the other peoples to join Israel and practice Israelite law. They could all become heirs of the promise to Abraham on their own basis, as Galatians, Philippians, and so forth. We can easily imagine that the message of Christ's humiliating crucifixion and divine vindication would have been a paradigm that resonated deeply with the cultural meaning of many subjugated peoples' situation of humiliation.

A second aspect is how "the social spaces where the hidden transcript grows were themselves an achievement of resistance ... won and defended in the teeth of power" (119). Paul indicates at several points that he, his co-workers, and the communities they catalyzed were under attack by the city authorities and/or other people in particular cities (see esp. 1 Thessalonians and Philippians). The magistrates of the various cities in which Paul and others carried out their mission apparently had semi-effective means of surveillance and repression. A key concern in some of Paul's letters is thus defense of the assembly-sites of the developing communities and their hidden transcript(s).

A third aspect is how a hidden transcript developed as the result of power relations among the subordinated themselves (118–19). In the assemblies started by Paul and co-workers not only did rival "apostles" introduce different "gospels," but the communities developed indigenous leaders of their own, who did not necessarily agree with or submit to the authority of the original agents of dissemination. In the Pauline letters that provide our only sources, moreover, Paul himself, as a self-designated authority figure of the wider movement of subordinated peoples, is attempting to shape the developing hidden transcript of the respective assemblies.

Judging from Paul's letters, the hidden transcript of the assemblies he and his co-workers catalyzed, like Mark and Q, included apocalyptic anticipations of historical transformation and reversal, specifically God's judgment of the Roman imperial order at the "day of the Lord," the "coming (parousia) of Christ," and the imminent establishment of the kingdom of God (cf. Scott 1990: 199). Paul's (and apparently other's) gospel included bold declarations of God's vindication (as the true emperor of the world) of the Messiah/Lord whom the Roman imperial authorities had crucified, but this was not boldly declared on the public stage. In his letters Paul boasts of his imprisonment and beatings, but we have no idea whether he boldly declared before the civil magistrates who arrested him that his Lord enthroned in heaven was about to "destroy every ruler and every authority and power" (1 Cor 15:24). The "breakthrough" of the declaration of the Galileans' and Judeans' hidden transcript had already been made by Jesus, and Paul and other apostles took as their point of departure God's vindication of the martyred messiah for the development of a new hidden transcript among other subjugated peoples.

Jesus, Paul, and the Arts of Resistance

Established biblical studies tends to reduce Jesus and the Gospels and Paul's letters and "churches" to their religious dimension. This is rooted in the Western separation of church from state, of religion from politics and economics. Biblical studies is, of course, not alone. As Indian historians involved in the subaltern studies project point out, Western colonialist and Marxist historians alike tended to dismiss Indian peasant movements as merely religious, with no relevance for politics (Guha). The Iranian revolution of 1979 may have been a wake-up call. In a context where the American-backed Shah had blocked all forms of ordinary political participation, traditional mourning rites for martyrs in the Shi'ite Muslim tradition became the occasions and form for the massive demonstrations that toppled the secular regime. These events caught American scholars in various fields totally off-guard, baffled that it defied all of their disciplinary models that did not take the people's grounding in traditional culture and religious seriously (Horsley 2003b). Previous attempts to overcome the religious reductionism in New Testament studies have tended to overemphasize the material dimension in popular discontent, as if poverty by itself could explain the origin of the popular movement touched of by Jesus. The work of James C. Scott can help New Testament interpreters understand how the material and political dimensions are interconnected with the emotional and religious dimensions.

The key to understanding the dynamics of power relations in Scott's reflections is the recognition that political resistance by the subjected is rooted in the off-stage hidden transcript. "So long as we confine our conception of *the political* to activity that is openly declared we are driven to conclude that subordinate groups essentially lack a political life or that what political life they do have is restricted to those exceptional moments of popular explosion. To do so is to miss the immense political terrain that lies between quiescence and revolt and that, for better or worse, is the political environment of subject classes" (199). Like other subjected peoples, Jesus and his followers and Paul and his assemblies were denied participation in official politics, which were controlled at the center by the dominant. Much of their behavior, which seems to have acquiesced in or even supported the dominant order, was coerced by the prevailing patterns of power.

Jesus, like other peasant leaders, however, further developed the people's hidden transcript in village communities in catalyzing a movement based in those sequestered sites. Scott argues that "we can view the social side of the hidden transcript as a political domain striving to enforce, against great odds, certain forms of conduct and resistance in relations with the dominant. *It would be more accurate to think of the hidden transcript as a condition of practical resistance rather than a substitute for it*" (191). In the case of Jesus and his movement we can perhaps go even further. Renewing those village communities in their covenantal cooperation and solidarity with one another (their traditional Israelite "moral economy;" Q/Luke 6:20–49; Mark 10:1–45) was already a significant form of political resistance to the Roman client rule of Herod Antipas and the Jerusalem temple-state, whose control was enhanced precisely by the disintegration in families and village communities caused by their economic exploitation. Then this renewed discourse of dignity grounded in covenantal renewal formed the basis for Jesus' bolder articulation of the now "well-cooked" articulation of Galilean peasants' indignation in parables and prophecies that condemned the rulers for their oppression of the people. Finally Jesus apparently dared to confront the Jerusalem rulers directly in a bold declaration of the people's discourse of indignation in the courtyard of the temple itself. Jesus, as represented in Mark and Q, engages in all of the varieties of popular political resistance that Scott outlines. Scott's illumination of these previously unrecognized forms of popular resistance makes possible a whole new understanding of Jesus as fully and actively engaged in the politics of Roman Palestine, but in the area between quiescence and active peasant revolt.

The swift act of repression by the rulers made him into a martyr, whom his followers believed had been vindicated by God, confirming his now "well-cooked" discourse of indignation, and further motivating organized long-range resistance by a wider movement of Israelite peoples that expanded into Judea and Samaria and to Diaspora Jewish communities, as well as among villagers in nearby areas. As Scott emphasizes, "It is only when this hidden transcript is openly declared that subordinates can fully recognize the full extent to which their claims, their dreams, their anger is shared by other subordinates with whom they have not been in direct touch" (1990: 223). It was in the Jesus movements in and beyond Galilee, apparently, that what became the elaborate hidden transcripts of those movements developed into regularly performed "texts" such as the Gospel of Mark and Q. They portray Jesus boldly declaring popular indignation in direct confrontation with the dominant in prime public space. Yet they are still hidden transcripts *and* they constitute political resistance, in the wide area between acquiescence and active insurrection. "No matter how elaborate the hidden transcript may become, it always remains a substitute for an act of assertion directly in the face of power" (114–15).

Paul and other Diaspora Jewish leaders then extended the movement(s) among non-Israelite peoples in the cities of the eastern Roman Empire, developing new but derivative hidden transcripts in newly formed "assemblies" of Philippians, Thessalonians, Corinthians, etc. The very formation of these household-based assemblies was a political move, an act of political resistance, as the very name *ekklesia* (the standard term for the public assembly of the Greek *polis*) indicates. Paul himself insisted that, while they were to interact with other urban residents in order to gain new recruits, members of the assemblies "in Christ" were not to have any other dealings with the dominant order, certainly not the city courts (1 Cor 5–7). Scott's statement cited just above also applies to Paul's assemblies: the social side of the hidden transcript is "a political domain striving to enforce, against great odds, certain forms of conduct and resistance in relations with the dominant" (191). "Under the conditions of tyranny and persecution in which most historical subjects live," the infrapolitics based on the hidden transcript "is political life" (201). Again, however, I believe we can say more about the assemblies catalyzed by Paul and his co-workers. They apparently constituted an alternative society with their own alternative "constitution" or "political order" (*politeuma*). The politics of resistance to the Roman imperial order in each city of the Pauline mission, moreover, given the surveillance and periodic repression by the authorities, "was conducted in more earnest, for higher stakes, and against greater odds than political life in liberal democracies" (200). Paul was spearheading an international movement of political resistance. The hidden transcript he helped develop envisioned a revolutionary transformation of the Roman imperial order. The movement's elaborate hidden transcript, however, remained "a substitute for an act of assertion directly in the face of power" (115).

The essays in this volume utilize the highly suggestive insights and theory of Scott to tackle key issues in interpretation of Jesus and Paul. All of the contributors, implicitly or explicitly, assume a stance sympathetic with subordinated peoples of the past and present. While all pursue primarily critical literary, historical, and social analysis on New Testament texts in historical contexts, some also examine illuminating historical and/or contemporary comparative materials. Some also find Scott useful in critical self-examination of our own scholarly motives, stances, and approaches in relation to texts and their uses.

Allen Dwight Callahan insists that, if only New Testament interpreters recognize historical realities in Palestine under the Seleucid and Roman Empires, Jesus acted in the context of a remarkably sustained "age of revolution." For three hundred years, from the Maccabean Revolt to the Bar Kokhba Revolt, Judeans and Galileans persisted not simply in rebellion, but in revolution aimed at an end to imperial domination. Their repeated revolutionary movements against Roman rule, unique among subject peoples, were deeply rooted in the Israelite tradition of resistance to oppression and heroic leaders of the people's persistent reassertion of their independent life under the rule of the God of justice. His focus on Israel's resistance to domination parallels Scott's larger agenda in his various books and articles. Yet Callahan finds some of Scott's basic conceptual apparatus inapplicable to the way that Israelite biblical tradition informed ongoing Judean and Galilean revolutionary movements. What may have originated as "little tradition" had become central to the standard Israelite biblical tradition. And the way that even priestly or scribal circles mobilized that tradition helped motivate movements that were revolutionary in their agenda.

William Herzog II uses Scott's work to illuminate two key passages in Mark's Gospel that provide windows onto Jesus' leadership of a popular movement of resistance. First he adapts Scott's earlier exploration of how peasants draw upon their own "little tradition" in protest and profanation of their rulers' "great tradition." This enables Herzog to key interpretation of Mark 2:13–17 on the historical class and regional differences between the Pharisaic retainers of the Jerusalem high priestly rulers and the Galilean peasantry, for whom Jesus is the spokesperson, and to move well past the dead-end debate about Jesus versus the Pharisees on the law. Herzog then draws on Scott's concept of the "hidden transcript" and his theory of popular resistance in disguised form to shed new light on the passage in which Jesus wriggles out of the trap set for him in the question about the Roman tribute. He demonstrates that far from fitting the modern Western division between church and state, Jesus' subtle reply to the attempted entrapment constitutes an unmistakable statement of resistance to the Roman imperial order in Palestine.

Richard Horsley explores ways in which Scott's appreciation of the cultural-and-emotional effects of and popular responses to the indignities that the dominant impose on them leads to a broadening of approach to the historical Jesus. If Jesus' sayings are not isolated from literary and social-political context, he can be seen to address and express Galilean peasants' indignation at their dehumanizing treatment by their rulers and to restore a sense of dignity. Scott's illumination of popular politics of anonymity and disguise, particularly the role of rumor, enable us to appreciate how Mark's narrative may provide a window onto how Jesus' proclamation of the kingdom and its manifestation in healings and exorcisms brought a long-anticipated renewal of Israel into expanding public expression. Finally, Scott's reflections on those rare moments when subordinates "speak truth to power" suggest that Jesus' bold confrontation with the Jerusalem rulers became the crucial moment of "breakthrough" to historical significance for the movement he was leading.

Neil Elliott suggests that Scott's work is applicable to Paul and the assemblies he helped catalyze in Greek cities of the Roman Empire as well as to Jesus movements among the Galilean and Judean peasants. The "new consensus" that the Pauline congregations consisted of a cross-section of Roman imperial society, including "middle-class" individuals concerned with "status ambivalence" is giving way, under critical reexamination, to a more realistic picture of life under the Roman Empire. The vast majority of the urban as well as the rural populace lived in rather severe economic circumstances. It may not be surprising, therefore, that Scott's work on the communal support strategies of agricultural communities helps illuminate Paul's advocacy of economic mutualism as a survival strategy for urban communities facing economic difficulties. Elliott illuminates Paul's strategy by comparison with a contemporary case of intentional peasant communities in Haiti. Elliott also finds further application of Scott's discussion of hidden transcripts of defiance in Philo's discussion of oppressive anti-Jewish violence in Alexandria and in Paul's peculiar language about authority in Rom 13.

Erik Heen, focusing on a particular aspect of the "hidden transcript" of the subordinated that Scott illuminates, that of "symbolic inversion," compares Paul's gospel message to accounts of the ancient Roman Saturnalia festival. He finds a remarkable similarity in their respective story-lines and in their criticism of the introduction of inappropriate social practices into their respective ritual meals. He suggests that both represent the reaction to the dominant timocratic culture of cities of the Roman Empire in the formation of "hidden transcripts" among various subordinated peoples. However, the Saturnalia had been domesticated by the overlay of the timocratic values operative through the patronage system through which subordinates were effectively controlled. By contrast, as evident in 1 Corinthians, Paul warns against the dangers of accommodation to the dominant patterns by focusing on the cross of Christ as the paradigm for believers.

Cynthia Kittredge argues that it may be more effective to use the lens of Scott's analysis of "hidden" forms of resistance on contemporary interpreters' own agenda of resistance, which often remains hidden behind Pauline texts that were or have become records of the "public transcript" through which the dominant order is maintained. She finds an affinity and potential alliance between Scott's perspective and approach and those of recent feminist interpreters in questioning the surface constructions of texts and exposing the complexity of domination. The letter to the Ephesians exemplifies a text with clearly dominant patterns of gender and master-slave relations while ostensibly opposing the overarching imperial pattern. The way interpreters read domination and resistance in texts such as Ephesians depends on their particular models of Christian history. It seems more effective at the outset therefore for interpreters interested in liberative or resistance readings to understand self-critically their own interests and concerns (e.g., economic justice; equal discipleship) that lead to the questions and approaches they bring to texts.

The respondents present far more than incisive comments on the articles. Warren Carter locates the discussion of using Scott's theory on the historical Jesus in the broader context of Gospel studies and explores possible applications of Scott uncovered by the articles. Susan Elliott carries Scott's theory a few steps further in relation to the interpretation of

Paul today, drawing on her own experience with communities of subjugated people. Finally, Gerald West, who had found Scott's critical reflection valuable for his own reflection on years of "reading with" communities of the poor and marginalized, presents a broader perspective both on reading biblical texts in such communities and on the role of professional intellectuals in that connection.

Those of us who were involved in these articles and responses are deeply appreciative of the work of James C. Scott, particularly for the ways in which it has stimulated our own critical rethinking of materials and issues involved in interpretation of Jesus and Paul. We believe that Scott offers many suggestive insights and important comparative observations that will enrich critical biblical interpretation.

PART 1

JESUS, HIDDEN TRANSCRIPTS, AND THE ARTS OF RESISTANCE

The Arts of Resistance in an Age of Revolt

Allen Dwight Callahan

Governments, Theocracies, and Armies are, of course, stronger than the scattered peasants. So the peasants have to resign themselves to being dominated, but they cannot feel as their own glories of a civilization that is radically their enemy. The only wars that touch their hearts are those in which they have fought to defend themselves against that civilization, against History and Government, Theocracy and the Army. These wars they fought under their own black pennants, without military leadership or training and without hope, ill-fated wars that they were bound to lose, fierce and desperate wars, incomprehensible to historians.

—Carlo Levi, *Christ Stopped at Eboli*

Being Dominated

James C. Scott has explained domination as a tacit schema of relations he calls the public transcript, "the open interaction between subordinates and those who dominate." To play their part, subordinates don a dissimilar mask of accommodation. The obverse of the public transcript is the hidden transcript, which "consists of those offstage speech, gestures, and practices that confirm, contradict, or inflect what appears to be in the public transcript." Scott theorizes that "[b]y asserting the discrepancy between the hidden transcript and the public transcript we may begin to judge the impact of domination on public discourse." Scott has developed his insightful analysis in several works, perhaps the best known of which is the modern classic *Domination and the Arts of Resistance* (1976, 1985, 1990).

Scott's theory treats of covert registers of discontent and refusal to buy into domination. In so doing, however, it in effect traces resistance in the absence of politics in any conventional sense: "The vast majority of people have been and continue to be not citizens but subjects. So long as we confine our conception of the political to activity that is openly declared we are driven to conclude that subordinate groups essentially lack a political life or that what political life they do have is restricted to those exceptional moments of popular expression" (1990: 199). Thus

Scott's analysis promises an impressionistic account of the otherwise secret struggles of those who do not rebel.

The study of Christian origins, however, combs the rubble of a revolutionary era in the history of Palestine, an era punctuated by "exceptional moments of popular expression." The Israelites had a robust collective memory of revolutionary resistance and divine deliverance from oppression. They were unlike that "vast majority of people" who, in Scott's words, "have been and continue to be not citizens but subjects." The Israelites possessed a traditional, collective self-understanding that they were not to be subjects ruled by men but citizens of a commonwealth ruled by God. That collective memory was a factor in indigenous unwillingness to countenance domination indefinitely and the Israelites' willingness to struggle, in the words of Josephus, "with more recklessness than science" (*Ant.* 17.274–76). Scott's theory, however, offers a science ill suited to help us to understand that recklessness.

Wars That Touch Their Hearts

In applying Scott's analysis to first-century Palestine, several New Testament scholars have posited that this memory was canonized in two traditions in post-exilic Judea. One, the "great tradition," was that of "the consciously cultivated ideas of professional scribes and priests." The other was that of the "little tradition," which was "the basic memories, tales, and ideals of the unlettered peasantry." [1] The "'great' or official tradition and the 'little' or popular tradition" are the poles of a fitful dialectic, "interaction" in Scott's terms; the two traditions "generally run parallel and influence each other while also standing in some tension" (Horsley 1994: 126).

For our study of revolutionary Palestine in the Common Era, however, the categories of "great tradition" and "little tradition" are of limited theoretical value, because Israel's "great tradition" has much in it that we would identify with a "little tradition." All its heroes, no matter how humble, have been taken up in what becomes the Israelite great tradition of sacred scripture. [2] The righteous indignation that we find in the

---

1. See Horsley (1984: 476), where he first applied this schema in the light of the work of cultural anthropological work by Redfield (1969; original 1956) and Wolf.

2. Horsley is aware of this. Thus his qualifications when applying this schema to Judea: "The two traditions will have been interdependent. The fact that the ruling elite sponsors literature does not mean that they originate all cultural traditions" (1984: 476). "The 'little tradition' cultivated among the peasantry and the 'great tradition' maintained by scribal circles often have common roots, parallel versions of common stories and laws, and have influenced each

"little tradition" is canonical in Israel's "great tradition." Israel's sacred literature occasioned a weaving together of critical, ambivalent, even contradictory traditions as its tradents sought to negotiate the conflicts of their own heritage in different historical moments with different interests. Such texture is the *raison d'être* of written traditions. Oral tradition is a story of conflicts; literary tradition, a conflict of stories.

So we must be cautious to avoid a simple correlation of great tradition with élite ideology and little tradition with subaltern insurgency. Israel's peculiar historical formation has brought the commoner to the court and the country mouse to the city in a tradition that confounds such tidy distinctions. Amos the Tekoan hillbilly is "neither the prophet nor a prophet's son," but a part-time shepherd—one of the most despised and degraded occupations in antiquity. Though this prophet without portfolio is unceremoniously turned out of the Samarian court by the priest Amaziah and told to take his oracles back down south, his complaint not only becomes a part of the Tradition, but becomes classic in it. As Samuel K. Eddy has observed,

> [In Palestine] the resistance [to the Seleucids] was not always the work of aristocrats.... While Judas, a Hasmonean of priestly rank, rebelled, so did the Hasidim, who had scarcely any rank at all. The sources of opposition in Judah were therefore unique. Among the Jews there was a persistent tradition that the peasant should remain free from exploitation, and that as prophet, like Amos the shepherd, he might talk back to his would-be oppressors ... men of slight social standing took an important part in resistance to the Greek kings. These were men like the authors of Zech 9–14, the compiler of Daniel, and Eleazar the Essene. (1961: 325)

The expression of resistance in ancient Israel is not a question of great versus little tradition, but of competing interpretations of one, complex common tradition.

In an age of revolt, it was the job of indigenous intellectuals to discern in Israel's tradition the appropriate script for their time. Daniel's mournful riverside meditation on the book of Jeremiah, one of the most poignant portrayals of an anguished intellectual in all of literature, signifies the earnestness that the *maskilim* invested in this task and foreshadows the intellectual work of resistance leaders under Roman hegemony. The *maskilim* are also important because they mark a moment

---

other" (2001: 118). He argues, however, we "have no reason to believe, either by direct evidence or by analogy from comparable peasant societies, that Galilean peasants would have known Israelite tradition in the form that we know it (the Hebrew Bible)" (2003: 62).

in Israel's history when a literate group of tradents defect from Jerusalem, the metropolis of the great tradition, and engage in protracted struggle with the Hasmonean tradents who remain. Eventually some of these dissenters boycotted the regime in Jerusalem, and ultimately some removed to the wastes of Qumran. Even as they left behind the temple and its reinstituted monarchic priesthood, with scrolls in hand they literally took the great tradition with them. The struggle was ultimately ideological: the *hadisim* were at odds with the Hasmoneans over the interpretation of the same complex, common tradition.

THEIR OWN BLACK PENNANTS

Hasmoneans and *hasidim* inaugurate the period that gives us the literature of the New Testament. Scholarship employs various circumlocutions that obscure what is obvious on any cursory review of events. "New Testament times," "the Second Temple period," and "the Second Commonwealth" are euphemisms for the ancient Near East in an age of revolt. One could object that the chronic disturbance that Josephus repeatedly reports are not revolutions but rebellions. Note the distinction between these two modes of resistance that Keith Bradley draws in his discussion of ancient slave uprisings.

> Indeed a clear conceptual distinction must be preserved between revolution and rebellion because the two are not at all synonymous. To argue for the establishment of a new state (as occurred in Haiti) is to argue for revolution, the creation of real change in society predicated on theoretical or intellectual assumptions and the substitution of one form of government for another, whether or not (in the event) for the benefit of a broader section of society. Rebellion, by contrast, although it might foreshadow revolution, is no more than violent protest against the established order of society by people reacting to their own victimization but not necessarily aiming to implement radical change in that society. (445–46)

Resistance in Palestine, however, was so intransigent because it sought "the creation of real change in society predicated on theoretical or intellectual assumptions and the substitution of one form of government for another." Its object was the establishment of an alternative order. In the Roman period some Israelites came to call that alternative order "the kingdom of God."

The period with which we have to do begins with a bang: the Maccabean Revolt. In the Hasmonean propaganda that we now call 1 Maccabees, we see that the revolt sets a precedent for following precedents of armed struggle. Mattathias, the priest who initiates the revolt against Antiochus IV, bequeaths the revolt to his sons in the testamentary bedside blessing recounted in 1 Macc 2. Mattathias commands his sons: "you shall join to yourselves all who observe the Torah, and take vengeance for your people. Bring retribution upon the Gentiles, and give heed to the commandment of the Torah" (1 Macc 2:67–68).

Throughout, 1 Maccabees styles the revolt as a recapitulation of the martial glory of Israel's ancient heroes. Most remarkable, however, is treatment of the figure Simon Maccabee in 1 Maccabees. Not initially a military leader, he is appointed by his dying father to be "father" and "a man of counsel" in the struggle (1 Macc 2). It is Simon who conquers the Jerusalem citadel (1 Macc 13) and is first to take power as high priest and as independent prince of a liberated Palestine. According to Mattathias's blessing, "Phinehas, our ancestor, through his act of zeal received a pact of priesthood for all time" (1 Macc 2:54). That pact is realized in Simon's accession to the high priesthood, corroborating the tacit claim of 1 Maccabees that Mattathias's priestly line is just as eligible for the high priesthood as that of the Oniads.

Simon's priestly destiny recapitulates the definition of religious zeal with martial resistance identified with the figure of Phinehas in Num 25:1–15. When Ben Sira praises famous men he recalls that "zealous for the God of all," Phinehas "met the crisis of his people and, at the prompting of his noble heart, atoned for the people of Israel. Therefore God conferred the right, in the covenant of friendship, to provide for the sanctuary and for his people, so that he and his descendants should possess the high priesthood forever" (Sir 45:23–24).[3] Simon the sword-bearing priest in turn comes to embody the tradition of resistance as sanctified violence. Just as 1 Maccabees styles Phinehas as the prototype of Simon Maccabeus, the militant heroine Judith appeals to "my father Simon" in the book of the Apocrypha that bears her name. During the Roman period others would follow in her train.

The memory of Maccabean victories was alive and well during the Roman imperial period. Three sources testify that Hanukkah, the feast of the Maccabean purification of the temple, was still being celebrated. Josephus (*Ant.* 12.7.7 ([§§323–326]) calls the festival *phos*, "Light." John 10:22, however, refers to it as *ta enkainia*, the festival of renewal, a name that signifies the historical event the festival commemorates. The third witness is the *Megillat Taanit* or "the Scroll of Fasts," which commemorated

---

3. This is the LXX text of Vaticanus, which understands Phinehas as a figure of both sacerdotal and secular power—my point here. By the time of Ben Sira's grandson and translator, however, Simon's son Onias III had been assassinated (2 Macc 4:34) and the line had in fact come to an end. Thus the emended version of 45:24: "May his [i.e., God's] kindness remain constantly with us, and may he save us in our day" (Skehan and DiLella: 514).

not only the "Feast of Dedication" but also other great moments of anti-Seleucid resistance, such as the day when "Antiochus the King was removed from Jerusalem."[4]

In 40 B.C.E. Herod received his kingdom from Augustus in the face of stiff native resistance that took the new monarch three years of pitched battle to put down. And when Herod was laid to rest in 4 B.C.E., his subjects were again up in arms. After his father's death, Herod's son Archelaus had to apply all his military muscle to crush a popular revolt. He also had to appeal to Quintilius Varus, the Syrian legate, for help. August granted Archelaus half the kingdom of his father and the title ethnarch, with the promise of a promotion to king if Archelaus proved himself worthy.

He did not. In a rare instance of accord, both Jews and Samaritans pleaded with the emperor to remove the ethnarch. In 6 C.E. Augustus deposed and exiled Archelaus, and his erstwhile possessions—Samaria, Judea, and Idumea—became the Roman province of Judea under direct imperial control. Judea was governed by a prefect of equestrian and not senatorial rank and policed with auxiliary units and not legions. But in other ways the Roman assumption of the political apparatus in Judea was more intrusive than in any other province of the empire. The Roman prefect not only expropriated the political administration, the royal buildings, and the royal army, but he also held the vestments of the high priesthood under lock and key: the high priest of Jerusalem could not even get dressed for the high holy days without the prefect's permission (Josephus, *Ant.* 17.4.3 §§93–94; Millar: 41–44). Nowhere else in the empire were Roman administrators so intimately implicated in the cultic life of a provincial community (Millar: 46).

While Judea and Samaria were under direct Roman administration with the priestly and other local élites as collaborators, each of the half dozen governors *ad seriatim* were faced with peculiar mass demonstrations and met them with bloody repression. The most notorious of those governors, Pontius Pilate, was recalled by the Syrian Legate Vitellius and sent packing to Rome because of his use of force in dispersing a mass of Samaritans gathered around a prophetic leader on Mount Gerazim. Pilate's vicious attack on the group with cavalry and armed infantry was judged excessive even by Roman reckoning.[5] In this thirty-five-year

---

4. For the text see Fitzmyer and Harrington, no. 150. In his classic study William Farmer showed that the Phinehas tradition of violent advocacy of Israelite law continued to be alive and well in the Roman Palestine (26–30).

5. Josephus himself goes on to report that the Samaritans went to the Syrian legate, Vitellius, and complained of Pilate's brutality. Vitellius agreed with the Samaritans and

period of social unrest and brutal imperial violence—from the death of Herod the Great to the end of Pontius Pilate's prefecture—Jesus of Nazareth lived and died.

After the brief reign of Herod's grandson Agrippa, mass demonstrations modeled on Israelite prophetic traditions again spring up and were again ruthlessly put down until the beginning of the first Judean revolt. Between 44 and 46 C.E., the Judean prophet Theudas led a multitude to the banks of the Jordan, where he claimed that the river would part at his command and allow the people to cross safely to the other side (*Ant.* 20.97–98). The Roman procurator Cuspius Fadus launched a surprise attack on them with a large cavalry force, killing many and taking prisoner those who survived the slaughter. Theudas was decapitated and his head was brought to Jerusalem. A prophet from Egypt (*Ant.* 20.169–1171 = *War* 2.261–263) led a massive crowd to the Mount of Olives. He promised that the city walls would fall at his command. Felix, Roman governor from 52–60, fell upon the crowd with cavalry and infantry, killed four hundred and took two hundred prisoners. The Egyptian escaped with his life and disappeared. Between 60 and 62 C.E., the Roman governor Festus sent out a force of cavalry and infantry to destroy a crowd that had followed an unnamed prophet into the Judean wilderness (*Ant.* 20.188). The prophet and his followers were massacred. Roughly a decade later a certain Jonathan the Weaver similarly led an unarmed mass of Judeans into the Libyan Desert to see "signs and apparitions" (*War* 7.437–450). The Libyan governor Catullus dispatched infantry and cavalry to attack them, and the hapless crowd was massacred.[6] In the summer of 67 the Samaritans gathered on Gerazim as they had in 36, and Vespasian slaughtered them there as had Pilate (Josephus, *War* 3.7.32 §§307–315). So determined was Vespasian to put an end to Samaritan aspirations that he founded pagan Neapolis virtually on top of ancient Shechem, much as Aelia Capitolina would be founded on top of Jerusalem after the second Jewish revolt. And at the outbreak of hostilities in Jerusalem in July or August of 70 C.E., Roman soldiers set fire to

---

dismissed Pilate and sent him back to Rome to explain his conduct to the emperor Tiberius. This incident ended Pilate's checkered career in Palestine. Josephus accuses the Samaritan mob of being armed (*en hoplois*) but this is very unlikely: Shaye Cohen (241) has shown that Josephus's *Antiquities* has a strong anti-Samaritan bias that may explain this incriminating claim (cf. Crossan: 161). It strains credulity that Vitellius would dismiss Pilate for attacking an armed and thus dangerous crowd. The accusation of brutality has merit only if the crowd was harmless.

6. Jonathan was captured and conspired with Catullus to discredit Jewish leaders in Alexandria and Rome. The conspiracy failed: the emperor Vespasian reprimanded Catullus, but had Jonathan tortured and then burned alive.

an area of the temple precincts where an unnamed prophet had collected over six thousand followers—many women and children—to await "tokens of their deliverance" (*War* 6.283–285). Roman infantrymen slaughtered those who escaped the flames.[7] It was in this incendiary ambient that Jesus' words and deeds were being remembered and interpreted in oral and written Gospel tradition.

Josephus' reports of prophetic activity suggest that due to direct Roman rule, Israelites shifted tactics to various modes of nonviolent mass organization. Thaumaturgical prophets pointed to a new regime. They were not mere wonderworkers: their miracles hearken to ancient Israelite antecedents of divine deliverance. Thus their penchant for wandering into deserts, parting rivers, and scaling mountains to await revelation as "the prophets of old," and doing so with a cast of thousands in tow. But violent resistance in the Maccabean style was neither forgotten nor foreclosed: indeed, when conditions were more promising Israelites had little difficulty shifting again to the martial paradigm of national deliverance. And Josephus tells us that just as the Romans were crushing banditry in Palestinian countryside, a small group of Jerusalem intellectuals, the *Sicarii* or "dagger men" waged a campaign of terror against the urban élites. They kidnapped and assassinated priests and nobles as retribution for complicity with imperial rule. Israelites variously drew on their communities' traditions of resistance and read the signs of their own times to discern when to work miracles and when to wage war, when to keep the flame, when to light the fuse.

Jesus was active during this period of the Roman "provincialization" of Judea and Samaria. Israelite populations had no apparatus for concerted opposition at the same time that imperial control had become direct yet disarticulated through three local regimes: the Roman prefecture of Judea and the respective tetrarchies of Antipas and Philip. This was a moment that demanded the cultivation of a collective consciousness of resistance: a necessary prelude to revolution. Thaumaturgical prophets read the "signs of freedom" that evoked collective memories of liberation. These prophetic agents were the vanguard of Israelite revolution. And the Romans recognized them as such.

---

7. This policy of provincial police action continued to characterize the Roman response to popular movements in the East. The bishop Hippolytus reports that a Syrian bishop led his congregation into the desert to prepare for the return of Christ, and says that the unarmed Christians were in danger of being massacred by the Roman governor (*Commentarium in Danielem* iv.18 GCS 250).

FIERCE AND DESPERATE WARS

Revolts are rare because they are dangerous, difficult, and require a complex formula of conditions to be possible, let alone practicable. Nevertheless, Israelites revolted more than any other people under Roman domination did, and more in the first century of the Common Era than in all other periods of their history combined. People of Israelite descent—and only people of Israelite descent—rose up in widespread, popular revolt against the Romans throughout disparate regions of Palestine. Josephus recounts separate military organizations in Idumea, Jericho, Peraea, the northwestern Judean hill country and the towns just north of Jerusalem, Lydda, Emmaus, and Joppa across the plain and toward the Mediterranean coast, and in Upper and Lower Galilee (Josephus, *War* 2.20.4 §§566–568; Millar: 363). Thus there were separate revolutionary commands in each of the ancestral territories to which ancient Israel laid claim through its biblical traditions. The revolt ended in Masada, in southeastern Idumea, which had been held by non-Israelites a mere two centuries before (Millar: 344–45). These revolutionaries could claim what Hasmonean propaganda had put in the mouth of Simon Maccabee: "We have taken neither foreign lands nor seized foreign property, but only the inheritance of our fathers, which at one time had been unjustly taken by our enemies" (1 Macc 15:33).

The ideological pressure of these common Israelite traditions also helps us make sense of the uneven Roman response to the revolt in its early stages. Imperial forces handily crushed open resistance—or, in the Samaritan instance, the threat of it—once the Roman military command resolved to do so. When the Roman general Cestus Gallus tried to withdraw after having made good headway against the revolutionary forces, the latter pursued him and routed his entire XII Fulminata legion, its auxiliaries, and civilian irregulars. Nevertheless, within a year the Romans had broken the back of resistance in Galilee and Samaria, and within two much of Peraea and Judea were again firmly under imperial control. The Romans suspended their operations in the summer of 68 at the news of the death of Nero: another reversal that was a boon to the fractious peasant forces holed up in Jerusalem. But in 69 Vespasian sent his son Titus to finish the job. Siege warfare further extended the life of the revolt in Herod's great southern fortresses of Herodium, Masada, and Machaerus. But by then Roman victory was a forgone conclusion.

The Roman response was fitful because in revolutionary Palestine Cestius Gallus, Vespasian, and Titus confronted something that Roman generals had never before faced: protracted, organized resistance at the hands of a popular force undaunted by Roman military superiority. Titus's triumph in 71, commemorated in Rome to this day on the arch that bears his name, is the only triumph in the history of the empire that celebrated the reconquest of an existing province (see Millar: 71–79). The ideological advantages of historical experience and collective memory in the war belonged to the Israelites—perhaps their only advantages. These were weapons alien to their adversaries, weapons continually sharpened by recollection of traditions echoed in their Scriptures.

Rebels lit the fuse in the world's largest communities of the Israelite Diaspora a mere two generations after the Egyptian prophet had drawn a mass following in Judea and Jonathan the Weaver had incited Judeans to look for a king in the Cyrenian desert. Revolt rocked Egypt and Cyrene in the in the first quarter of the second century, then Palestine exploded again less than twenty years later. This second revolt was led by a messianic central command. The Torah, enjoining strict law observance of the Sabbath and celebration of the feasts, became its constitution. At its head was a *nasi'*, a prince, named Simon bar Kokhba. None less than Rabbi Akiba acclaimed him the "son of the star" of Num 24:14, for centuries interpreted as a messianic oracle. Silver and bronze coins of the Bar Kokhba regime dated Years 1–5 featured the following legends in Paleo-Hebrew script: "Simon, Prince of Israel," "Simon ben Kosiba, Prince of Israel." Other legends proclaimed the political will of the revolutionary government: "Shekel of Israel," "Holy Jerusalem," "Freedom of Zion," and "For the Redemption of Zion." This last-mentioned legend is especially poignant: it is the same palaeo-Hebrew legend featured on a crude coin found in Gamla in the Galilee dating from the first year of the first revolt (Freyne 2001: 302–3). Silver tetradrachms show the Temple and the legend "Jerusalem" on the obverse, with a palm branch—the symbol of Maccabean resistance—on the reverse (Millar: 367). History was repeating itself—again.

And again the lofty aspirations of revolution crashed and burned under the withering assault of Roman military might. In the first revolt the Judeans lost their temple; in the second they lost the very land on which it had stood. By the second half of the second century, rabbinical consensus disavowed revolution as folly contrary to the laws of God and the lessons of history. The *Megillat Taanit* celebrating Israel's martial valor would not be included in the canon of rabbinical literature. With the rise of the Amoraim, the Great Assembly claimed the mantle of the prophets, and the rabbis came to see not Roman imperialism but Jewish messianism as the source of Israel's problems. Yohanan bar Nappaha, the great rabbi of the second half of the second century, argued that revolt had proven futile and that Israel's only hope was divine intervention. *Midrash Psalms* 36:6 accredits to him the following parable.

A man once tried to light a lamp, but every time he lit it it went out. Finally he exclaimed, "How long shall I waste my effort on this lamp? I shall wait for the sun to shine, and then I shall have light." So it is with the Jews. When they were enslaved in Egypt, Moses emerged to redeem them, but they were enslaved again by the Babylonians. Daniel, Hananiah, Mishael, and Azariah emerged to redeem them, but they were enslaved again by the Elamites, Medes, and Persians. Mordecai and Esther emerged to redeem them, but they were enslaved again by the Greeks. The Hasmonean and his sons emerged to redeem them, but they were enslaved again by the evil Edomites [viz., the Herodians]. Finally the Jews exclaimed: "We are tired of being continually enslaved and redeemed, only to be enslaved again. Let us pray for redemption not through human agency, but through our Redeemer, the Lord of Hosts, the Holy One of Israel. Let us pray for light not from man, but from God."

Asked about the Messiah, Yohanan is reputed to have replied, "Let him come, but let me not see him" (b. Sanh. 98.b).

BOUND TO LOSE

The first chapter of Domination and the Arts of Resistance opens with an Ethiopian proverb: "Bow low and fart silently." As long as flatulent subalterns bow downwind no one is the wiser, and both resentment and regime remain intact. In this way the hidden transcript tacitly reinscribes the public transcript. The inner life of the subordinated, however violent its fantasies and however seething its outrage, by its very secrecy and subterfuge confirms the relations of domination and subordination. As Scott has observed, "The goal of slaves and other subordinate groups, as they conduct their ideological and material resistance, is precisely to escape detection.... In this respect, subordinate groups are complicitous [sic] in contributing to a sanitized official transcript, for that is one way they cover their tracks" (1990: 87). This tacit reinscription, however, is not to be confused with the open, principled Israelite resistance that marks the spirit of Jesus' age. "Acts of desperation, revolt, and defiance can offer us something of a window on the hidden transcript," writes Scott: in first century Palestine, Israelite rebels threw that window wide open.

At no moment in the Second Temple period was Israelite resistance waged with silent flatulence: it was expressed in the public actions of peasants, princes, and priests. And a string of revolutionaries named Simon: Simon Maccabee, Simon ben Giora, the outlaw rabbi Simon bar Yohai,[8]

---

8. In b. Šabb. 33b one reads the following story about Simon bar Yohai's famed hatred of Rome. "Rabbi Judah, Rabbi Yose, and Rabbi Simon were sitting and talking.... Rabbi

and Simon bar Kokhba. And between the respective revolutions of the first Simon and the second, two others: Simon the zealot and Simon ben Jonah, also known as Peter and remembered among other things for his sword-wielding zeal. It was apparently a matter of public record that Jesus of Nazareth freely associated with men of revolutionary sentiments. Upon a careful sifting of our sources in the light of all we know about Palestine the two centuries before and the two centuries after the turn of the Common Era, this is not surprising. These men, after all, lived in an age of revolt.

Judah began: 'How splendid are the works of this people [i.e., the Romans]. They have built marketplaces, baths, and bridges.' Rabbi Yose said nothing. Rabbi Simon bar Yohai answered him: 'Everything they have made they have made only for themselves: marketplaces, for whores; baths, to wallow in; bridges, to levy tolls.'" Rabbi Simon openly hoped for a Parthian invasion on the Roman Empire's troubled eastern frontier. *Lamentations Rabbah* 1.13.41 attributes to him the saying, "If you see a Persian horse tethered in Palestine, look for the feet of the messiah." Simon bar Yohai went into hiding after the Romans condemned him to death for sedition.

ONSTAGE AND OFFSTAGE WITH JESUS OF NAZARETH: PUBLIC TRANSCRIPTS, HIDDEN TRANSCRIPTS, AND GOSPEL TEXTS

William R. Herzog II

This essay will explore how the work of James C. Scott may contribute to an understanding of some of the cultural and political dynamics at work in the public activity of the historical Jesus. To do this, the essay will draw on three core concepts found in Scott's work: (1) the profanation of the great tradition as a form of protest against the elites who would use it to erase the little tradition which governs the lives of peasant villagers (Scott 1977); (2) the presence of public and hidden transcripts in the discourse between classes in agrarian societies (Scott 1990); and (3) the identification of weapons employed by the weak in their everyday forms of resistance to those who would exploit and oppress them (Scott 1985). Given the limited scope of this inquiry, it will be possible to do little more than suggest how Scott's perspectives and analyses can inform a reading of the work of the historical Jesus by applying them to specific texts from the Synoptic tradition. The proof of the pudding is in the tasting.

DEFINING AND DEFENDING WORLD: THE ROLE OF PROTEST AND PROFANATION IN THE CLASH BETWEEN THE GREAT TRADITION AND THE LITTLE TRADITION (MARK 2:15–17)

Jesus conducted his public activity in a world of advanced agrarian societies. (Lenski and Lenski; Lenski; Hanson and Oakman; and Stegemann and Stegemann.) Such societies are characteristically divided between a small class of ruling elites who have almost everything and a peasant base that has practically nothing. The ruling class lives in luxury while the vast majority of the population lives at a subsistence level or worse, at the edge of destitution and ruin. The peasant class produces the wealth on which agrarian societies are based, primarily through their cultivation of crops, orchards and vineyards. Yet, through a redistributive economy, the rulers claim the lion's share for themselves, the so-called surplus, while leaving barely enough for peasants to maintain their subsistence existence. This redistribution of wealth takes place primarily through the taking of tribute. It is important not to equate tribute with what we call taxation. Taking tribute was an economic expression of domination because it established the ability of the ruling class to take the yield of the land from the hands of those who had produced it and appropriate it for their own political purposes and social ends. In Palestine, these dynamics apply whether we are discussing the client kingship of Herod Antipas in Galilee or the rule of the high-priestly families in the subprovince of Judea under the control of a Roman Prefect. The references to the Herods as client kings and to the high priestly families being under a Roman Prefect indicate that the peasants of Galilee and Judea were subjected to more than one level of tribute. Peasants in Galilee were subjected to the tribute demanded by imperial Rome, the tribute taken by Herod Antipas to maintain his own rule and, finally, to the tribute called tithes demanded by the high priestly houses who controlled the temple in Jerusalem. There is some debate about the total amount of tribute that Galilean peasants were forced to pay but the estimates range from 20 percent to as high as 40 percent of their harvests and herds each year (Borg: 47–49; Horsley 1987: 29–33; 1995: 216–21; Stegemann and Stegemann: 114–25). Fiensy (99–101) estimates that Roman tribute on the land, the *tributum soli,* amounted to 12.5 percent but could, in some instances, range as high as one-third of grains and one-half of fruits. In addition, all subjects paid the *tributum capitis* or a tax on one's person. The philosophy behind the head tax was clear. "Just as all land was considered as belonging ultimately to the Roman Empire, and thus, subject to taxation as a kind of rent, so also did one's body belong to Rome" (Fiensy: 101). Peasants were probably assessed one denarius per year. Whether we accept the lower or the higher figure, or some estimate in between, the impact on the peasantry was the same. They were being forced to pay more than their subsistence existence could absorb.

Since the continuing rule of agrarian elites depended directly on their ability to extract tribute and keep the peasant class in subjection to them, and since peasants did not accept their oppression and exploitation without resistance, conflict was built into the very structure of agrarian societies. One form this conflict took was the struggle between the great tradition and the little tradition (Scott 1977).

The great tradition contained the construction of the world as seen by the rulers. It was usually centered in urban areas and propagated from there to the villages of the countryside. More often than not, it was written down. In an illiterate culture, writing has power; so the fact that the great tradition was written tended to enhance its authority. Of course, the great tradition had its guardians who controlled its parameters and determined its interpretation. These guardians might be hereditary sacral elites (e.g., high priests) or their retainers (e.g., scribes or a political faction like the Pharisees). The great tradition while propagating a "social ideology of patronage," would usually legitimize "inequalities in material and cultural resources as fore-ordained" and celebrate "the positive value of stratification" (Scott 1977: 14).

In Jesus's day, the Torah functioned as the great tradition whose influence extended throughout Palestine from Jerusalem into Galilee, even though it was ruled by Herod Antipas and not under the jurisdiction of the temple in Judea. To put the matter more precisely, a particular reading of the Torah functioned as the great tradition which sustained the rule of the high priestly families in Jerusalem, along with a lay aristocracy in Judea, and the rule of the Herods in Galilee. This "oral tradition" or "tradition of the elders" specified what in the great bulk of Torah was "binding" and what could be "loosed," that is, what was negotiable or nonbinding. It was very likely the case that the great tradition focused primarily on matters of purity and how they should be applied to the people of Israel, since this issue could be used to maximize the social distance between elites and peasants while reinforcing the control of the few over the many. The attempt to force peasants to adopt the great tradition would actually serve to intensify their marginalization, for "whether it is a matter of knowing the sacred texts, of speaking and dressing properly, of performing the elaborate ceremonies of initiation, marriage, or burial, peasants are asked, in effect, to revere a standard which is impossible for them to achieve" (Scott 1977: 17). The same holds true for the rituals of purity surrounding the consumption of meals and the temple's demands for tithes.

For all of these reasons, the great tradition could neither support the lives of peasant villagers nor serve their interests. As Scott has noted, the farther down the scale of social stratification one moves, the less binding the great tradition becomes (1977: 7). In similar fashion, the farther one moves away from the center toward the periphery, the weaker the great tradition becomes. This cultural and geographical distance provides space for the little tradition to take root and grow. Scott defines the little tradition as "the distinctive patterns of belief and behavior which are valued by the peasantry of an agrarian society" (8). The little tradition expresses the values of peasants and incorporates their grasp and selective appropriation of the great tradition in a way that sustains their life, culture and values. In this fashion, the little tradition becomes a source and a resource for resisting the imposition of the great tradition by the ruling elites. In spite of their determined efforts, elites are usually unable to impose their definition of reality and social world on peasant villagers. Peasants find ways to manage what Scott calls a "negotiated subordination"; that is, they can neither deny nor disregard the imposition of the great tradition by ruling elites, but they can and do resist. More often than not, the little tradition encourages this resistance. By combining elements of the great tradition with its own indigenous characteristics, the little tradition will be more local and syncretistic than the great tradition, which strives to define common norms as perceived by the ruling powers that be. In short, the little tradition will be "arrayed against the ideology and institutions of urban elites" (7). But what forms might this resistance take? Scott identifies one of those paths of resistance as the formation of a "shadow society, a pattern of structural, stylistic and normative opposition to the politico-religious tradition of ruling elites" (4). In a strange way, the emergence of this shadow society reflects the way hegemony engenders its opposite, or as Scott puts it, "what matters for our purposes, however, is that the material and symbolic hegemony normally exercised by ruling institutions does not preclude, but rather engenders, a set of contrary values which represent in their entirety a kind of shadow society" (19). This society comes to expression in a variety of social and cultural scenarios, both onstage and offstage, such as "millenial dreams ... popular theatre, folk tales, folk sayings, myths, poetry, jokes and songs" (20).

Using Scott's work as a guide, it may be possible to catch a glimpse of what this conflict might have looked like in the context of first-century Palestine. Mark 2:15–17 depicts a conflict between Jesus and "the scribes of the Pharisees" over eating with "toll collectors and sinners." The Pharisees were, to some extent, a table companionship group who aspired to eat every meal in a state of ritual purity equal to that of the priests performing sacerdotal duties in the temple. Neusner has observed that "Pharisaic table-fellowship required keeping everywhere the laws of ritual purity that normally applied only in the Jerusalem Temple, so Pharisees ate their private meals in the same condition of ritual purity as did the priests of the holy cult" (67). This meant that the Pharisees were oriented to the temple in Jerusalem as the center of their symbolic world. They took their models of purity from the Torah's concerns about the ritual purity of priests in the temple and attempted to apply them to all Israel. The way to be the people of God was to become a nation of priests. The crucial link that joined temple to household was the table and the meals consumed at the table.

> But the Pharisees held that even outside of the Temple, in one's own home, the laws of ritual purity were to be followed in the only circumstance in which they might apply, namely, at the table. Therefore, one must eat secular food (ordinary, everyday meals) in a state of ritual purity *as if one were a Temple priest.* The Pharisees thus arrogated to themselves—and to all Jews equally—the status of Temple priests.... The

table of every Jew in his home was seen as being like the table of the
Lord in the Jerusalem Temple. (Neusner: 83)

This required what Neusner calls a "perpetual ritualization of daily life
and constant, inner awareness of the communal order of being" (90).

That perpetual ritualization included the food that was prepared, the
pots and pans in which it was prepared, the dishes in which it was
served, as well as the hands and bodies of those who reclined at table
together. In addition, to be clean, all food had to be tithed to the temple.
This included all food purchased in the public marketplace because the
purchaser could not be certain that the original growers of the food had
tithed it properly to the temple. As a result of these concerns, tithing
came to occupy a central place in Pharisaic theology and practice. As Saldarini (2001: 213) notes, the holiness agenda of the Pharisees was
appropriate for a colonized people who had lost control of their political
life, for it allowed them to refocus their attention on those areas of domestic life "that can be controlled by people out of power in their own
society: food, sex and marriage."

Saldarini contends that the Pharisees were more than a table companionship group. They were also a political interest group with a
political agenda for Judea and Galilee centered in great tradition readings
of Torah that left the peasantry utterly incapable of fulfilling the practices
and commitments articulated by those great tradition versions. (Saldarini
2001) This is a dilemma common to peasants, as Scott has already noted.
To the degree that they embrace the great tradition, they are enforcing
their own marginalization. Still, the very act of carving out an area of
ritual purity created a space that the colonizer could not easily penetrate,
and offering tithes replicated the demands for tribute but in a context of
support for the temple. So the Pharisees' agenda could be read as covertly
political. It is clear, however, that the Pharisees were not members of the
ruling class. They achieved what influence they did have by attaching
themselves to powerful political patrons who shared their agenda of a
temple-centered holiness for Judea and Galilee.

Seen in this perspective, the table companionship group and the
political interest group come together to form a coherent view of the
Pharisees. I have argued elsewhere that the Pharisees were also the rule
creators and rule enforcers who traveled from the center (Jerusalem) to
enforce conformity with the great tradition centered in Jerusalem
(Herzog: ch. 7). In this capacity, they moved between the center
(Jerusalem) and the periphery (Galilee) to extend the reach of the great
tradition and to monitor compliance with it.

It is in this context that Jesus' reclining at table with toll collectors and
sinners made a serious symbolic statement about the Pharisees' project.

According to the Pharisees' version of the great tradition, the meal that mattered most occurred when priests gathered in the temple, and it was meant to be replicated at all the tables of those who followed the great tradition or aspired to follow it. But the very conditions that led to pure table companionship excluded the peasants of Galilee as well as other assorted toll collectors and sinners. If emulation was not a possibility, subversion still was. Jesus joined toll collectors and sinners in an onstage act of popular political theater that "engenders a set of contrary values which represent ... a kind of shadow society" (Scott 1977: 19).

The clash between traditions is echoed in the conflict between Jesus and "the scribes of the Pharisees." Jesus provokes the hostile exchange by reclining at table with toll collectors and sinners. Toll collectors (*telonai*) were at the very bottom of the economic scale. (see Donahue: 39–61) They worked the toll booths and cheated as many as they could in order to earn money for the chief toll collector under whom they worked. Because they were conveniently visible figures, they received the lion's share of the hostility and anger intended for the more invisible elites whose dirty work they did. The term "sinners" here probably refers to those who were chronically negligent of the Torah's purity codes and concerns. From the point of view of this reading of the great tradition, uncleanness could be contracted through touch, so Jesus was rendering himself unclean just by reclining at table with sinners. Every time he broke off a piece of bread and dipped it in a common dish, he would contract the impurity of anyone else eating from the same dishes. Jesus apparently did not view the matter in the same way. At table with outcasts, Jesus was acting out an alternative political vision for the renewal of Israel, which included the ingathering of those who were made outcasts by the elite reading of the great tradition. What is at stake is who will be welcomed to the table and who will be included in the meal? If Jesus gathers with toll collectors and sinners, he is announcing by means of this enacted parable that the purity codes of the Torah are irrelevant at best and an obstruction at worst to the work of the covenant-renewing God. The meal not only lampoons the meals that attempt to replicate the holiness of the temple but may reflect a theme of social reversal when the outcasts will feast while the elites are excluded (see Q 13:28–29).

This is why the scribal Pharisees respond to the challenge posed by his behavior. Given their concern for the purity codes of the Torah as interpreted in the great tradition of the oral Torah, their question, "Why does he recline at table with toll collectors and sinners?" is an entirely reasonable one. It also poses a political challenge to which Jesus must respond, and he does by using a proverb and a sharp retort. The proverb appeals to common sense. Where should a physician be if not with the sick? The retort appeals to Jesus' own interpretation of the work of the covenant-renewing God and reveals his understanding of the meal. Both N.T. Wright and John Meier think that the "symbolic praxis" of eating with all sorts of people was a regular part of Jesus' activity, but they relate it to Jesus' own theological convictions. Meier elaborates the theological point of such meals more fully when he suggests that "his meals with sinners and the disreputable were celebrations of the lost being found, of God's eschatological mercy reaching out and embracing [sinners]. His banquets with sinful Israelites were a preparation and foretaste of the coming banquet in the kingdom of God" (Meier: 303). What is clear is that Jesus used the meals as opportunities for the inclusion of the very folk who were excluded from the Pharisees' table gatherings. In this regard, Wright is also convinced that table companionship was intimately related to Jesus' announcement of the coming reign of God and represented an acting out of its future banquet. But notice that both Meier and Wright sublimate the political and economic dimensions of this conflict in order to develop their theological reading. Emphasizing the future or eschatological nature of the meal leads them to overlook its more immediate social and class significance. For them, the meal is more like an anticipation of the Christian eschatological banquet than a class conflict in which the great and little traditions confront each other.

Seen through Scott's eyes, the meal with toll collectors and sinners is a profanation of the great tradition represented in the oral Torah of the Pharisees. Such a profanation provides a glimpse into the religion of the dominated class.

> The radical strain of little tradition religion may take the form of rituals of reversal in which, for a time, the poor become aristocrats; the prevailing hierarchy of power and piety are openly mocked; and deference is suspended. Popular sacrilege is at the core of these "moments of madness." (1977: 29)

Jesus' table companionship represents just such a "ritual of reversal" in which those invited to the table are those who are normally rejected as table guests. The hospitality of the reign of God mocks the concern for purity that dominates the Pharisaic table gathering. Normally, elites try to control such profanations, limiting them to particular occasions and places in the hope that they may act "to drain off the tensions which any political or moral order engenders," especially a ruthlessly exploitive and oppressive political order and its accompanying moral sanctions.

However much the rulers try to control these unsanctioned forms of the little tradition, these profanations serve as a constant reminder that "the symbolic hegemony of ruling groups is not complete" while revealing "an alternate moral universe" and "a latent normative subculture" that cannot be completely controlled (1977: 29). In this context, it is possible that every time Jesus gathered at table with toll collectors and sinners, he was enacting out of an alternate moral universe that refused to be controlled by the normative order of the great tradition that prevailed in Judea and Galilee under the temple-state ruled by the high priests and the client kingship of the Herods. This sense of just such an alternative reality underlies Jesus' last remark: "I did not come to call the righteous, but sinners." His aphorism has a playful, perhaps a mocking tone, for Jesus does not deny the label "righteous" to the scribal Pharisees, but declares that their status is irrelevant to what God is about. The reign of God and the renewal of Israel is about sinners, not the righteous. The righteous are simply beside the point; therefore, their purity concerns cannot be determinative for Jesus' table companionship. If they were, he would be gathering at table with scribes and Pharisees.

Scott's analysis has provided a context in which to understand the social meaning of Jesus' reclining at table with toll collectors and sinners as a profanation of the great tradition's understanding of meals as occasions for the households of Judea and Galilee to model themselves on the meals served in the temple and consumed by ritually pure priests. These banquets of exclusion are not so subtly subverted by a meal that gathers the excluded into a shadow banquet embodying the values and vision of a very different social world, what Jesus called the reign of God as an expression of the renewal of Israel. These shadow banquets were held onstage and drew the attention of scribal Pharisees who perceived the profanation of the tradition of the elders implied by such gatherings. In a social world in which peasants were increasingly subjected to the purity demands of the temple while simultaneously being excluded by its demands for tithes that they could not afford, they found in Jesus a prophetic figure whose praxis of inclusion stood in sharp contrast to the exclusive gatherings of scribal Pharisees. Nowhere was this more evident than the gatherings of common people at table. That Jesus understood the significance of these meals is implied in numerous sayings and parables found at several levels of the Jesus tradition (Q/Luke 7:31–35; Mark 7:1–12; Luke 13:28–29; Matt 8:11–13; Luke 14:15–24; 16:19–31). It is also evident that the depiction of these subversive meals has been crafted for Mark's community. As such, they are neither snapshots of what might have occurred in Jesus's day nor verbatim reports of public dialogues, but the conversation among the characters in the story quite likely does depict the issues underlying Jesus table companionship and the dissent that it sparked.

DISSEMBLING, A WEAPON OF THE WEAK:
PUBLIC AND HIDDEN TRANSCRIPTS IN MARK 12:13–17

It has long been recognized that the question about paying tribute to Caesar was a loaded question but few have pursued the implications of that insight. Once the observation is made, interpreters revert to the usual reading of the passage as counseling how Christians are to adjudicate the competing claims of church and state. In other words, it is treated as a brief treatise on Christian citizenship. But this ignores "the imperial situation" (Horsley 1987: 3–19) in which the encounter occurs. Caesar was interested in obedient subjects, not active citizens. Nor is the inquiry addressed to Jesus an attempt to gather information; it is rather an attempt at entrapment with serious consequences. If we are to understand the incident, we need to place it in an appropriate context and take into account its political dynamics. In this encounter, power relations are asymmetrical, so it is reasonable to assume that the political speech of Jesus will dissemble by feigning obedience to rulers and loyalty to the colonial overlords while pursuing his own hidden agenda and communicating other more subtle messages.

Scott (1990) frames the matter in this way. In a political environment where an oppressive ruling class dominates a suppressed population, there will be a "public transcript" of events controlled by the ruling elites and a "hidden transcript" of the same events as seen through the eyes of the peasants. The public transcript is "a shorthand way of describing the open interaction between subordinates and those who dominate," whereas the hidden transcript is what characterizes the "discourse that takes place 'offstage,' beyond the direct observation of the power holders." (Scott 1990: 2, 4) Put differently, the hidden transcript contains what the oppressed say to each other and what they really think about their rulers but are too intimidated to express openly. The public transcript of the elites is "the *self*-portrait of dominant elites as they would have themselves seen" (18). Quite clearly, there will be a significant discrepancy between the public transcript of the dominant elites and the hidden transcript of the oppressed.[1]

---

1. The following analysis will focus on the public transcript of the elites and the hidden transcript of the oppressed. But this is only a part of the whole picture, since each group will have both a public and a hidden transcript. The public transcript of the dominated class, for instance, will appear to conform to the world created by the elites and will contribute to their "flattering self-image." For the oppressed, this feigned compliance and show of loyalty is simply a matter of survival. This is the communication that occurs "onstage" where the controlling elites write the script and choreograph the political play. In their public self-portrait, elites will depict themselves as generous patrons, often depicting their relationship

This discrepancy would appear to create a chasm as great as the one that separated the rich man from Lazarus. How can one ever get from one to the other? What makes the difficulty even greater is that the public transcript of the elites may appear in a variety of written forms but peasants are usually illiterate and live in an oral culture, so their perspectives are even harder to discern and define. The task would be impossible were it not for a third form of political discourse found among oppressed classes. Scott describes this as "a politics of disguise and anonymity that takes place in public view but is designed to have a double meaning or to shield the identity of the actors" (1990: 18–19). This means that "a partly sanitized, ambiguous and coded version of the hidden transcript is always present in the public discourse of subordinate groups" (19).

The following study of Mark 12:13–17 suggests that the conflict between Jesus and his opponents is an example of this ambiguous and coded political speech. It appears to support the hegemonic powers but conveys other more elusive and subversive messages. In an extended field study of a Malaysian village, Scott identified what he called "the weapons of the weak" which lurk beneath the "rituals of deference" and "symbolic compliance" demanded of the weak as part of the onstage political play (Scott 1985). These weapons support the "everyday forms of peasant resistance—the prosaic but constant struggle between the peasantry and those who seek to extract labor, food, taxes, rents and interest from them." Such weapons include "foot dragging, dissimulation, false compliance, pilfering, feigned ignorance, slander, arson, sabotage and so forth" (29). I have added dissembling to this list. If it is simply too dangerous for the oppressed to disclose their hidden transcripts onstage, they will dissemble when they are entrapped or choose to play out a public transcript under the scrutiny of their rulers. When confronted by enemies who try to force the hidden transcript of resistance to Roman rule into the domain of the public transcript, Jesus dissembles because he is a rural peasant artisan who belongs to the dominated class, not to the elites who control the empire and (so they fancy) rule the world. In this incident, it is no accident that Jesus is dealing with tribute, a primary focal point for everyday resistance. As Scott notes, peasant resistance tends to form around "the material nexus of class struggle—the appropriation of land, labor, taxes, rents and so forth" (33). The following reading of the question about the payment of tribute will suggest that Jesus was no stranger

---

with the oppressed in kinship terms (the elites as parents and the peasants as children or grateful clients). Onstage the elites always show class solidarity, although their offstage hidden transcript would reveal the endless competition for status and prestige that marks the "intraclass" warfare of ruling class political infighting.

to the weapons of the weak and knew how to employ a "politics of disguise" while inscribing in his debate with the Pharisees and Herodians an ambiguous and coded version of the hidden transcript of resistance to Roman colonial rule.

From Bultmann to the present, form critics have agreed that Mark 12:13–17 is an integral unit of tradition and that 12:17 never circulated as an independent saying. Nor did Bultmann think the passage was a creation of the early church (26). In this, Taylor agreed when he noted, "of its genuineness there can be no question" (478). It is equally clear that Mark placed the incident on the Temple Mount. There is nothing in the pericope itself to suggest that it belongs there, and the presence of Herodians (if a historical reminiscence) may indicate a Galilean context. Since the setting does not appreciably affect the reading of the incident proposed here, the question of location can be left unresolved.

Whatever its original context, the incident depicts a conflict disguised as an inquiry. Mark is as clear about this (12:13) as Jesus is (12:15b). This is no civics class discussion about the duties of citizens in a democratic society; it is an attempt at political entrapment with lethal consequences. Every element in the encounter points in this direction: (1) the political context of entrapment; (2) the flattery of the Pharisees and Herodians; (3) the explosive question about tribute; (4) the use of the denarius; and (5) the rapid-fire exchange culminating in Jesus' aphorism. It will be useful to examine each element briefly.

The Context of Entrapment

Working with the Lukan version of the story (Luke 20:20–26), J. Duncan M. Derrett has argued that the description of the people's response in 20:26 contains a verb (*apokrisis*) that became "a technical term for a *rescript*; it is what we lawyers call a *responsum,* a technical answer to a technical question, particularly in the field of behavior." (Derrett: 38–48, esp. 39) He finds support for this position by noting the reference to Jesus as teaching "the way of God" (20:21). Jesus is not being asked to render a personal opinion but to speak as a rabbi and interpreter of the Torah. More precisely, the question is: what does the Torah say about paying tribute to Caesar? Following these leads, Derrett builds his case that Luke is portraying Jesus as God's appointed emissary who, in the tradition of Moses, declares God's will before the people. Therefore, he concludes, Jesus' response is decidedly "not merely a piece of evasion"(40). If it were, it would defeat its purpose as an update on the Torah for the age of Tiberius.

The difficulty with Derrett's reading is that it tends to overlook the elements of entrapment that surround the account and enliven its conflict because he views the question as an earnest inquiry into the meaning of Torah. The scene, however, is neither a courtroom nor a public covenant-renewal ceremony but one of political intrigue. Using Scott's language, we can say that the Herodians and Pharisees are trying to goad Jesus into revealing the hidden transcript of resistance to Roman rule as that resistance expressed itself in opposition to the tribute and, in Mark, the issue is very pointedly the *kensos,* the poll tax or the *tributum capitis.*

Malina and Rohrbaugh propose reading the encounter as an example of a "challenge-riposte encounter" (256). In the ancient world, enemies engaged in verbal challenges in order to expose their opponents and shame them publicly. This encounter begins with just such a recognizable agenda even though it is disguised as a form of flattery that fools no one. Indeed, it was not employed for that purpose. Rather than responding to the trap laid down by the flattery, Jesus "answers with an insulting counter-question" because an honorable man cannot cede the terms of the debate defined by his opponent's initial challenge but must establish them on his own terms. This explains, in part, why Jesus neither quotes Torah nor debates its meaning (*pace* Derrett). He knows this is not a disinterested question but a challenge and a trap in the form of a familiar social challenge. The challenge was a zero sum game; someone won and someone lost, and the winner prevailed at the expense of his opponent. In this way, a figure like Jesus could acquire honor even though he was born into a peasant family without much ascribed honor. Since honor challenges normally occurred between social equals, Jesus and his movement were probably seen as similar to a political interest group like the Pharisees.

The problem with this reading of the conflict is that it minimizes the political and economic dimensions of the public encounter. In their reading, the challenge and riposte is part of a battle to preserve or gain honor and to avoid being shamed, but this reading loses track of what is at stake politically in this clash between a public transcript that justifies paying tribute and a hidden transcript that resists paying tribute. The temple-state's retainers who initiate the conflict with Jesus are ultimately beholden to Rome for their power and prestige, and they know that the system of imperial domination is dependent upon the orderly and timely payment of tribute. The tribute was a symbolic form of subjection, so the question about the payment of tribute is politically loaded. One could add to this dynamic the asymmetrical power relations between the rulers who demand tribute and the ruled who pay it, another aspect of the debate that Malina and Rohrbaugh omit. Since they believe that the encounter is between those who are roughly social equals, they miss the class conflict implicit in the debate between the proxies of the ruling class and the prophet who speaks for the people of the land. An analysis like that of Scott brings these dimensions of the encounter to the surface.

Flattery

The initial flattery may appear to be ineffective because it fails to deceive Jesus, but it was not intended for Jesus' ears but the ears of the crowd. The flatterers are preparing the crowd for Jesus to disavow the tribute. By describing Jesus as a teacher who does not judge people by their social standing or curry the favor of the rich and powerful, they are "daring Jesus to commit himself in this loaded political situation" (Myers: 311). Every seemingly complimentary reference raises the stakes by forcing Jesus to "save face" before the crowd by opposing the payment of tribute. The flattery throws down the gauntlet by attempting to force Jesus to deny the payment of tribute.

The Question about Tribute

The question posed by the Pharisees and Herodians was not a general question about taxes; it was a specific question about paying tribute. The payment of tribute to Rome had been a volatile issue since Pompey laid Jerusalem and Judea under tribute in 63 B.C.E., mainly because it was a symbol of Rome's supremacy. The Romans collected tribute on land and people as their way of asserting their domination over the bodies and lands that they had conquered. When Augustus converted Archelaus's failed kingdom into a Roman province in 6 C.E., he conducted a census in order to develop an inventory of assets on which tribute could be calculated. "The census constituted the numerical basis (computed in hectares and human heads) from which the Romans levied their so-called poll (or head) tax" which all nonelites were expected to pay in "imperial specie" (Finney: 632). It was this census that provoked the "fourth philosophy" led by Judas of Gamala to organize resistance to the tribute by arguing that "the payment of tribute to the Romans was incompatible with Israel's theocratic ideals" (Bruce: 254–55; Horsley and Hanson: ch. 5; Horsley 1987: ch. 10; cf. Josephus, *War* 2.118; *Ant.* 18.4–6, 9–10, 23–24). From the inception of the "fourth philosophy" and what Bruce judges to be its unprecedented position with regard to paying tribute to pagan rulers, the issue became a permanent bone of contention (Abrahams: 62–65; Bruce: 255–56). Josephus reveals what is at stake in the conflict when he depicts Judas of Galilee as "upbraiding his countrymen as cowards for consenting to pay tribute to the Romans and tolerating mortal masters, after having God for their lord" (*War* 2:118). Myers highlights the conflict in the sharpest of terms when he declares that the encounter was "a test of loyalty that divided collaborators from subversives against the backdrop of revolt" (310). At its most basic level, the conflict reflected the Israelite covenantal insistence that God alone should rule Israel, a claim that excluded all other rulers, whether Roman, Herodian, or priestly.

The Denarius

When the tribute was collected in Roman coinage, it was part and parcel of Roman political propaganda. The denarius was the stable and durable coin of Tiberius's reign, and wherever Roman power subjugated provincial peoples, the denarius was certain to follow (Hart: 248; Stauffer: 122–28). The obverse of the denarius contained a profile of Tiberius's head "adorned with the laurel wreath, the sign of divinity" (Stauffer: 124) and was inscribed with the epigram (abbreviations written in full), *Tiberius Caesar Divi Augusti Filius Augustus,* a clear claim for the divinity of both Augustus and his divine son Tiberius. The reverse depicted the emperor's mother, Livia, "sitting on the throne of the gods, in her right hand the Olympian scepter, in her left hand the olive branch to symbolize her incarnation as the heavenly *Pax,* the divine counterpart to the *Pax Romana."* It was inscribed with the phrase, *pontifex maximus,* or high priest (Stauffer: 125). The enduring presence of the denarius and its ubiquity throughout the empire made it a familiar symbol of Caesar's presence and power. It was no ordinary Roman coin. The Roman denarius was a piece of political propaganda that staked Rome's claim to rule the cosmos. It legitimated Tiberius by relating him to Augustus and asserted that the "peace of Rome" was mediated by the gods through their high priest who was a member of the ruling family. The coin reinforced the ideological basis of Roman domination.

Against this background Jesus' demand for a denarius makes sense. To deflect his opponents' momentum and to defuse their question, Jesus combines a counterquestion with a demand to find a denarius. In doing so, he takes the initiative from his interlocutors and determines the terms of the encounter. This is why the coin is so crucial. Numerous commentators have recognized the centrality of the coin but few have pursued the implications of their observations (see Belo: 187; Bruce: 259–61; Finney: 631–32; Myers: 311; Stauffer: 121–28; see also Kennard: 73–102). Finney is correct when he observes that the request for the coin "interrupts the dialogue and redirects its flow" (631). By calling attention to the coin, Jesus seems to refocus the controversy away from the Torah. He does not intend to debate Torah because he knows his opponents' interest in "the way of God" is a ruse. Better to establish other ground. Besides, if he argues Torah then he is on the grounds of his opponents who represent the interests of the great tradition. It would be better to find some other ground, more compatible with the little tradition, on which to stand.

The denarius also distinguishes Jesus from his adversaries. By the way they have formulated their question they have implied that they are actually on Jesus's side: "Should we pay [tribute] or should we not?" By asking for a denarius Jesus reveals that he does not have the coin, but his opponents are able to scurry about to find one. Whether they have a denarius among themselves or have to search for one is unclear. By procuring the denarius, the Pharisees and Herodians have separated themselves from Jesus. They have access to a denarius; Jesus does not. As Belo noted, the coin marks "the uncleanness inflicted on the country by the occupying power," and, as such, it mirrors the economic exploitation and political suppression of the *pax Romana* (187).

The Entrapping Question and Final Riddle

The movement escalates as soon as the Pharisees and Herodians pro-duce the denarius. Jesus asks a nasty question: "Whose image (*eikon*) and inscription (*epigraphe*) is this?" If the act of producing the coin did not shame his opponents, the question did. Everyone knew what was on the hated coin. It was a statement of blasphemy and idolatry rolled into one, and his opponents knew it. They seek the most innocuous answer possi-ble because they cannot refuse to answer the question for fear of being seen as ashamed of Rome in which case their role as collaborators could be compromised. So they have to answer the question, however embar-rassing it might be to do so and however much it puts them in a negative light, and they do so by muttering "Caesar's."

The very act of holding up the coin and playing dumb borders on the sarcastic, as Kennard noted long ago (113–20). Imagine a teacher holding up the denarius and asking innocently of the most powerful man in the Mediterranean world with the most familiar profile, "Who is this guy? And what does he say about himself here?" Playing dumb can be an effective weapon of the weak. It is also possible that this is an example of the jokes used by the weak. Humor can be a most engaging way to undermine the strong while denying any such purpose. Just kidding! Both the image and the epigram condemn the coin; it violates Deut 8:5 which forbids making any graven images of things on the earth, below the earth or in heaven. More importantly, the coin violates the first and the second commandments of the Decalogue (Exod 20:1–6). The coin is a living disavowal of the covenant found in Torah. Above all, the coin iden-tifies Jesus' enemies with the idolatrous coin. Even though he may be holding the coin that his opponents procured for him, Jesus has distanced himself from it by forcing his opponents to procure it and acknowledge what is inscribed on it. They have been skewered, but Jesus is still on the spot. He has, in a sense, already prevailed in the political debate. The

Pharisees and Herodians have discredited themselves through their association with the coin and clear knowledge of its claims. But the public challenge by the Pharisees and Herodians has set up an expectation that Jesus would address the question of tribute. The disguised hostile challenge pressed by the Pharisees and Herodians has evolved into an expectation that Jesus will use the little tradition to defuse the claims of the great tradition.

Jesus responds to the challenge with an aphoristic riddle. "Pay back to Caesar what is Caesar's and to God what is God's." Until more recent times, the majority opinion has been that Jesus counseled paying tribute. Bruce compares Jesus's "counsel on non-resistance to Rome" with Jeremiah's "counsel of submission to Babylon" (Bruce: 260). As Jeremiah advised Judah not to resist the Babylonian Empire, Jesus counsels cooperation with Rome by paying tribute. The reason lies with the coin itself, "a coin which by its very form and appearance contravenes [God's] law and cannot be regarded as [God's]." Throughout his discussion, Bruce assumes that Jesus would be more aligned with the long standing tradition of the prophets rather than the newly emerging "fourth philosophy" which considered any payment of tribute a compromise with Israel's theocratic ideal, namely, its insistence that God alone was Israel's true sovereign, and no human ruler could take God's place. He does not seem to think there is another position. Stauffer, who agrees with this basic conclusion, proceeds to parallel the two halves of the saying. Just as Jesus counseled paying tribute to Caesar, he supported paying the temple tax as well. This is what belongs to God (Stauffer: 129–34). In a variation on this theme, Kennard believes that Jesus limited his advice to those who originally asked the question, "the upper-class quislings" and aristocrats who collaborated with Rome and benefitted from their collusion (113–19). Since they possessed the denarii, Jesus advised them to repay Caesar whose policies had brought them so much wealth. All of this is in keeping with rabbinic thought and the prophetic tradition, according to Abrahams (62–65), who is convinced that rabbinic teaching counseled support for foreign monarchs unless they forced the Jewish community to compromise on matters of Torah.

But the issue may not be so easily resolved, since the Roman denarius did involve a Torah issue and, therefore, a political one. More to the point, Jesus' aphorism implies a conflict. Tannehill entertains the notion that the statement of Jesus is in the form of an antithetical aphorism, but he eventually changes his mind in the light of his conviction that Jesus was staking out a political "middle position" according to which it is permissible to pay tribute but even more important to contemplate the things that are owed to God (Tannehill: 173–76). In short, he thinks that Jesus answered the question while minimizing its importance by introducing the more momentous issue of the debts owed to God. The difficulty with Tannehill's position is that it seems to be governed by his prior conviction that Jesus was a centrist politician and, in light of that view, he seems to abandon his careful analysis of the antithetical nature of Jesus' aphorism. Having made a convincing case, he then abandons it. Belo would reject all of the views addressed so far. They are, from his perspective, "a non-reading of the narrative, an act of ideological blindness imposed by the interests of those who make it" (Belo: 187).

Whether or not one accepts Belo's harsh judgment, there are good reasons for questioning the readings that attribute to Jesus' support for paying tribute. Taking a cue from Tannehill, Myers has argued persuasively that Jesus did utter an antithetical aphorism that set competing loyalties in sharp contrast to each other. The tribute laid a heavy burden on the peasantry who were exploited to raise the tribute and whose lands could be expropriated when it appeared that it could not be met. Since Jesus devoted so much of his public activity to the very people who would be most adversely affected by tributary demands, he would not readily accept their validity. With this conclusion, Horsley agrees (1987: 308–314). Scott has also argued that the ideological fractures in agrarian societies more or less follow class lines.

The shift of verbs from the initial challenge to Jesus' response is significant. The challenge frames the question in the following manner: "Should we give [dounai] tribute to Caesar?" The retort speaks of paying back [apodote] to Caesar what is his. Apodidonai refers to paying back a debt that is owed. As Horsley notes, the verb evokes "the imperial situation of domination and subjugation" (1987: 309). This is in keeping with what Lenski calls "the proprietary theory of the state" common to agrarian rulers who view their conquered domains as their personal estates to exploit and dispose of as they choose (Lenski: 214–19). Because they rule, they can demand from their subjects whatever they require to maintain themselves in power. Tribute is but one expression of this right. The significance of this proprietary right for the political process is great. In order to pursue their political goals, rulers of agrarian societies required enormous amounts of wealth, and they could accumulate that wealth in one of two ways: internal tribute through exploitation of a peasant base or booty accumulated through conquest. So the question of whether it was theologically correct to pay tribute struck at the very heart of the legitimacy of the Roman Empire by addressing its most essential function. The question of whether tribute was compatible with the theocratic ideals of Israel functioned as a thinly disguised effort to reinforce the public transcript, promoted by Rome and reinforced by collaborating Israelite ruling elites, on the right of Rome to occupy Judea and Galilee.

For this reason, Horsley is convinced that Jesus escalated the issue from the question of tribute to the question of lordship where the conflict is even more sharply drawn. What "things" do not belong to God? Kennard has rightly seen that all things belong to God, the land, the earth and the fullness thereof, the heavens and the riches of the earth (123–25). What then can belong to Caesar? One thing only. The coin which he minted in his image and likeness. That can be given back to Caesar because it came from Caesar. Indeed, it must be given back because it is blasphemous and idolatrous; therefore, it symbolizes "the uncleanness inflicted on the country by the occupying power; what Jesus is rejecting is the occupation" (Belo: 187).

But that is exactly what cannot be said openly in the form of a public transcript. The Pharisees and Herodians have attempted to force Jesus to disclose and declare the hidden transcript of resistance to tribute as a form of resisting Roman rule. Jesus responds with an aphorism that functions like a riddle. It is his version of that third kind of speech, a disguised, ambiguous and coded way of maintaining the hidden transcript of resistance while leaving a public transcript that is in no way actionable. Jesus seems to be saying: "return the coins to Caesar. Caesar imposed the coins on the land; pay him back in the same coinage." But this is not a call to pay tribute as a recognition of Rome's right to rule. Tannehill's instinct was right. It is an antithetical aphorism but it is uttered in a way that raises as many questions as it answers.

Jesus has been forced to play a role in a political drama whose purpose was to reinforce Rome's right to take tribute. Impressed into the role of an actor in this type of political street theatre, Jesus seemingly has to choose between deference to Rome and its prerogatives, which would alienate him from his base of support among the peasantry, or denial of tribute, which would subject him to immediate arrest and execution. Somehow, Jesus manages to balance seeming deference to the powers that be with a coded message of resistance. He dissembles in order to avoid entrapment, and the history of the interpretation of this passage bears out the success of his efforts.

Jesus's adversaries were supposedly "astonished" at his answer because they understood what he was doing. His dissembling left them powerless to arrest him while permitting him to speak the coded hidden transcript to those who had "ears to hear." Make no mistake about it. The peasants and common people of the land who heard Jesus' aphorism knew exactly what he was saying. His coded message was an encouragement to resist. Yet his statement, as it was heard on the public stage, was in no way actionable . On the one hand, Jesus publicly revealed the hidden transcript by declaring that the people of the land did not owe Rome a thing. Thus, Jesus' response offered both an inducement to resistance and the encouragement to resist by using the full arsenal of the weapons of the weak. On the other hand, Jesus never answered the question posed by his opponents: "Is it lawful to pay tribute to Caesar?" Why? Because he recognized that they were acting out of their role in the imperial order, not as Israelites seeking to abide by the Decalogue. The Pharisees who posed the question already knew the answer. It was a violation of Israel's heritage and covenant to pay tribute to Rome but their place in the impe-rial scheme of things prohibited them from telling the truth. This put Jesus in the dangerous position of witnessing to that truth, but in a dis-guised and coded fashion.

It could easily be argued that nothing changed as the result of Jesus's deception. The triumph was a pyrrhic victory that changed nothing. True, peasants still had to pay tribute, but now they could pay their denarius poll tax or *tributum capitis* not as an act of acquiescence but as an act of resistance, even defiance. They were returning the denarius to the blasphemer who had minted it without acknowledging Rome's claim to rule either their bodies or their land. Jesus' hidden transcript of resistance reinterpreted their actions while maintaining the façade of conformity to the colonizer's demands. In societies where peasants have so little control over so much of what happens in their lives, this little tradition reading of the payment of tribute offered a source of encouragement and resolve. Now the payment of the denarius was not a test of Rome's right to rule but removing blasphemous coins from the land.

CONCLUSION

This essay has argued that the perspectives found in the work of James C. Scott can offer new insights into familiar texts while providing a glimpse into the activities of the historical Jesus. When Jesus reclined at table with toll collectors and sinners (Mark 2:15–17 and parallels), he may have been making a theological statement about the inclusive character of the covenant God who was reconstituting the people of Israel, but the occasion can also be seen as an act of protest and profanation. It could equally well be that Jesus and his table companions were acting out a prophetic critique of the great tradition based on a purity reading of the Torah while providing a little-tradition version of the holy meal. In this ritual of reversal, the hospitality of the reign of God is offered to sinners, toll collectors and other outcasts. In similar fashion, Jesus' debate over the payment of tribute to Rome (Mark 12:13–17 and parallels) can be seen as a political debate in which Jesus is forced to play a role in a form of polit-ical theater controlled by the elites and their retainers. Trapped into making a statement about the payment of tribute, Jesus uses a coded, ambiguous and elusive form of speech that communicates in the hidden transcript of resistance while appearing to show appropriate deference to Rome and its quislings.

In each case, Scott has shown how important it is to understand the social dynamics and cultural contexts in which speech occurs, especially when we are trying to understand the situation of peasants, artisans and other nonelites. This means that many texts cannot simply be taken at face value. It is important to understand the political situation in which people speak and act, and this includes the historical Jesus. Scott has contributed to our understanding of both the public and hidden dimensions of Gospel texts by attending to the public and hidden transcripts contained in them. He has also reminded us of the strength and importance of the little tradition that appears in so many forms, even in great tradition texts. After reading Scott's work, reading the Gospels will never be the same.

The Politics of Disguise and Public Declaration of the Hidden Transcript: Broadening Our Approach to the Historical Jesus with Scott's "Arts of Resistance" Theory

Richard A. Horsley

It is difficult to imagine that American historians would construct "the life" of "the historical Abraham Lincoln" or "the historical Martin Luther King" by focusing on their sayings removed from the contexts of their speeches. Indeed, in approaching a figure such as Lincoln or King, historians consider far more than their speeches. They rather analyze and bring together several interrelated facets of (1) their subjects' relations with the particular historical crisis in which they operated and its historical roots, (2) the cultural ideals and traditions out of which they operated, (3) the particular offices they held or roles they played, (4) the ways they interacted with and affected their contemporaries, particularly their immediate associates and followers, and (5) the impact and historical significance of their actions (see further Horsley 2003: ch. 3). Critical historians' approach to a figure of historical significance is usually relational and contextual.

The purposeful isolation of Jesus sayings from their literary contexts (in order to ascertain their "original form" and "authenticity") so basic to the standard approach to the historical Jesus has become severely limiting to a historical understanding in at least three interrelated ways. First, the isolation of Jesus' sayings from their literary contexts blocks access to Jesus' historical impact and the historical significance of his speech and action. The only sources for the latter are the texts derived from communities of Jesus' followers, mainly the Gospels (non-canonical as well as canonical). Second, a separate saying has no meaning in itself, since meaning depends on context (Halliday). But the only sources which can guide us toward the ancient historical meaning-context of those sayings are the Gospels. Third, no one communicates in isolated sayings, which are not intelligible units of communication. Isolated individual Jesus sayings are merely like artifacts displayed in museum cases. Jesus emerged as a catalyst or leader of a significant historical movement by interacting and communicating effectively with other people who became motivated into action in the problematic historical circumstances of their lives. Jesus and his followers, moreover, were rooted in and acted out of the Israelite cultural tradition, perhaps even by adapting certain "scripts" deeply ingrained in those cultural traditions (Horsley 2001: ch. 10).

For a defensible historical inquiry, therefore, we must not dispense with but work from the only sources that provide indications from close to the historical situation of the significance and meaning-context of Jesus' speech and action. It would seem most appropriate to work from Gospel documents such as the Gospel of Mark as a complete story and the whole series of Jesus' speeches in Q (which is not a collection of sayings but a sequence of discourses; see Horsley 2001; Horsley and Draper). At the very least we must work from the infrastructural components of Mark and Q, such as the parallel chains of miracles in Mark and John or the parallel discourses in Mark and Q, which also provide indications of meaning-context. It so happens that Mark's story and the Q series of Jesus' speeches and their intermediate length components, also apparently constituted the basic units of communication about Jesus. Those same fundamental units of communication that also provide our only ancient indicators of meaning-context and historical significance also display a figure fully engaged in political-religious conflict. Since individual sayings are meaningless outside of a meaning-context, the only viable historical approach appears to be "backing up," as it were, to the earliest Gospel sources. We can first discern their respective representations of Jesus-in-context in the earliest Gospel sources (or Jesus-in-relationship-with...) and then "triangulate" back to the leader-in-movement-in-context.

Many previous constructions of the historical Jesus have concluded that since Jesus' "authentic" sayings, as isolated from literary contexts, do not indicate that he was engaged in any direct, active revolt against the rulers, he was therefore relatively innocuous politically, quiescent and perhaps even an advocate of nonresistance. If, instead of focusing on isolated Jesus-sayings, we attend to the literary forms that constituted the means of communication, such as Q speeches and Mark's narrative, which portray Jesus engaged in political conflict, we are forced to deal with the concrete historical context, which was also rife with political-religious conflict. For an adequate historical approach, we must attend not only to Jesus' context in a movement of followers but also to the cultural tradition in which they are embedded, as well as the historical conditions of and for his work and the movement he catalyzed (Horsley 1999; 2001; Horsley and Draper).

The work of James C. Scott, particularly *Domination and the Arts of Resistance* (1990), can help us move toward a more adequate approach to the historical Jesus in many ways. Principal among them, Scott's work can help us contextualize Jesus' speech and action in historical social-political relations and can help us better understand how the movement(s) that developed indicate his historical significance. Scott opens for fruitful investigation the usually unrecognized emotional-cultural dimension of peoples' subordination to power that mediates between political-economic conditions and peoples' consciousness.

Jesus scholars generally have reached an impasse on Jesus and politics, partly because, reflecting the views of their own culture, they view politics as separate from religion, and partly because they understand politics in the relatively narrow terms of public affairs on the public stage. If Jesus had engaged in political activity, it would have to have been in the form of revolt. Since Gospel sources give little or no indication of Jesus as leading or advocating a revolt, then he must have been engaged in religious activity, with little or no implications for political-economic power relations.

Scott's work can help us move past this impasse by discerning an ordinarily unrecognized area of political activity and forms of popular resistance to power present in many historical circumstances. In Scott's terms, Jesus operated in this area between quiescence and revolt, (1) by cultivating the "hidden transcript" of Galilean and other villagers, (2) by spearheading peasant politics of anonymity and disguise, and (3) by bold declaration of the "hidden transcript" in the face of power—that is by exercising three of the four types of the politics that Scott suggests are available to subjected people (18–19).

JESUS' TEACHINGS AS A "HIDDEN TRANSCRIPT"
OF POPULAR INDIGNATION AND DIGNITY

As discussed in the introduction above, Scott (1990) devises the concept of "hidden transcript" for the "discourse of dignity" developed by subordinated peoples in sequestered sites off the public stage to counter the regular indignities of domination. The public actions and behavior of slaves, serfs, and peasants are coerced by the forces of domination arrayed against them. Evidence from a wide variety of historical situations, however, indicates that domination and exploitation generate a set of counter-values. Regular experience of degradation and insult generates a "hidden transcript" of indignation among groups of slaves or peasants determined to preserve their own dignity, resist the worst effects of domination, and insist on justice (114). Beside and behind the many hidden and disguised forms of resistance stands a popular ideology that comprises an alternative to the values and view articulated in the official public transcript controlled by the dominant. "In as much as the major historical forms of domination have presented themselves in the form of a metaphysics, a religion, a worldview, they have provoked the development of more or less equally elaborate ideologies that justify inequality, bondage, monarchy, caste, and so on. . . . Resistance to ideological domination requires a counter-ideology—a negation—that will effectively provide a general normative form to the host of resistant practices invented in self-defense by any subordinate group" (118).

Scott's analysis highlights several interrelated features of the "hidden transcript." It is cultivated beyond the effective reach of the eyes and ears of power in sequestered sites such as slave-barracks, ale houses, and village communities. As resentment and anger are articulated in language, they acquire disciplined forms, indeed can even acquire relatively "cooked" articulation in sophisticated and stable cultural forms. Insofar as humiliation and fantasies of justice are always experienced within a cultural tradition and social framework, a discourse of dignity that becomes "the property of a whole category of subordinates" must develop and resonate with that cultural tradition as it responds to developing dynamics of power (119). And, "like folk culture, the hidden transcript has no reality as pure thought," but continues effectively as it is regularly articulated, disseminated, and enacted in the secure off-stage sites (119).

When examined with fresh eyes, Jesus' teaching exhibits all of the features of what Scott discusses as a "hidden transcript." Not only do the earliest Gospel sources Mark and Q portray Jesus as delivering most of his teaching as a hidden transcript, but the Gospel texts themselves can only be understood as hidden transcripts, albeit very "well-cooked" ones. Although in later centuries Mark became part of the official scripture of the established church, hence part of the official transcript, in its origins the Gospel derived from and was addressed to communities that were "off-stage." Far from being public document addressed (also) to the high priests, Pharisees, Herodians, and Romans, Mark and Q were produced by and performed in small communities of popular movements meeting apparently in houses and villages.

To start with, as represented in Mark and Q, Jesus delivers his teaching in sequestered sites. His teaching assumes relatively elaborate and sophisticated cultural forms. The substance of his teaching combines sharp declarations of God's judgment against the forms and practices of domination and hopeful declarations of the sufficiency and justice possible under the direct rule of God. His speech resonates vibrantly with Israelite popular tradition (Horsley and Draper: ch. 5). And, far from being "pure thought" or "theology," Jesus' teaching displays features of regular performance in community settings, even in some cases of "performative speech."

When Jesus scholars purposely isolate the sayings of Jesus from their literary contexts in the Gospels, they wind up with no social location and no historical meaning context for the communication that was presumably happening in Jesus' speech. But those literary contexts in the Gospels provide the only possible indications from close to the historical context of Jesus of the communication and meaning context needed to investigate Jesus' speech. If we proceed rather by beginning with the literary contexts, they give indications aplenty of the social location and historical circumstances of Jesus' speech (Horsley and Draper; Horsley 2001). The Gospel of Mark, by consensus the earliest Gospel, portrays Jesus and his disciples as teaching and healing in village communities, particularly in the synagogues, which were local village assemblies, not religious buildings. Once we inquire into the basic form of society in Galilee and the surrounding rural areas where Jesus operated, Mark's historical verisimilitude is obvious, for the fundamental societal form was the village community (Horsley 1995). The only episodes in Mark that lack this historical verisimilitude are the disputes with the Pharisees (mainly in 2:1–3:5), for rulers of agrarian societies do not generally delegate their retainers to maintain such close surveillance on village affairs. The non-Markan Jesus-speeches that can be identified through the parallel speech material in the Gospels of Matthew and Luke, moreover, are clearly addressed to agrarian people who are poor, hungry, and heavily in debt, i.e., peasants living in village communities. The context of Jesus' teaching is consistently the local village community. And that is precisely where he sends his envoys to heal and teach, in the parallel "mission" speeches in Mark 6:6–13 and Q/Luke 9:57–10:16.

Correspondingly the substance of Jesus' teaching fits what Scott calls a "discourse of dignity," the "hidden transcript" that is cultivated precisely in "sequestered sites" as the village communities where Jesus taught. The elaborate and sophisticated forms of a well-"cooked" discourse of dignity combining judgment and justice, and resonating with the forms and contents of Israelite popular tradition, can be discerned in any number of Jesus' speeches and debates.

It is now increasingly being recognized that the speeches of Jesus paralleled in Matthew and Luke took the form not of a collection of separate sayings (like the Gospel of Thomas) but of a sequence of speeches on various issues of concern to communities of a Jesus movement (Kloppenborg; Robinson et al.: introduction; Horsley 1991; Horsley and Draper: ch. 4). Some of these speeches focus only on encouragement of the people, such as assurance that if they focus single-mindedly on pursuit of the kingdom of God subsistence food and shelter will somehow materialize (Q/Luke 12:22–31). Many of them, however, combine blunt statements of God's judgment against the wealthy, unjust, and arrogant rulers with statements of deliverance and justice for the people. God's prophet is at hand with baptism of both Spirit (renewal of social life) and fire (judgment; Q/Luke 3:7–9, 16–17). Indeed Jesus is that prophet, who brings personal and social healings with the good news for the poor, set over against those who wear "soft raiment" in their luxurious palaces, in a contested struggle entailed in the advent of God's kingdom (Q/Luke 7:18–35). The rhetoric of divine judgment heats up in speeches such as the prophetic woes that Jesus declares against the Pharisaic retainers of the Jerusalem rulers for their scribal practices that exacerbate the exploitation and suffering of the people through tithing and other mechanisms. That Jesus is articulating long-standing grievances and anger at the rulers and their retainers is vividly articulated in the next to last "woe" and declaration of sentence: because earlier generations of Jerusalem rulers had consistently killed the prophets God sent to pronounce judgment, "the blood of all the prophets, shed from the foundation of the world, will be required of this generation!" (Q/Luke 11:47–51). Similarly, God, like a mother hen solicitous for the welfare of the people, is about to destroy the Jerusalem ruling house because of its violence against the prophets sent to warn them, and while Israel is finally gathered together in the feast of the kingdom, those who presumed on their illustrious ancestry will be weeping and gnashing their teeth in outer darkness! (Q/Luke 13:28–29, 34–35).

These prophetic declarations of fulfillment (Q 7:18–35) and judgment (Q 11:47–51; 13:28–29, 34–35) not only perpetuate and resonate with the strong Israelite tradition of prophecy, but they also assume distinctive prophetic forms familiar from that cultural tradition. Beyond the earlier Israelite prophets known from the canon of the Hebrew Bible, sources are scarce in the extreme. Yet the fragmentary sources for the oracular prophets John the Baptist and Jesus son of Hananiah, as well as for the prophetic leaders of popular movements such as Theudas and the Egyptian Jewish prophet, indicate that prophetic figures were still periodically emerging from and renewing the "hidden transcript" of the Galilean and Judean peasantry (Horsley 1985, 1986). The appearance of other such prophetic figures contemporary with Jesus of Nazareth lends further credence to our discernment that the latter was rooted in and creatively generating a discourse of dignity in Galilean villages.

Most striking of all the Jesus-speeches in Q in terms of its creative adaptation of traditional Israelite cultural forms and its resonance with Israelite tradition is the renewal of the Mosaic covenant that Jesus enacts in performative speech in Q/Luke 6:20–49. Because of the standard focus on individual sayings, interpreters have not often considered this speech as a whole, much less recognized that it follows and adapts the standard formal components of the Mosaic covenant at the core of Israelite cultural tradition. The parallel adaptation of the same covenantal components and overall form in the *Community Rule* (and the *Damascus Rule,* to a degree) from the scribal-priestly community at Qumran now confirms that covenant forms and covenant renewal were still alive in late Second Temple Palestine (Baltzer; Horsley and Draper: ch. 9). As in the covenant-renewal ceremony at Qumran (1QS 1–2), so also Jesus transforms the blessings and woes that originally functioned as sanctions on covenant keeping (but had come to be instruments of self-blame for the people's historical suffering) into new declarations of deliverance, only now in the present or imminent future rather than the distant past. The effect of the declaration, "Blessed are you poor, for yours is the kingdom of God ... [but] woe to the rich, for they have received their consolation!" (Q 6:20–26), was to restate the dignity of the peasantry, over against the injustices emanating from the wealthy and powerful. The ensuing restatement of covenantal principles, deeply rooted in traditional Israelite covenantal teaching, then provided guidelines for the restoration of covenantal justice in the village community. Bolstered by the opening declaration that God was again responding to their distressed conditions with new deliverance, the people could now regain the spirit of mutual sharing, cooperation, and solidarity traditional in their covenantal "moral economy," as they cancelled each others' debts, again lent freely, and broke the cycle of petty local quarreling and disputes (Q 6:27–38; Horsley 1987: 255–75; cf. Scott 1976).

Similarly in the Gospel of Mark, Jesus' teaching, often in dispute with the Pharisees or in dialogue with the disciples, comes alive as a discourse of dignity that resonates deeply with Israelite popular tradition, over against the behavior of the wealthy elite and the exploitative practices of the ruling institutions. In Mark 2:2–12, in the context of a healing, Jesus declares that "humanity" has the authority to forgive sins, over against the sacrificial apparatus of the Jerusalem temple, for which the people paid dearly. In Mark 7:1–13, set up by a mocking dispute with the Pharisees and their temple-based purity codes cultivated by Pharisees and other elite scribal circles, Jesus declares that the demand for peasant support of the temple apparatus (Korban = "dedicated" produce/property") was a violation of the basic (Mosaic) "commandment of God" to "honor your father and mother." That is, against the attempts of the temple-state's retainers to secure support for the temple, Jesus insists that the people reject the efforts of the Pharisees and retain locally, in their own households, the scarce economic resources they needed to support their families.

In Mark 10:16–31, using as an example a wealthy man who claims to be keeping the Mosaic covenantal principles while all the time gaining his wealth by defrauding the peasants (presumably through [forbidden] interest on loans), and declaring it impossible that the rich could get into the kingdom of God, Jesus insists upon the Mosaic covenantal "moral economy" as the principles that should guide local social-economic life. And in the next dialogue with the disciples (10:32–45) he similarly insists upon egalitarian political leadership, in pointed contrast with "the [imperial] nations" who have kings and emperors who lord it over them. Throughout these dialogues Jesus sets the restoration of the people's dignity and independent social-political-economic life over against the practices and institutions of the exploitative wealthy rulers. And in every case he is drawing upon and creatively adapting the Israelite cultural tradition, especially the Mosaic covenant that articulated what Scott elsewhere calls the "moral economy" under the exclusive rule of God.

Two decades ago, Werner Kelber, in a telling critique of the print-culture assumptions of Bultmann's form critical approach, pointed out that the Jesus-teachings that survived were what resonated with the people (Kelber 1983). In his reflections on the "hidden transcript" Scott offers a way of appreciating the concrete situation and relations in which this happened and of explaining why certain Jesus teachings survived: because they expressed collective indignation and restored people's dignity. In particular, Scott brings into focus the emotional energy that lies behind and finds expression in Jesus' teachings, which both resonate with long-standing Israelite traditions of resistance to oppressive power and bring creative new developments of traditional Israelite prophetic forms and principles. Adapting Scott's reflections on the "hidden transcript" to the teachings of Jesus enables us to discern a whole area of political resistance in between quiescence and revolt, and to discern that many much-discussed teachings of Jesus can be seen as aspects of resistance to domination.

The teachings of Jesus, however, form only part of the activities in which Jesus engaged and of the effects and significance of his activities that resulted in ongoing Jesus-movements. Scott's reflections on other forms of popular political resistance also illuminate these other aspects of Jesus' overall conflict with the rulers, as portrayed in the Gospel sources.

THE POLITICS OF DISGUISE AND ANONYMITY:
JESUS' CAMPAIGN IN GALILEE AND BEYOND

On occasion groups of subordinated people move their continuing struggle against domination beyond the confines of their specially sequestered sites into "a politics of disguise and anonymity that takes place in public view but is designed to have double meaning or to shield the identity of the actors" (1990: 18–19). One of the principal modes of the politics of anonymity is rumor. Rumor travels in a process of elaboration in which it is adapted to the hopes and fears of those who hear it and retell it (145). Scott provides several illustrations that are suggestive for the Gospel of Mark and, through Mark, for Jesus-in-movement. Prior to the French Revolution, when the king finally summoned the Estates General for the first time since 1614, the peasants eagerly anticipated their imminent liberation. According to contemporary sources, they went home from assemblies called to elect representatives and to draw up their concerns believing that they were now at last free from tithes and feudal dues and that the king wished everyone to be equal, with no more bishops and lords (145–46). "In the [Caribbean] slave rebellions in the late eighteenth and early nineteenth centuries, there was a fairly consistent belief that the king or British officials had set slaves free and that the whites were keeping the word from them" (147). The many parallels from Russian serfs, Indian untouchables, and cargo cults among peoples overwhelmed by Western conquest, says Scott, "are too striking to ignore." Believing that God or the authorities had granted their dreams "vulnerable groups express their hidden aspirations in public in a way that both enables them to avoid individual responsibility and aligns them with some higher power" (148).

Scott's list of parallels can be expanded from cases of peasant movements in first century Palestine. The first that immediately come to mind are the prophetic movements led by Theudas and "the Egyptian" in midcentury Judea, both of which involved large numbers of Judean peasants in a remarkable collective anticipation of divine deliverance, judging from the hostile accounts of Josephus. In a popular movement significant enough that it was remembered in tandem with the "revolt" against the tribute led by Judas of Galilee (Acts 5:36), Theudas "persuaded most of the common people to take their possessions and follow him to the Jordan River, saying that at his command the river would be divided." (Ant 20.97–98). "The Egyptian false-prophet" led "the mass of the common people [about thirty-thousand] to go with him to the Mount of Olives, just opposite the city, from where, at his command, the walls of Jerusalem would fall down [and the Roman garrison overpowered]" (Ant. 20.169–171, cf. War 2.261–163). That the Roman governors sent out "a cavalry unit" and/or "heavily armed Roman troops" to slaughter hundreds of these evidently nonviolent seekers of deliverance may be another indication of their numbers, that is, an indication of how far the rumor of imminent deliverance had spread among the Judean peasantry. These collective anticipations of God's new acts of deliverance were clearly resonating with the Judean peasants' hidden transcript, the popular memory of the "little tradition" of Moses/Joshua leading the people across the (Red Sea/Jordan) water into their wilderness preparation for the entry into their land and of Joshua's leading the miraculous battle against Jericho. As Scott comments, "a powerful and suppressed desire for relief from the burdens of subordination seems not only to infuse the autonomous religious life of the oppressed but also to strongly color their interpretation of events" (147).

New Testament scholars have labeled these movements "apocalyptic" (Crossan 1991) or their leaders "sign prophets" (Barnett). The latter label says too little, while the former is much too broad and synthetic a concept. The principal sources for the broad general concept of "apocalypticism" used for late second temple Palestinian materials are the literary products of Judean scribal circles. I have cautioned elsewhere about presuming that elite scribal literature can be used to project popular thinking and action (Horsley 1987:140–43). Compared with the synthetic modern scholarly construct of "apocalyptic," Scott's discussion of hidden transcript gets us more deeply into the motives and the dynamics of dignity and indignity, of oppression and subordination and resentment. The popular prophetic movements are not the "apocalypticism" expressed in literary apocalypses, but peasant yearning or desire touched off by a symbol or reports of an event. "A powerful and suppressed desire for relief from the burdens of subordination seems not only to infuse the autonomous religious life of the oppressed but also to strongly color their interpretation of events" (Scott: 147).

Another ancient Palestinian collective action in which rumor must have shaped events according to popular interests was the massive strike by Galilean peasants over the emperor Gaius's plan to place an image of himself in the Jerusalem temple. There is no reason to believe that Galileans peasants would have had any reason to defend the sanctity of the temple itself, one of the principal political-economic-religious institutions of domination to which they were partially subjected. But the rumor of the impending invasion of their territory by a huge Roman military expedition, the effects of which they knew only too well from previous Roman military slaughter, enslavement, and devastation, apparently motivated them to take collective action. Saying "we will die sooner than violate our laws" (according to Josephus), they refused to plant their crops. Herodian officials and the Roman Legate of Syria knew exactly what the result would be: "there would be a harvest of banditry, because the requirement of the tribute could not be met" (*Ant.* 18.261–274).

The occurrence of several other Judean and Galilean popular movements in which the spread of rumor of anticipated divine deliverance (or impending invasion) makes all the more intriguing the Gospel of Mark's portrayal of the rapidly widening popular response to Jesus' preaching of the kingdom of God and manifestation of God's enabling power in exorcisms and healings. Jesus came to Galilee, proclaiming "the time is fulfilled, and the kingdom of God is at hand." He summoned disciples to assist in his mission, taught and performed exorcisms in village assemblies and healings in assemblies and houses. His fame quickly spread throughout Galilee, crowds of increasing size gathered around and soon expanded into "a great multitude" and "great numbers" from Judea, Idumea to the south, and even from the region around Tyre and Sidon to the north (Mark 1:27–28, 32–33, 37–39, 45; 2:1–2, 13; 3:7–10, 20; 5:20–21, 24; 6:33, 54–56). People came bearing their friends and relatives for healing. A woman who had been hemorrhaging for "twelve" years touched him from behind and was instantly healed, not by his word or action, but through her own trust (faith) that power was working through him. In several motifs in the story, such as the appointment of the Twelve as representative figures and miraculous actions of a new Moses (sea-crossings and wilderness feedings) and new Elijah (healings), Mark indicates that Jesus was spearheading a renewal of Israel based in its village communities, a renewal that expanded into nearby regions to include other villagers as well.

Mark's portrayal of Jesus' mission in Galilee and beyond thus resembles other peasant movements that spread through rumor, movements where subordinated peoples' long-suppressed yearning for liberation that had been cultivated in their hidden transcript suddenly, in response to a rumor or a prophet's promise and miraculous actions, bursts forth in rapidly spreading collective anticipation that the hour of deliverance is at hand. Earlier generations of critical New Testament scholars, reacting against the naïve assumption that the Gospel of Mark constituted a reliable historical record from which to reconstruct the history of Jesus' ministry—and finally assimilating the historical skepticism of Enlightenment reason—rejected Mark's narrative as historically worthless "framing" and much of the contents of Mark as historically worthless "miracle" stories and "mythology." Indeed, the Markan framing, along with miraculous stories, was seen as an obstacle to historical reconstruction. Critical scholars focused mainly on the sayings of Jesus, which ostensibly offered greater possibilities for establishing at least some authentic fragments of Jesus' teaching. For the last century liberal scholarship has presented Jesus as primarily a teacher, lately even stripped of prophetic judgment and reduced to a sage or a Cynic-like philosopher. It is hardly considered that Jesus himself was connected with a movement — that was what the disciples founded in response to the resurrection faith. While still dismissing the value of particular healing or exorcism stories as historical information, scholars have come to believe that Jesus did perform healings and perhaps even exorcisms. But that is usually

consigned to a separate, less important chapter in Jesus-books, which
focus on his sayings. It has been almost impossible to discern how Jesus'
healings and exorcisms fit together with his teaching about the kingdom
of God—except in a very general way as apparent manifestations of the
kingdom that he preached as imminent.

Scott's presentation of the politics of disguise and anonymity as one
of the modes of popular resistance to domination offers comparative
material as a helpful model on which we can reimagine, as components
of a larger picture, the Jesus-materials that atomizing analysis of Jesus as
teacher has rejected. For example, parallel to belief among Caribbean
slaves that the distant British king had set them free, Jesus' preaching that
the kingdom of God was at hand and its manifestation in exorcisms
touched off a movement of people who believed that God was liberating
them from domination by the Romans and their client rulers (Scott 1990:
148). Perhaps Mark "knows what he is talking about" after all, given how
similar his narrative is to many other historical cases of rapidly spreading
popular movements that Scott cites as "too striking to ignore." Mark's
narrative turns out to be remarkable for its historical verisimilitude.

This seems to open the possibility of taking Mark's narrative seriously as an historical source, but in a way very different from its naïve
nineteenth century use as a direct historical record for a sequence of
events. The sequence of episodes in Mark has been narratively plotted by
Mark's composer(s)/performer(s). But the artfully composed narrative
represents the way such a prophetic figure's message of God's imminent
action and his manifestation of that action in healings and exorcisms
would have resonated with the people on the basis of their shared hidden
discourse of indignation and yearning.

We cannot understand Jesus except in the context of the movement of
the people who responded to and interacted with him. And Scott's exposition of the hidden transcript enables us to appreciate how that
interaction worked on the basis of Israelite popular tradition in the context of Galilean villages. The hidden transcript, however, does not always
remain confined to the secure sites in which it is regularly cultivated.
Subjected peasants' indignation overflows the borders of their villages in
other forms of popular politics, usually in various forms of disguise and
anonymity. Mark presents a story of considerable historical verisimilitude of how Jesus' preaching and healing touched off a seemingly
spontaneous movement of renewal that generated divinely inspired popular power opposed to and threatening to the dominant rulers and their
representatives. Mark does not provide evidence for any particular healing or exorcism or speech before a Galilean village assembly—nor does it
matter that we establish historical verification for any particular incident
and the way it actually happened. But Mark does provide a credible

account of the relationship between Jesus' proclamation of the kingdom, his practice of healing and exorcism, and the resulting renewal of personal life and village community in Galilee. By thus creatively adapting the central scripts and patterns of popular Israelite cultural tradition, (Mark's) Jesus thus brought political expression of the hidden transcript to public expression and public view.

JESUS' BOLD DECLARATION OF THE HIDDEN TRANSCRIPT IN THE FACE OF POWER

The standard liberal approach to Jesus, focusing on atomized sayings of Jesus, grouping them into topics like artifacts in museum display cases, tends not to ask questions of historical significance and historical explanation. Martin Luther did not simply write up some theses, but nailed them to the church door—and was brought to trial where he firmly declared his stand. Martin Luther King Jr. did not simply make some memorable statements, but led marches in the face of the municipal and state police, their attack dogs, water hoses, and truncheons—and was eventually assassinated. Modern Western interpreters constructed a Jesus who was politically innocuous. He is confined largely to cultural-religious affairs. His sayings were pithy and countercultural, and the table-fellowship he shared was inclusive (Crossan 1991). Any of his declarations or actions that might seem politically challenging are effectively depoliticized, either "cleaned up" (the obstructive prophetic demonstration against the temple was only a "cleansing") or blunted (rendering unto God and Caesar reduced to church versus state). But Jesus would have had little historical impact, and no one would have remembered those sayings or continued the table-fellowship, had he not carried out some public confrontation of the rulers and ruling institutions in Jerusalem—and been executed as an insurrectionary (by crucifixion) by the Romans. This is both suggested and can be explained by Scott's exposition of the fourth variety of the popular politics of resistance, the public declaration of the hidden transcript in the face of power.

Jesus' confrontation with the rulers in Jerusalem, perhaps mainly his condemnation of the temple and high priests, as compounded by his crucifixion, appears to have been the breakthrough event that led to the sudden expansion of the movement he had inaugurated in Galilee, ensuring that he became a significant historical figure. And the expansion of that movement, in turn, did not merely remember his teachings and deeds, but perpetuated, cultivated, and consolidated his speech and program of societal renewal.

The breakthrough that consolidated his mission and energized the expansion of his movement(s) was the result of a conjunction of factors.

Because of the methodological individualism of New Testament studies and its focus on meaning abstracted from political context, it is important to learn from social-political historians the importance of structural factors. Jesus' (-with-followers') "pilgrimage" to Jerusalem juxtaposes the prophetic spokesperson and catalyst of an Israelite peasant movement from Galilee and the (lavishly rebuilt) temple and high priesthood, the ruling institutions that had taken over and ruled that distant district for a hundred years prior to the lifetime of Jesus—in Scott's terms, a spokesperson of the subjugated and the dominant ruling institution and rulers. Scott, however, insists on including key factors often ignored by social scientists as well as humanists, the emotional dynamics of domination and subjugation. The indignities imposed by domination induce in the subjugated a deep-running indignation that has not only produced a certain oppositional ideology, but an oppositional tone or mood of some intensity, the expression of which is ordinarily blocked by the (potential) coercive power of the dominant. Because that indignation desires expression, however, a spokesperson's bold defiance of the dominant can transform the collective indignation into an excitement and energy that drives events, a political breakthrough can escalate rapidly into a significant movement. Such charismatic acts, says Scott, "gain their social force by virtue of their roots in the hidden transcript of a subordinate group" (1990: 203).

"The moment when the dissent of the hidden transcript crosses the threshold to open resistance is always a politically charged occasion" (207). The occasion of the "politically charge occasion" in Jesus' case, moreover, was itself the politically (-religiously) charged occasion of Passover. We should remind ourselves that we cannot simply read a public declaration of the hidden transcript directly off of the Markan or other Gospel text. Mark, the Gospel of John, and Q must apparently be taken as hidden transcripts, although they portray forays by Jesus into public to make prophetic condemnations of the dominant. Generations of previous criticism of Gospel accounts of Jesus' face-off with the Judean and Roman rulers in Jerusalem have resulted in critical consensus on a number of related matters: that Jesus and some followers did go, at Passover time, to Jerusalem, where he carried out a demonstration and/or prophetic statement (of destruction) against the temple, was arrested, apparently by betrayal, and tried before a high-priestly court, and sentenced by Pilate and crucified by the Romans. As we know from Josephus's account of a major riot and massacre under the governor Cumanus, the celebration of liberation from foreign rulers at Passover was carried out literally under the watchful eye of Roman troops posted on the temple porticoes to intimidate the celebrants. As Scott's material suggests, however, such intimidation also effectively evoked indignation, which would have been all the more intense at such a moment of celebration of God's previous action in liberating the people from foreign rule.

The various aspects of the moment of breakthough, which were inseparable in the event, can be pulled apart only momentarily for analysis. The energy generated by the event results from "the sense of personal release, satisfaction, pride, and elation" experienced in the moment of public challenge to domination, the moment when someone speaks truth instead of submissive lies and equivocation (1990: 208). Scott suggests that there is a double release that corresponds to a double frustration involved in subordination. In addition to the release of finally resisting rather than submitting to domination, there is the release of finally being able to express the response initially choked back to avoid repressive consequences (213).

Given the methodological individualism of American New Testament studies in particular, we should take special note of Scott's point that the breakthrough act of defiance must be public in order to have any impact (1990: 214–15). The individual and collective loss of dignity of the subordinated is public loss in which they must continually kowtow to power, including in ancient Judea and Galilee the established ritualized mechanisms by which their produce is expropriated and their community and family life disintegrated, as well as the periodic predatory actions in which the Herodian and priestly aristocracy engaged. If his prophecies or demonstration against the temple are included at all in the "data base" for the historical Jesus, they are often pictured as the statements of an individual prophetic reformer or mere symbolic gestures. Yet whatever his precise actions, which took place in the public space of the city, they did have a public impact, which is why the Jerusalem rulers needed to crack down and the Roman governor needed to make an example of him. The impact of his action derived from its having been a public defiance that matched the people's public humiliation.

Besides being public, Jesus' breakthrough act of defiance took the cultural form of "a public breaking of an established ritual of public subordination" (1990: 215). As specialists on the original establishment of the "Second Temple" have more consistently explained in recent decades, the Jerusalem temple-state was from its origin the local face of the imperial order established by the Persian regime and perpetuated by the Ptolemies, Seleucids, and the Romans, as well as the institutionalized means by which the goods of the Judeans and other peoples were expropriated by the Jerusalem aristocracy (articulated in Ezra and Nehemiah). But the cultural form was that of a temple and sacred priesthood that mediated between the people and "the God who is in Jerusalem" (Ezra 1:3). By the time of Jesus, Herod had dramatically expanded and rebuilt the temple complex in grand Hellenistic style as one of the wonders of the (Roman imperial) world, augmenting its already considerable sacred aura, at least in the minds of those who performed the public rituals of order and obedience (Josephus, *War* 1.401; *Ant.* 17.162; Richardson 245–49). As we know from severe criticism of the temple and incumbent high priests even among scribal circles who were politically-economically dependent on the temple-state, opposition was strong even while compliance was forthcoming (e.g., sharp criticism of the "Wicked Priest" and the incumbent Jerusalem priesthood in several the Dead Sea Scrolls, and the protest of Herod's Roman eagle over one gate [Josephus, *War* 1.648–55; *Ant.* 17.149–67]). For Jesus to utter a prophetic condemnation of *the* super-sacred institution of (supposed) hoary antiquity and to conduct some sort of disruptive demonstration in the courtyard of the temple would have been the utmost in acts of profanation and blasphemy (Scott 1977). The witnesses at his trial in Mark's portrayal may have been false, but the charge was right on target. "The successful public breaking of a taboo imposed by the dominant ... is an extremely efficient means of encouraging a conflagration of defiance" (Scott 1990: 215). Whatever he did and said in the temple, Jesus' demonstration was far more ominous than the typical form of peasant or slave defiance such as refusing to salute or bow one's head.

Further, Jesus' public act of defiance had such evocative power because it was an irrevocable step. It was a direct, blatant challenge not only to the sacred power base of the rulers of Jerusalem but also to the Roman imperial order represented by the Golden Roman eagle that Herod the Great had erected above the principal gate and the daily sacrifices to Rome and the emperor conducted at the altar (*War* 1.648–655; 2.197, 409). There was no going back, no withdrawal again to confinement in the villages of Galilee. In such an act of defiance, "even if it is beaten back and driven underground, something irrevocable has nonetheless occurred" (1990: 215). Even when the stories of Jesus' temple demonstration and prophecies and parable against the high priests were consolidated back in the hidden transcript of the Gospel tradition (behind Mark), something irrevocable had occurred that helped motivate the expansion of the renewal of Israel over against the temple-state that Jesus had inaugurated in his program of preaching the kingdom and manifesting it in healings and exorcisms. His action in the temple was a breakthrough event.

As Scott explains, however, to more fully understand such breakthrough acts of defiance we must be able to discern how they arise from and derive their power from their relation with the hidden transcript that has long been cultivated in the secure sites of the subordinated (1990: 214). Jesus' prophecy against the temple and prophetic demonstration in the temple did not come "out of the blue." From the previous and subsequent outbursts of popular protest against the high priesthood by Galileans and Judeans mentioned by Josephus (Horsley 1987: 33–43, 90–99) and reflections of Galilean laxity in rendering dues to the temple in later rabbinic literature (*m. Ned.* 2:4; *t. Sanh.* 2:2; *y. Sanh.* 1.18d; *y. Ma'aś. Š.* 5.56b) we can deduce that a great deal of resentment against these ruling institutions festered in village communities. Galilean laxity on tithes and other dues, for example, suggests the kinds of "hidden" forms of resistance to domination that Scott documents for other peasantries. Jesus' preaching and healing in Galilean and other villages, moreover, had focused and articulated the resentment against the ruling institutions in Jerusalem. Many of the "typical" stories from Jesus traditions that made it into Mark or Q give expression to popular indignation at the temple, priesthood, and their representatives. Jesus "teaches" with power/ authority on behalf of the people in way that the scribes had never done (Mark 1:22–28). Jesus heals or "makes clean" the "leper" in a way that does not require offering to the temple (Mark 1:40–45). In his healing Jesus mediates God's forgiveness of sins in sharp contrast to the temple-based system that emphasizes sin in order to enhance motivation for recourse to its services as indispensable for salvation (2:2–12). Jesus insists that local family (and village) resources be deployed for local family subsistence in accordance with the covenantal commandment of God ("Honor father and mother") instead of being siphoned in support of the temple (*korban*), as urged by the Pharisees (7:1–13).

The cumulative impact of all these stories is to indicate that Jesus' program of the renewal of Israel in the local village communities that constituted its primary social form was pointedly over against the Jerusalem ruling institutions long before he made any move toward a confrontation in the capital city. That is, popular indignation against the temple and high priesthood was focused and articulated in the special development of the Galilean villagers' hidden transcript spearheaded by Jesus' mission. There was no occasion for a dramatic declaration of that indignation so long as he remained in Galilee. The cultivation of that indignation in the Galilean hidden transcript, however, accounts for the latent energy that is suddenly released by Jesus' bold condemnation of the temple in the very center of that sacred public stage. One might say that Jesus' confrontation in Jerusalem was already well rehearsed in his distinctive development of the hidden transcript. But rather than diminish the effect of the breakthrough, it enhanced it because it had been keenly anticipated by a movement already in the making.

A further and closely related aspect of Jesus' breakthrough is illuminated by Scott's distinction, borrowing the terms of Levi-Strauss, between relatively "raw" and relatively "cooked" declarations of defiance. As represented in the Gospel of Mark, Jesus' declaration of the hidden transcript on the public stage is not an impulsive expression of blind fury but a measured symbolic action and a formal prophetic pronouncement. "Cooked declarations are more likely to be nuanced and elaborate because they arise under circumstances in which there is a good deal of offstage freedom among subordinate groups, allowing them to share a rich and deep hidden transcript. In a sense ... [it] already has a quasi-public existence" (1990: 216). In the relatively secure sites of Galilean villages, which were historically not under regular surveillance by the Pharisees or Herodians (contrary to the picture of Mark 2–3; 7), Jesus had plenty of opportunity to voice condemnation of the temple and high priests (as suggested just above). Because Galilean and Judean and Samaritan villagers had long cultivated versions of Israelite "little tradition" (to utilize another concept that Scott utilized earlier [1977] to illuminate peasant "protest and profanation"), moreover, Jesus could draw upon the forms and themes of Israelite prophetic lore. His lament over the impending destruction and desolation of the ruling house of Jerusalem takes the traditional form of a prophetic lament, as evident in Amos 5:2–3. In Mark's account of the demonstration in the temple, not only does Jesus cite Jeremiah's famous prophecy of the (original) temple's destruction in punishment for violating the covenantal commandments (Jer 7; 26), but his action is patterned after prophetic symbolic actions (Isa 20; Jer 27–28). Israelite tradition thus provided forms of protest and condemnation that already carried ominous denotations of divine judgment. And it gave the breakthrough declaration of condemnation all the more resonance with the people, who were rooted in this prophetic tradition.

Scott's discussion of the "public declaration of the hidden transcript," finally, illuminates more precisely how the concept of charisma can be used to understand (or misused to misunderstand) Jesus-in-movement. Jesus' development of the hidden transcript constituted and prepared "the social production of charisma." Charisma has often been adduced to explain the significance of Jesus. Insofar as the concept was taken in its popular sense of an unusual quality possessed by (or divinely bestowed upon) a leader, however, it served simply to further mystify Jesus. And insofar as "charisma" is an abstract concept, without any particular context and cultural content, it does nothing to illuminate Jesus in particular, but only dissolves him into a trans-historical class of figures. Sensing the distortion and mystification in application to Melanesian cargo cults and other such resistance movements, Peter Worsley (1956) carefully explained how the concept is relational. The people who project their desires or yearnings onto a leader or his or her message in a crisis situation are just as important as the figure who speaks their mind and leads their action in that intolerable situation. Recognizing the importance of the hidden transcript as the basis on which a breakthrough of defiance takes place and empowers people to wider protest and even wider development of a movement both restores the relational dynamics at the center of the concept of charisma and the cultural specificity of charisma.

Periodically in his discussion of the hidden transcript Scott finds a telling example in the character of Mrs. Poyser, who in exasperation finally spoke her mind to Squire Donnithorne in George Eliot's novel *Adam Bede.* In speaking truth to power, "the role of heroine in this case is to a large extent scripted in advance offstage by all members of the subordinate group, and the individual who fills that role is that one who somehow—through anger, courage, a sense of responsibility, or indignation—summons the wherewithal to speak on behalf of others" (1990:222). With respect to Jesus of Nazareth in ancient Palestine, this is an understatement. Jesus was challenging not a single "squire" but the whole political-economic-religious dominant order. And Jesus' prophetic condemnation of the temple was far more "cooked," a well-planned performance more than a sudden outburst. Jesus, moreover, was adapting a well-known cultural script deeply embedded in the Israelite popular tradition in which the people were rooted. He was not only the new Moses and/or Elijah but the new Amos or Jeremiah who dared march directly into the temple courtyard and pronounce God's condemnation. The charismatic charge of those earlier prophetic breakthroughs carried over onto Jesus' action in the temple and its resonance with the people. Jesus not only "wills the general will" so that he speaks for the crowd of pilgrims in Jerusalem and other Galilean and Judean villagers. He also again, with Amos and Jeremiah, speaks out the indignation of all those earlier generations of Israelite peasants and his speech and symbolic prophetic action resonate with Israelite tradition which has compounded and given particular cultural form to the hidden transcript of his Galilean and other followers. The specific contents and dynamics of the charismatic relation between Jesus and his movement was "the shared discourse of the hidden transcript created and ripened in the nooks and crannies" of the Galilean village communities where they were free to rehearse their indignation. That is what underlies and explains the instantaneous mutuality that comes to expression in Jesus' breakthrough.

In "the highly charged atmosphere created by the open declaration" of defiance, "a subordinate group learns ... that they may now, more safely, venture open defiance" (1990: 222). The last several episodes in Mark's narrative may seem to contradict this in the case of Jesus' followers. "They were afraid!" Mark, however, has his own distinctive agenda in having the twelve all abandon Jesus, in addition to the betrayal and denial by some (Kelber 1979; Horsley 2001). It is now commonly sensed that Mark is summoning the hearers of his Gospel back to "Galilee" (where Jesus has preceded them) to continue the movement. Thereafter, in every performance of the Gospel, particularly Jesus' bold declaration of defiance, his followers were emboldened to continue the movement. Every performance of Q speeches, particularly the woes against the Pharisees and the prophetic lament over the Jerusalem ruling house, was a repeat performance of Jesus' breakthrough. Jesus' breakthough act in Jerusalem was thus the decisive event that led to the rapid expansion of his movement through Palestine and beyond, "a crystallization of public action that is astonishingly rapid" (1990: 223). *It is only when this hidden transcript is openly declared that subordinates can fully recognize the full extent to which their claims, their dreams, their anger is shared by other subordinates with whom they have not been in direct touch"* (223, italics original).

Toward the end of his discussion of "public declaration" Scott comments on the relation between the hidden transcript that develops in sequestered sites over a period of time and the public breakthroughs that ignite wider resistance, that the process "is more one of recognizing close relatives of one's hidden transcript rather than of filling essentially empty heads with novel ideas" (223). This comment brings us full circle to where we started, with the recognition that Scott's discussion of the hidden transcript enables us to move from the "revelation" model of Jesus as a religious teacher of individuals to a "relational" model of the historical Jesus as communicating with other Galileans in a crisis situation on the basis of their shared Israelite tradition—and pursuing several interrelated forms of popular political discourse that express the people's dignity as well as indignation.

James C. Scott and New Testament Studies: A Response to Allen Callahan, William Herzog, and Richard Horsley

Warren Carter

The discipline of New Testament studies has, since the enlightenment, cast its lot predominantly with things historical. The historical critical method has provided the means by which the inquiry has been conducted. It has stimulated the development of various new methods either as allies, such as form and redaction criticisms, or as critics, as with some feminist and postcolonial approaches. It has been the conversation partner with which other forms of inquiry such as New Testament theology must dialogue, and the mark by which the legitimacy of other methods and their proponents (e.g., narrative criticism and critics) have been determined. Of course, historical criticism has been unable to maintain its hegemony for various reasons, one of which has been its inability to answer all the questions it has posed for itself.

Historical inquiry, though, has not been static as the emergence of disciplines such as new historicism and ideological criticism (along with feminist and post-colonial work) that critically reframe the enterprise attests. Social science criticism in combination with various forms of historical inquiry has blossomed in recent biblical studies in part because it addresses some previously unanswerable questions, offering insights and correctives to previous scholarship that had constructed an early Christian movement largely comprising minds without bodies, ideas without social interaction, and texts without communities.

At a time, then, when New Testament scholars generally hold historical inquiry to be important but often conduct it with an array of critical approaches, what might the work of James C. Scott on the interaction between exploitative ruling elites and exploited nonelites, between forms of domination and forms of resistance, offer New Testament scholars and in particular those who investigate the historical Jesus and the Synoptic tradition?

In his introductory essay, Richard Horsley argues that Scott's attention to the power dynamics of elite and nonelite interaction in an imperial world, predicated on the interconnection of politics, religion and culture, provides a corrective to much New Testament work that often concentrates its attention on religion and texts in isolation from larger sociopolitical and cultural realities. More specifically, in both his introduction and essay on the "Politics of Disguise," Horsley attacks features of the "unhistorical quest for an apolitical Jesus": isolating sayings of Jesus from their literary contexts, interpreting sayings without reference to an exploitative imperial sociohistorical context of domination and resistance, constructing Jesus as a figure interested only in religious matters without perceiving his embeddedness in and engagement with sociopolitical contexts. Such generalizations do not apply to all historical Jesus work but there is no denying the tendencies.

Horsley and Herzog rightly value Scott's work as a means of analyzing the power dynamics of elite/nonelite interaction in the imperial world from which the New Testament originates. It is one thing to know, as "everybody knows," that Jesus and the traditions and texts about him originate when Rome's empire rules supreme. It is quite another to press this observation to understand the structures and dynamics of such a world, especially its means of establishing domination as well as the opportunities and means for resistance. It is a further step to overcome our contemporary separation of the religious from the political and press the historical inquiry to examine the interaction of Jesus and his followers with such a world. Gerhard Lenski's work on social stratification in agrarian empires has provided New Testament scholars with a very helpful framework for understanding Rome's world, as Herzog rightly notes. But Scott opens up further dimensions with his attention to the means of domination and the resistance, both open and, especially, concealed, that they provoke in societies such as the Roman imperial world in which there are massive power inequalities.

Immediately helpful is Scott's identification of three means or spheres by which and in which a small elite extends its domination and exploitation of a population (Scott 1990: 198). One sphere is the material (appropriation of grain, taxes, etc.), another comprises matters of status (acts of humiliation and assaults on dignity), and the third is ideological (justification by elites for their practices: coins, inscriptions, buildings, texts, ceremonies, personnel, speeches, etc.) Each sphere of domination does not, despite the claims of the public transcripts crafted by elites (coins, rituals, texts, etc.), create grateful and blessed submission throughout the populace. Rather, it creates both compliance and numerous forms of resistance that Scott organizes into two basic categories, "forms of public declared resistance" and "forms of disguised low profile undisclosed resistance or infra-politics." He catalogues examples of types of resistance appropriate to each arena. Public resistance to material domination may comprise boycotts or open revolt. Public responses to status domination or humiliation involve public assertions of worth and dignity in gestures, clothing, speech, or violation of symbols. Public responses to ideological domination comprise counter-ideologies that negate an elite's claims with counter visions and claims. In the second category, disguised forms of resistance to material domination may involve pilfering, foot-dragging, poaching, evasion, anonymous threats, and the like. Disguised forms of resistance to status domination comprise anger and retaliation in rituals, tales, rumor, autonomous space, and so forth. Disguised forms of resistance to ideological domination involve the development of a dissident subculture such as millennial religions, social banditry or world-upside-down imagery. Scott's discussion of individual aspects of this summary is rich, offering insight into imperial dynamics both from above and below.

The essays of Horsley, Herzog, and Callahan engage Scott's insights in relation to the historical Jesus. Horsley's approach is heuristic, ranging across Q and Mark. His central task is to expose the inadequacies of the common view that, because Jesus did not advocate open revolt, he must be "innocuous politically." Attention to the dynamics of domination and resistance engages the "concrete historical context" of Jesus and his followers and identifies Jesus' primary conflict with the Jerusalem and Roman rulers (Horsley: 62, in this volume).

Horsley insightfully reads through the lens of Scott's four forms of political discourse found among subordinate groups (Scott 1990: 18–19): appeals based in the flattering self-image of elites; the hidden transcript or dignity-restoring counter-ideology that negates the dominant paradigm and expresses anger, revenge, and self-assertion; the politics of disguise and anonymity that comprises words and actions of double meaning; and the rupturing of the political order with direct attack, challenge and defiance. Horsley finds Jesus to be involved in articulating a hidden transcript that expresses "God's judgment against the forms and practices of domination and hopeful declarations of the sufficiency and justice possible under the direct rule of God." Jesus also exemplifies the politics of disguise and anonymity, notably through the resonating rumor of God's imminent establishment of God's reign in his words, exorcisms and healings. And Jesus ruptures the political order with direct challenges to the ruling institutions and Jerusalem and Roman leaders who respond by executing him. Here the public temple conflict is critical. Horsley rightly recognizes that the temple was not primarily or solely a religious institution isolated from sociopolitical and economic forms of domination. Nor was the Jerusalem leadership primarily or solely interested in isolated religious matters, stereotypes that seem especially entrenched in New Testament scholarship that has not engaged the work of scholars such as Lenski, Scott, Saldarini, Hanson and Oakman, and Horsley. Jesus' action grows out of, resonates with, and expresses the indignation and humiliation of a wider subordinated society.

Horsley's analysis is compelling in its capacity to locate Jesus in the midst of imperial dynamics of domination and resistance, to interpret Jesus' teaching and actions in these concrete sociopolitical dynamics, and to account for Jesus' death. But while he effectively employs three of Scott's forms of political discourse, the omission of Scott's first form (discourse based on the flattering self-image of elites) is interesting. Horsley does not explicitly address this omission. Its absence invites some explanation. The most likely reason concerns the absence from Q or Mark of obvious signs of Jesus or his followers appealing to the authorities for actions that cohere with the (conflicting) commitments of both parties. Rather, Jesus' encounters with authorities are marked by contests and conflicts where his hidden transcript collides with the public transcript and where statements and actions of double-meaning and ambiguity are to the fore. In fact, an appeal of any sort, even for their lives, is precisely what John does not make before Herod Antipas (Mark 6:14–29) nor Jesus before the Jerusalem elite and its ally Pilate (14:55–65; 15:1–5). Nor in his conflicts with the Jerusalem elite does Jesus exploit the domination system to try to gain material favors. What, then, might be the significance of the absence of this form of discourse? One response would be to argue that its absence points to a completely unbridgeable divide between the elite and Jesus. The absence reinforces the Gospel's presentation that the elite, responsible for the current social structure, has no role in God's purposes (see Mark 7:13; Q/Luke 11:47–51) while underlining a link between Jesus' articulation of the hidden transcript and the divine will for transformation.

There is a further at least interesting if not disturbing implication of articulating the hidden transcript that Scott identifies but which Horsley does not engage. In discussing "Social Control and Surveillance from Below: Defending the Hidden Transcript" (Scott 1990: 128–34), Scott argues that "members of a dissident subordinate subculture can act informally to foster a high degree of conformity to standards that violate dominant norms" (129). By using "social incentives and sanctions" to reward or punish group members, the subordinate group can counter the public transcript and effect a high level of conformity to the hidden transcript. Mutual surveillance, small indicators of disapproval, slander, insults, shunning, physical intimidation, and violence denote but some of the spectrum of means available to secure words and actions that constitute a social solidarity and express and thereby reinforce the hidden transcript.

Scott would suggest that we imagine considerable communal pressure exerted on followers of Jesus and expressed among themselves in similar sorts of words, gestures, and actions. While we have no other access to such informal communal pressure, we do have access to the social pressure that the traditions of Jesus' teachings themselves exert in creating social solidarity and alternative social interactions. The traditions pressure community members to share available material resources (Q/Luke 6:30; 12:33–34), forgive debts (Q/Luke 11:4), show mercy and not judge (Q/Luke 6:36–38), and offer forgiveness to effect reconciliation (Q/Luke 17:3–4). Discernment in evaluating the actions of others is valued (Q/Luke 6:43–45) as is conformity to Jesus' teaching/hidden transcript since circumstances will expose, and thereby publicly honor or shame, those who are genuine and those who are not (Q/Luke 6:46–49; 12:1–3). Required behavior receives social honoring (Q/Luke 14:7–11). But not only is social pressure to conform exerted; so too is divine pressure. Divine approval is evoked for faithful following (Q/Luke 9:57–62), as is divine blessing (Q/Luke 12:22–32). Followers are reminded of their privileged identity as recipients of divine revelation (Q/Luke 10:21–22, 23–24). Conversely, divine judgment is evoked on those who do not live accordingly (Q/Luke 11:29–32), who fail to be loyal "before people" (Q/Luke 12:8–9), and who do not live in a way ready to give account (Q/Luke 12:39–40). Imitation of the practices of the dominant elite means being cursed like them (Q/Luke 11:39b–52). Conformity to Jesus' behavior as one who serves, rather than conformity to the way of domination embraced by "the kings of the Gentiles and those in authority," results in a reversal of status by being honored in the kingdom (Q/Luke 22:24–30). Eschatological accountability offers great rewards for faithfulness and punishment for nonconformity (Q/Luke 17:22–37). A similar catalogue could be assembled from Mark.

It must be recognized that any community needs some sort of communal discipline and that other traditions highlight divine rewards (Q 6:20–49) and care (Q 12:22–31) as incentives for faithful discipleship, as well as encourage conflict resolution (Matt 18:15–20). Nevertheless, such sayings exert considerable pressure on community members to live in ways consistent with the alternative or hidden transcript while engaging the public transcript. Ironically, the hidden transcript, the means or resisting societal domination, functions, at least in part, as a means of exerting pressure or bullying to foster conformity in the lifestyle of resistance. In such a function, the subordinate subculture's dissident transcript—the traditions of Q and Mark—disturbingly imitates some features of the society of domination that it resists. Frantz Fanon (1968) identifies such internalization and imitation of imperial ways as a feature of imperial societies in his work on French-dominated Algeria.

William Herzog's essay utilizes a different approach in that he employs three of Scott's core concepts in discussing two pericopes (Mark 2:15–17; 12:13–17). Herzog examines the scene in which the "scribes of the Pharisees" oppose Jesus' eating with tax collectors and sinners (Mark 2:15–17) in terms of the clash between what Scott calls the great tradition ("the construction of the world as seen by the rulers" [42]) and the little tradition ("distinctive patterns of belief and behavior which are valued by the peasantry of an agrarian society" [43, quoting Scott]). The great tradition is akin to what Scott identifies as the "public transcript" or the forms of interaction determined by the elite to shape and control social interaction and stratification to their own ends. The little tradition, which Jesus employs, is an alternative, resistant, or "hidden transcript" that exists among subordinate groups but is not usually announced explicitly to the elite because of fear and/or sagacity, but takes expression in disguised and ambiguous statements and actions. It envisages different forms of interaction and so contests the public transcript in a calculated and often disguised or hidden manner.

In this scene, according to Herzog, the "scribes of the Pharisees" represent a great tradition that requires, according to their "oral Torah," table purity for all meals, something that peasants were unable to attain (e.g., range of utensils; tithing; association with the pure). Jesus enacts the little tradition, "an alternative political vision for the renewal of Israel which includes the ingathering of those who were made outcasts by the elite reading of the great tradition." The two traditions or transcripts collide as Jesus "lampoons" and "mocks" the great tradition and challenges and exposes the limits of the scribes' authority with an alternative and independent social experience in a "ritual of reversal."

Herzog's analysis of the scene in Scott's terms of clashing traditions is insightful and illustrative of the usefulness of Scott's material for this New Testament material. Two points, though, need further attention. Herzog's analysis of the operative "great tradition" in terms of purity requirements misleadingly suggests that the "great tradition" is monolithic. Further exploration suggests that the great tradition is neither monolithic nor fixed in its content, but it is multistranded and complex as Callahan points out. In his analysis, Herzog focuses on the scribes and their great tradition of purity, yet pays no attention to the presence of tax collectors in the scene. The scene does not specify either the collectors' social rank (upper level of low-level subcontractors) or the agent(s) they represent (the Jerusalem high priesthood and/or Antipas), but ultimately in the Galiilean tributary economy all tax dollars lead to and work for Rome. They represent (whether by conviction or expedience or association) a further great tradition of a quite different cultural origin, namely Roman sovereignty of the land, its production, and people. In Rome's imperial theology, this sovereignty derives from Jupiter who has entrusted a commission of *imperium sine fine* (Vergil, *Aeneid* 1.279) to Rome as Jupiter's chosen agent (Carter 2001: 9–34). Material domination, status humiliation, and ideological domination combine. The claim of eternal Roman sovereignty of course evokes, and surely conflicts with, a central affirmation of Israel's traditions, God's gift of the land to the chosen people. Clearly the scribes, conventionally collaborators (at least in part) with the ruling power and so (sub)scribers at least in function to Rome's great tradition, do not (predominantly) represent this part of Israel's traditions in the scene. But Jesus does. Mark's previous chapter contains Jesus' declaration of God's empire or sovereignty (1:15), establishing Jesus, not the scribes, as the representative of this part of the tradition. But since Jesus is not among the elite, this central claim of the tradition now functions in a liberative and contestive manner as part of Jesus' "little" tradition. Yet he dines with taxcollectors, in a sense allied with him against the scribes, but who are also associated with the Roman tradition that Jesus resists. Identifying the great tradition, then, is some what slippery. Great traditions seem to be fluid, diverse, multilayered, composite, selectively constituted and represented, and common to several of the parties in conflict. Function as well as content plays a part in identifying them. The same applies to little traditions. Both great and little traditions draw selectively from a larger cultural repertoire of available traditions.

Second, Herzog castigates Meier and Wright for sublimating the "political and economic dimensions of the conflict" to their theological, especially eschatological, readings. He is quite correct and insightfully demonstrates the importance of the context of agrarian empires and contested domination for the scene. However, Scott's work, as do various discussions of Roman imperial power and theology, also cautions against driving the political-versus-theological division too hard. Eschatological scenarios can be part of the hidden transcripts, offering a political vision of another way of organizing the world, negating the elite's attempt to circumscribe it, promising the defeat of the elite and its claims. It is no accident that eschatological scenarios in a wide spectrum of first-century writings emphasize reversal of current circumstances by imagining worlds of abundant food and physical wholeness. Such scenarios of reversal provide trenchant commentary on the elite's agenda.

In the second part of his essay, Herzog insightfully discusses the incident in Mark 12:13–17 concerning paying tribute to Caesar. Herzog applies Scott's categories of the public and hidden transcripts to make explicit the setting of class conflict and domination in which Jesus' saying about rendering to Caesar and to God is "an example of this ambiguous and coded political speech," the speech of double meanings, that marks the discourse of subordinate groups. When faced by an attempt to force him publicly to renounce the public transcript and to articulate the hidden (alternative) transcript thereby condemning himself, Jesus dissembles and resorts to "public disguise" and ambiguity, appearing not to denounce the status quo while offering coded resistance to it. Jesus reframes the action of paying the tax from "a test of Rome's right to rule" (public transcript) to an action that signifies "removing blasphemous coins from the land."

While Horsley and Herzog find Scott's work to be illuminating, Allen Callahan is not persuaded of its appropriateness. While Scott talks "resistance," Callahan talks revolution. While Scott employs proverbs of peasants who by bowing and farting refuse open revolt but express covert opposition, Callahan encounters the foul stench of complicity and the reinscribing of the patterns of domination. Callahan focuses instead on Israel's legacy of open, public, revolutionary resistance that sought "real change" in replacing a dominating power with another form of government.

In detailing these challenges grounded in Israel's memory and identity of revolutionary resistance to oppressive powers, Callahan is critical of attempts to employ Scott's notion of "the great tradition" (stereotypically cultivated by scribes and priests) and "the little tradition" (stereotypically the ideals of peasants). Israel's traditions are not so easily divided but present common protagonists for both elite and poor. As befits the nature of written documents, they comprise complex and even contradictory traditions. These factors of commonality and complexity invalidate attempts to equate the great tradition with elite ideology and the little tradition with subaltern ideology. Rather, it is a matter of "competing interpretations of one, complex 'great tradition'," of discerning the appropriate script for particular circumstances.

Callahan styles the period that produces the New Testament as "an age of revolution" that sought "the establishment of an alternative order." He briefly evokes a series of revolutionary acts: the Maccabean revolt, sword-wielding zealous priests, confrontations with Herod and Pilate, demonstrations of mass protest led by figures modeled on Israelite prophetic traditions, violent and nonviolent acts. Various traditions inform and interpret the actions: "popular messianism, subversive prophecy, militant martyrdom." Thaumaturgical prophets perform "signs of freedom." Callahan locates Jesus' ministry in this context of revolt and vicious Roman retaliation and enforcement of control.

Callahan's essay provides a helpful corrective to misapplications of the "great tradition/little tradition" dynamic, lifts up the dynamic of appropriate interpretation, recalls the overt and public acts of (frequently militaristic) rebellion that pervade the first-century world of the emerging Jesus movement, and underlines the important contribution of various traditions and ideologies. But there are several major problems with his discussion.

One is that in correctly recognizing the complex and common nature of Israel's traditions, he does not pursue his insight that conflicts over interpretation mean that in effect at various times parts of this common tradition do function as a great tradition to legitimate systemic exploitation (e.g., the temple sacrificial system in the hands of the Jerusalem elite allied with Roman power), while parts of it function at times to legitimate opposition (little tradition). Callahan emphasizes the shifting and partial nature of the parts, but cannot thereby eliminate their variable functions as great and little traditions.

A further problem concerns Callahan's overstatement of the nature and extent of the first-century quest for revolution. There is no doubt that there were significant levels of violent and public resistance that contested Roman domination. Nor is there doubt that there were outbreaks in disparate regions. But to emphasize that "people of Israelite descent ... rose up in widespread, popular revolt against the Romans" (37) is to give a partial and conventional picture at best. Callahan acknowledges accommodation, complicity, and nonviolent resistance in passing but he is quite dismissive of ineffective "flatulent subalterns bow[ing] downwind" (39) while concentrating his attention on public and violent resistance and revolution.

It is precisely this emphasis on violent, public revolt as the only or predominantly, legitimate, or worthy form of resistance that Scott's work counters. There is no denying Israel's long ideological tradition of resistance and a series of revolutionary actions, but Callahan misses Scott's central point that such public, visible, and "mass" violent and nonviolent revolutionary acts are not the only means by which resistance is expressed in contexts of domination. Callahan does not define the numerical (rather than geographical) extent of those who engaged in violent revolt, nor does he bother with those who did not engage in public acts. Moreover, he seems dismissive of concealed acts of resistance because they are more complicit than corrective, more expressive than effective in accomplishing change. But revolution may not be the goal of every act of resistance, violence may not be the means, and domination and subordination may not be redefined, but resistance is nevertheless expressed. Callahan gives little consideration to the dignity-bestowing and life-sustaining role of such acts of resistance. And further, as Callahan's own catalogue of public resistances to Roman domination graphically illustrates, an appeal to effectiveness provides no warrant for focusing only on public acts of resistance and dismissing the discrete and nondetectable. When subalterns embrace violence and militarism against Rome rather than only emit flatulence, "resentment and regime remain intact" (39) well into the second half of the second century, at least among the living. That is to say, an antithetical or binary understanding of revolt (only this but not that) is inadequate for identifying the copious and shifting ways subalterns negotiate imperial power.

In failing to recognize and value "nonpublic" acts of resistance, Callahan fails to locate a significant portion of Jesus' ministry in this spectrum of negotiated interactions. In asserting the empire of God, Jesus too seeks a new regime but he refuses violence as a means of establishing it (Wink 1992, discussion of Matt 5:38–48). As Horsley and Herzog show in this volume, Jesus' words and actions of resistance comprise much more than the public and violent confrontations with elite power that attract Callahan's interest. In attending exclusively to these public outbursts—important in their own right—Callahan ignores both the imperial structures that pervade much of daily peasant life as well as Scott's emphasis on the everyday, covert, expressions of resistance in socioeconomic interactions. These hidden and calculated acts also contribute to and express the web of dissatisfaction with the alliance of Roman and Jerusalem power. While the quest to resist *and* escape detection does reinscribe and confirm the public transcripts of domination and ensure complicity, such acts and words of "secrecy and subterfuge" also inscribe different ways of imagining and structuring the world. They encourage different practices that enact alternative social interactions (however shortlived), thereby elaborating and emphasizing resistant models and ideology in the common and complex tradition.

What Is Not Investigated

These three essays focus on the historical Jesus and the early Jesus traditions, notably Q and Mark. In relation to this focus, they offer both persuasive demonstrations of the usefulness of Scott's work as well as salutary warnings about its limits. Elsewhere in this volume, Paul's writings are engaged in the similar context of the conflict between domination and resistance.

Are the remaining New Testament texts amenable to such analysis? Horsley seems unconvinced:

> At least some materials in some books in the New Testament are evidently records of the hidden transcript of Jesus movement(s). ... The later literate leadership and literary products of what had become "early Christianity," such as Luke (Luke-Acts) and those who claimed to be writing in Paul's name (the Pastoral Epistles) ... have clearly acquiesced in various ways to the dominant order. But the earliest documents later

included in the New Testament clearly represent movements of resistance. (Horsley: 14, in this volume)

Presumably, it is partly for the reason that the passing of time means a
move to acquiescence that this volume does not include any essays on
Matthew, Luke-Acts, and John.

Setting aside any consideration of the later pseudo-Paulines for the
purposes of this discussion, I am not yet persuaded that this distinction
between early resistant writings and later acquiescent post-Markan
(canonical) Gospels can be sustained, at least as a blanket generalization.
Charisma can be regenerated and maintained through the passing of time
by means of ongoing traditions. And several other factors suggest the
generalization should not be too quickly embraced.

For one thing, several of these Gospels have not yet been the focus of
the detailed analysis framed and informed by Scott's work evident in the
essays in this collection. Gospels such as Luke and John have not been
closely read in terms of the great and little traditions, the public and
hidden transcripts, words and gestures of disguise and ambiguity, the
forms of public political discourse, and the dynamics and means of domination and resistance. Certainly the imperial world has not disappeared
between approximately 30 and 80 C.E., though the absence of attention to
it in much Gospel scholarship suggests it does not exist. In fact, imperial
power has been publicly reasserted in the defeat of Jerusalem of 70 C.E.
Until scholarly work on Gospels takes interaction with the imperial
world seriously, it would seem to be too soon to announce a verdict of
acquiescence (Carter 2003).

Moreover, several later New Testament writings immediately undermine the hypothesis that early equals resistance and late (for New
Testament writings) equals acquiescence. Ongoing work on Revelation
certainly does not support that claim (Howard-Brooks and Gwyther
1999). The document contests the public transcript of Rome's sovereignty
with its hidden transcript of God's sovereignty manifested in the slain
but standing lamb. It urges the rupturing of the public order, the exposing of the public transcript, and the direct challenge to the status quo
regardless of the cost. First Peter's command to submit to every authority
(2:13), honor the emperor (2:17), obey masters (2:18), and obey husbands
(3:1) seems the model of acquiescence to cultural norms of sacrifice to
household, city and imperial gods. Yet three times the letter adamantly
identifies the heart's commitment to Christ as the defining factor for the
existence of the letter's audience (1:22; 3:3–4, 15). Scott's third form of
political discourse among subordinates that emphasizes the exploitation
of public deference yet hidden and anonymous acts of resistance to deny
elite claims offers significant insight about 1 Peter's apparent submission.

In this context of expressed public deference and masked resistance, 1 Peter's strategy enables the letter's hearers to live, apparently compliantly, in an oppressive context that they cannot change, while embracing a hidden transcript of participation in God's yet-to-be completed salvific work (1:23; 4:7) that constitutes their identity in ways that contest and supercede restrictive elite categories of "wife," "slave" and "subject of the emperor" (1:1–2:10; Carter forthcoming).

Further, my own work on the Gospel of Matthew has demonstrated the importance of the context of imperial domination and resistance for this Gospel (Carter 2000; 2001). A reasonable guess locates the Gospel's audience in Antioch, the capital of the Roman province of Syria, a city in which there were numerous displays of the public imperial transcript. That transcript claimed that Rome exercised sovereignty over the world, that Rome and the emperor manifested the presence of the gods, that the emperor and imperial officials were agents of the gods, and that Rome manifested the gods' blessing in constituting societal well-being. Significantly, Matthew's Christology contests every aspect of this public transcript. It resists Rome's ideological domination with an alternative framework, and offers an alternative societal experience marked not by domination and death but by service and transformation (10:7–8; 20:25; 25:31–46). Thus the Gospel's hidden transcript announces God's sovereignty, "Lord of heaven and earth" (11:25), manifested in Jesus who announces and displays God's reign or empire (4:17). Jesus manifests God's saving presence as "Immanuel" (1:21–23); as God's Son (2:15; 3:17), he and not the emperor is God's agent. Through him God's blessing is manifested (5:3–12)—bad news for the elite but good news for the poor. They will inherit the earth, thereby ensuring access to adequate resources. Jesus' healings and feedings repair the damage of imperial rule on human health and anticipate the eschatological establishment of God's purposes marked by abundant food and wholeness (11:2–5; Isa 35:5–6; 25:1–10).

Practices of resistance are part of this way of life that is designated as the way of the cross (16:24). That which is supposed to terrify and conform, that which is the ultimate means of rejecting those who do not conform, is reframed as a sign that God's purposes embrace those brutalized by imperial power and that God's life overcomes imperial death. Violent resistance is forbidden, but acts that resist humiliation and assert dignity are normative (5:38–43; Wink 1992). Acts of mercy that relieve suffering and embody a different way of life are also normative, and assessed in the judgment (25:31–45). The community must pay the tax that Vespasian imposed on Jews post-70 (17:24–27). This apparently external act of conformity to Rome's regime is reframed, however, as an expression of God's sovereignty that is asserted over even the fish of the sea (Carter 2001: 130–44).

Much more could be said about Matthew's participation in this struggle of domination and resistance. Scott's work will broaden the horizons of scholars trained to think that the only social experience on Matthew's horizon is that of the synagogue. It will enable them to move beyond a rigid separation of religion from the sociopolitical, to engage Matthew's world on its own terms of massive inequalities of power and resources, and to understand the Gospel narrative as a hidden transcript of resistance, as well as an instrument of complicity and imitation.

While Horsley has demonstrated the importance of Scott for Mark, and my work has demonstrated his value for Matthew, what then of Luke and John? Even a cursory glance suggests Scott's work may be illuminating. Though there have been some brave detractors (Green 1997), a long tradition has viewed Luke as very conformist, either apologizing for or to the empire. But it is hard to reconcile such passages as Mary's Magnificat in Luke 1:46–56, or the angelic proclamation in 2:8–14 and Jesus' Nazareth sermon from Isa 61 in Luke 4:18 with such a view. These passages sound much more like hidden transcripts that resist the dominant transcripts. Of course it is not as simple as that, but even that recognition complicates much contemporary work.

And what about John? Is the "spiritual" or "mystical" Gospel so utterly untouched by the imperial world, as most contemporary scholarship assumes, that it knows nothing of a sociopolitical world of domination and resistance? I do not just have the Pilate scene in mind (Carter 2003). Perhaps Jesus' signs involving physical wholeness and material abundance point not just to Jesus' identity but also to a little tradition that affirms God's very material purposes for a different world? Perhaps the initial placement in the Gospel of the story of the temple scene, Jesus' rupturing of the domination world with a challenge that exposes one of its means of exploiting peasants, signifies from the outset of the narrative the Gospel's engagement with and resistance to the imperial world that scholars, ironically, have not yet adequately understood? Is "eternal life" part of the hidden transcript, offering a vision and way of life that differs greatly from that offered by the eternal empire (*imperium sine fine*), by the *urbs aeterna*, the eternal city?

Horsley, Herzog, and Callahan are to be commended for the significant and insightful discussions that they offer in investigating aspects of the historical Jesus and early traditions. In so doing they also provide a significant challenge to investigate the rest of the New Testament writings in relation to Scott's work. Where are these writings to be located on a spectrum that ranges from sustaining the arts of resistance to maintaining the arts of domination?

One final matter. The three essays are, as befits this task and their context of origin, rigorously historical in their investigation. As such they are very instructive. But these writings that we know as New Testament texts are also central texts for contemporary Christian communities. At least in the United States, these communities are located at the center of the most powerful economic, cultural, and military empire that planet earth has ever experienced, an empire well practiced in the arts of domination. What implications for churches, both the mainstream and the culturally minority and marginal, might there be if Scott's work is in play as a reading partner or as a set of lenses? What implications might there be if churches, shaped by such reading, enter into discourse in the public arena with public transcripts?

PART 2

HIDDEN TRANSCRIPTS AND THE
ARTS OF RESISTANCE IN PAUL'S LETTERS

STRATEGIES OF RESISTANCE AND HIDDEN TRANSCRIPTS IN THE PAULINE COMMUNITIES

Neil Elliott

James C. Scott's work on "everyday forms of peasant resistance" and on "hidden transcripts" of defiance among subordinate classes (1977, 1985, 1990) has begun to have a welcome impact in biblical studies, especially as we continue to open our scholarship to the important questions arising out of postcolonial criticism. It's not surprising to find enthusiasm for Scott's work among scholars exploring the social currents around Jesus in agrarian Palestine: Richard Horsley (1987) and John Dominic Crossan (1991) have set Jesus squarely in the context of Galilean peasant unrest and social banditry. Gerald O. West has discussed some of the political implications of Scott's work for teaching the Bible (1990, 1999b).

The case appears quite different, at first glance, with regard to the letters of the apostle Paul. With the possible exception of Galatians, these letters are addressed to communities gathered in urban centers in the Roman world. We are now quite used to a standard picture (Malherbe 1977 called it a "new consensus") of Paul's context as a richly textured urban society, characterized by a complex interaction of very different measures of social status. According to this now conventional view, Paul's congregations were populated by a cross section of first-century urban society, made up of individuals enjoying very different levels of wealth, legal status, education, and other status indicators. The interaction of these different indicators is supposed to have resulted, for many of Paul's contemporaries, in a profound and pervasive sense of "status ambivalence" (Meeks 1983). The one group we should clearly not expect to find in these congregations, according to this consensus, is peasants; and the last person most of us would think of associating with the "hidden transcripts" of an underclass would be Paul himself. The apostle's reputed Roman citizenship (see Acts 16:37–38; 22:25–29; 23:27), apparent training in rhetoric, and what is often taken as thinly disguised condescension to the poor (what Theissen 1982b called Paul's "love patriarchalism"), surely betray an élite background and sympathies (see also Judge 1960, 1972, 1980).

My argument here, nevertheless, is that Scott's work on grassroots resistance and "transcripts" of defiance to hegemonic social pressures are of great value for our efforts to contextualize Paul's praxis and rhetoric. In what follows, I observe, first, that recent critiques of the just-sketched "new consensus" accompany suggestions that Paul's assemblies practiced alternative economic relationships at odds with the dominant patronage networks of the Roman Empire. I then address the methodological difficulty of appropriating Scott's work in peasant societies for the study of a different social reality, first-century urban centers. Finally, I discuss a surprising case—Rom 13:1–7—where Paul's letter provides a glimpse into the sort of "hidden transcript" of defiance that Scott has so ably described.

PAUL AND THE PLIGHT OF THE URBAN POOR

Aspects of the received wisdom regarding the social circumstances in the Pauline congregations have recently been questioned. Insight regarding the "steep social pyramid" of Roman society (MacMullen 1974) has been buttressed by studies of the fundamentally "parasitic" nature of the Roman economy (Garnsey and Saller 1987; De Ste. Croix; Alcock). Drawing on that scholarship, others have questioned conventional generalizations about social status in the Pauline churches. Justin Meggitt's monograph on "Paul, Poverty, and Survival" (1998) is a particularly important example of this trend. Meggitt describes a globalizing Roman economy in which agriculture remained predominant, nearly 90 percent of the population living on or from the land, their labor harnessed by a form of "political capitalism" in which profit-making was squarely "in the hands of the élite" (47). In this economy, anything approximating a "middle class" was relatively insignificant (49); a wide gulf separated the very few rich and the very many poor. The vast majority endured at subsistence level—or below it—enduring an "absolute poverty" in which "the basic essentials necessary for supporting human life are not taken for granted but are a continuous source for anxiety" (5). The urban slums teemed with semiskilled and unskilled workers, scrapping for occasional work to keep them just above the level of beggary and destitution. On Peter Garnsey's analysis, the provision of a regular grain dole in Rome, benefiting only male citizens—at most, a fifth of the population—highlights the general destitution in the city: most Romans were poor (Garnsey 1993; 1991). Meggitt concludes that similar mass urban destitution would have been the case throughout the cities of the Empire (1998: 51–53; see De Ste. Croix: 371).

Most important for my purpose here, Meggitt shows that common generalizations about Paul's own social location, relative prosperity, and privilege have too often been based on anachronistic assumptions about Paul's social mobility and independence (75–97). The same is true of the assemblies he served (97–154). A wealth of close observations leads Meggitt to conclude that in absolute terms, *"Paul and the Pauline churches shared in this general experience of deprivation and subsistence. Neither the apostle nor any members of the congregations he addresses in his epistles escaped from the harsh existence that typified life in the Roman Empire for the non-élite"* (75, italics original); "the Pauline Christians *shared fully in the bleak material existence which was the lot of more than 99 percent of the inhabitants of the Empire"* (153, italics original).

This is of course a conclusion very different from the older consensus that continues to dominate Pauline studies, and so Meggitt devotes an excursus to criticizing the methodology that informed that consensus (97–154). The cumulative effect of his case is clearly to shift the burden of proof onto those who would continue to present a "status-ambivalent," relatively middle-class portrait of the first urban Christians. Even with respect to Corinth—where the rhetoric of 1 and 2 Corinthians clearly addresses tensions running along a fault line of status and social power— Meggitt argues against the popular notion that the church included a significant number of wealthy, high-status individuals. Other interpreters have reached similar conclusions regarding the Corinthian congregation in particular, describing social conditions as more difficult than earlier scholarship allowed, and highlighting the desperation that could feed tensions within the congregation. Richard Horsley, for example, describes Corinth as "the epitome of urban society created by empire," suggesting that Paul's congregation was drawn from

> a conglomeration of atomized individuals cut off from the supportive communities and particular cultural traditions that had formerly constituted their corporate identities and solidarities as Syrians, Judeans, Italians, or Greeks. As freedpeople and urban poor isolated from any horizontal supportive social network, they were either already part of or readily vulnerable for recruitment into the lower layers of patronage pyramids extending downwards into the social hierarchy as the power bases of those clambering for high honor and office expanded. (1997: 243)

ECONOMIC MUTUALITY VS. PATRONAGE

These recent studies not only relocate the Pauline congregations "downward" in social class but also describe a deliberate economic practice fostered within and among these congregations as an alternative to the pervasive patronage system. Horsley (1997: 249–50) finds the roots of the early Jesus movement's economic practice in "the horizontal economic reciprocity of village communities following the traditional Mosaic covenantal ideal of maintaining the subsistence level of all community members" as enjoined in Lev 25. He suggests that Paul's own refusal of support, deviating from the usual practice of the Jesus movement, may be ascribed to Paul's sensitivity, "as a former scribal 'retainer,'" to living off poorer communities (250). In Corinth, Paul confronted individuals "still attuned to the values of the patronage system." Beyond his personal refusal of patronage, however, "his larger concern may have been to prevent the assembly he was attempting to 'build up' from replicating the controlling and exploitative power relations of the dominant society." Paul's collection for Jerusalem indicates the *international* dimension of the practice he seeks to put in place (251).

Meggitt provides a more detailed description of the economic practices in the Pauline congregations as a survival strategy of "economic mutualism," characterized by relationships of mutual interdependence within and between communities and aimed at "promoting *material well being*" (163–64). This mutuality was embodied in relations of "horizontal reciprocity," as opposed to the "vertical reciprocity" of the patronage system (157–58; compare Crossan 1991: 48–71). Like Horsley, Meggitt also considers Paul's collection for Jerusalem the prime exhibit in the case, for it not only embodies direct relief to the economically poor in Jerusalem, but is "thoroughly *mutual* in its character." Paul makes the case clearly in his defense of the collection in 2 Cor 8:13–14: "I do not mean that there should be relief for others and pressure on you, but it is a question of fair balance between your present abundance and their need, so that their abundance may be for your need, in order that there may be a fair balance." Contributing to the needs of the Jerusalem church establishes a mutual relationship that could be reversed, should the precarious balance of food security shift and the Corinthians find themselves in need. Thus, Meggitt writes, "by meeting the needs of the Jerusalem congregation, the communities were contributing to their own long-term, economic stability" (1998: 159–61). To similar effect, Sze-kar Wan has argued that the collection for Jerusalem expressed an alternative sociopolitical vision for a community "with its own economic principles and bases for structuring life." That vision "stood in opposition to and criticism of" the "political, social, and cultural hegemonic forces, expressions, and institutions" of dominant Roman society, "including the patronage system" (Wan 2000: 196).

It is just here, in the opposition between economic mutualism and patronage, that we find an important point of contact with Scott's work. These were not neutral alternative modes of social and economic organization, after all; rather, they served different and opposed interests. Much has been written about the ubiquitous *ideology* of benefaction (euergetism) and patronage in the ancient Roman world, an ideology that Meggitt observes was "created and practiced for the benefit of the élite, and not for the poor" (1998: 166; see De Ste. Croix: 334, 341–43, 362, 364–67, 372). Peter Garnsey (1988) has reminded us that common people very rarely appear as clients in the literary sources available to us; unless the poor had something the rich wanted, patronage relationships simply did not materialize. Meggitt declares (1998: 166–69) that from the point of view of the poor, patronage relationships were "at best non-existent and at worst exploitative": they were "certainly not the all pervasive phenomenon so often assumed" in much New Testament scholarship, nor did they afford any "real opportunities to engender effective strategies for survival." Nevertheless, the *ideology* of patronage—the (usually false) promise that individuals could better their lot by resorting to dependence on their superiors—was pervasive. Crossan described it as "the dynamic morality that held society together" (1991: 40); De Ste. Croix called it "the mainspring of Roman public life" (65).

The ideology of patronage rests on the maintenance of a perceived universal social competition for resources. As Scott observes, this perception of social reality is represented as justifying systems of socioeconomic relationships structured on vertical reciprocity, such as patronage, within the ideological construction of the dominant class:

> If the logic of a pattern of domination is to bring about the complete atomization and surveillance of subordinates, this logic encounters a reciprocal resistance from below. Subordinates everywhere implicitly understand that if the logic of domination prevails, they will be reduced to a Hobbesian war of all against all. Individual strategies of preferment are a constant temptation to members of subordinate groups. It is, in part, to encourage normative and practical defection [i.e., from solidarity within the subordinate community] that elites call forth the public acts of compliance that represent their authority. Also by such means elites create the loyal retainers, "trustees," and informers on whom they can rely. (Scott 1990: 128–29)

Scott continues that given the pressure of a dominant culture to coerce conformity, mutuality within subordinate communities must rely on "social incentives and sanctions." He refers to a "patrolling" within the social sites where resistance is imagined, a discipline exerted against "anyone who puts on airs, who denies his origins, who seems aloof, who attempts to hobnob with elites." In this way subordinate groups police conformity of speech and sanction "a wide range of practices that damage the collective interest of subordinates" (129–30).

We can recognize immediately the applicability of Scott's observations to the Pauline congregations. Paul sought to enforce an ethos of mutuality with specific sanctions, for example enticing the Corinthians with the promise of praise if they contributed, threatening them with humiliation if they failed (2 Cor 9:1–5). Scott describes such "imposed mutuality" as a "form of daily resistance" on the part of the subordinate community to outside pressures on relations of production and exchange (1985: 261–65; 1990: 128–35).

It follows that in the context of the ancient Roman city, we should expect economic mutuality as a survival strategy to involve some specific form of resistance to the social and economic pressures embodied in the ideology of patronage. Recent scholarship on Paul provides evidence of just such resistance. We have already noted Sze-kar Wan's argument that the collection for Jerusalem involved a specific repudiation of the ideology of patronage. Peter Marshall (1987) has provided a careful analysis of the social conventions of "enmity" in 2 Corinthians, showing that in fact Paul strenuously resisted pressures from individuals in the Corinthian congregation to accept their patronage (see also Chow 1992). Mark Reasoner (1999) finds a similar repudiation of Roman codes of honor for the powerful and shame for the powerless behind Paul's talk of "strong" and "weak" in Romans. Moreover, I have argued elsewhere, in general terms, that the rhetoric of Paul's other letters served similar purposes, reinforcing an egalitarian practice of mutuality in deliberate contradiction of the prevalent ideology and iconography of Roman power (Elliott 1994: 181–216; 2002a).

Is Economic Mutuality "Resistance"?

Even if we allow Meggitt's general case regarding the poverty in which most members of the Pauline congregations lived, however, we still face methodological challenges to moving from Scott's work on resistance *in peasant societies* to the sort of economic mutuality Paul encouraged in an *urban* social environment.

In the latter case, first of all, we are reading ancient letters: the sort of "thick" description and analysis of social interaction that an astute observer like Scott might carry out in a contemporary peasant society is not possible with regard to the Pauline congregations. We *believe* we are reading Paul's strategic response to one or another particular situation, based on his construal of the issues involved. Moving from text to situation is a very precarious enterprise, however. We are constantly reminded how much we do not know, and how much we can never learn without the methods available to participant observers. We cannot know what reactions these letters actually provoked in their intended audiences. Did Paul's hearers in fact realize the mutualism Paul urged on them? What did that look like? Did Onesimus's master accede to Paul's request, whatever that was? Did Paul's would-be patrons in Corinth have a change of heart?

We cannot answer those questions. Observing Paul's rhetoric is simply no substitute for a "thick" description of the common life of the Pauline congregations. Nevertheless, aspects of his rhetoric would have constituted a clear *ideological* assault on the values of the patronage system. His letters manifest a more ideologically "condensed" form of intervention than the Malaysian practices Scott describes precisely because the forms of exchange Paul seeks to promote are *not* already embedded in a community's life. To be sure, Paul's drawing on traditions of "horizontal reciprocity" from a village-based society may have evoked significant resonances for any of his readers familiar with such traditions in their own backgrounds. But judging from Paul's rhetoric, the practices he advocates are being formed *de novo,* in an urban context where otherwise unaffiliated individuals are gathering in private households to live out a *new* form of community.

Once we notice the frequency with which Paul evokes a clear social break with the past for individuals who have joined these communities (e.g., "turning to God from idols," 1 Thess 1:9), we will recognize that the mutuality being "preached" here is, in a sense, experimental. In this regard, Meeks speaks of the breaking of former social ties in the Pauline congregations and the establishment of "a new, fictive kinship," a transition that he remarks would have seemed "terribly subversive to the basic institutions of society" (1983: 85–89). We should expect this project to depend on more explicitly ideological appeals (that is to say, "theo-logical" or "christological" appeals), rather than on the sort of implicit shared norms and practices that might be assumed by an established peasant community.

Another challenge is that, since Paul's letters address not peasant communities but congregations of *urban* poor, we should expect their strategies for survival to have been structurally different from those that established agrarian communities (such as those that Scott studied) would find workable. Meggitt himself makes the point. Referring to Peter Garnsey's work on famine and food in the Greco-Roman world, he observes that

> the poor who lived in cities could take only very limited *direct* action in the face of subsistence risk. For the most part they were reliant upon markets and market dependent shops for their foodstuffs and were therefore passive victims of problems of supply (whereas peasants had a number of adaptive agricultural mechanisms—risk buffering tech-niques—which could allow them to maintain better some kind of consumption stability). (1998: 164–65)

For example, city dwellers were unable to rely on even modest food stockpiles to the extent peasants could have done. They could reduce their "liabilities" by removing dependents from their households; they could try to barter whatever meager possessions they had. But these were hardly reliable long-term strategies for survival.

By contrast, Scott (1985) could describe everyday routines of resistance in an established agrarian society, the forms of noncompliance and sabotage that constitute resistance against structural exploitation by landlords and employers. Part of the power of his analysis is that by numerous measures, Malaysia is, in his words, something of an "ideal" case, characterized by "an open, buoyant, capitalist economy with an abundance of natural resources," a relative absence of overcrowding, and "a state that is less predatory than most of its neighbors"—indeed, a state that works to moderate market pressures so as to maintain a domestic supply of rice, and at least to a modest degree, to redress poverty. In Scott's words, "If one had to be a peasant somewhere in Southeast Asia, there is little doubt that Malaysia would be the first choice by nearly any standard" (1985: 50–53).

In the local agrarian society Scott studied, there were "no riots, no demonstrations, no arson, no organized social banditry, no open violence"—none, that is, of the open forms of conflict we routinely associate with the term "peasant resistance." Malaysia did not offer examples of formally organized peasant resistance movements, and for just this reason could serve as an exception proving the rule that was the heart of Scott's argument: that resistance, or in the strongest terms, class struggle at the ideological as well as the material level, was the fabric of a "hidden transcript" in peasant society, well prior to its public expression (241–303). "The stubborn, persistent, and irreducible forms of resistance" Scott examined "may thus represent the truly durable weapons of the weak both before and *after* the revolution."

By way of contrast, the economic pressures on the urban poor gathered in various first-century Roman cities were stark, and mass violence a regular occurrence. The chronicle of conquests in Augustus' *Res Gestae* hints powerfully at the social dislocation and economic disruption that military conquest, mass enslavements, and the subsequent "globalization" of the economy (i.e., the assimilation of local economies into the imperial economy) must have occasioned. Horsley observes that the relations between Rome and Corinth, in particular, "exemplify the most extreme forms of Roman imperial practice and of the imperial society it produced," namely, the sacking of Corinth in 146 B.C.E. and Julius Caesar's repopulation of the city with "large numbers of urban poor from Rome" (1997: 242–43). Similarly harsh measures produced the Romanized economy in other cities, including Roman Judea, where the social dislocation was a major contributor to insurrection and revolt (Goodman 1987). Stephen Dyson (1971) has shown that native revolts against Rome could erupt in the interval between Roman military conquest of a territory and final administrative consolidation of the area's resources into the Roman economic system.

In Rome itself, De Ste. Croix described rioting as the primary means through which the Roman *plebs urbana* could function as a "pressure group" (357). The notorious examples of civic violence in Alexandria in 38–41 and, later, in and around Rome itself, involved a volatile mixture of resentment of taxes and resentment of the Roman ruling class. That resentment could be shifted, with disastrous results, onto the most vulnerable population in the urban environment, an easily identifiable ethnic group caricatured in satire as rootless indigents: the Jews (Gager 1981; Schäfer 1997; Slingerland 1997).

It appears, then, that the Malaysian situation studied by Scott and the Roman urban context of the Pauline congregations might be placed at some distance from each other on what Scott himself describes as a "continuum of situations," from more to less explicit repression, allowing or evoking different forms and measures of resistance (1985: 286). Paul's strategy, so far as we can tell from his letters, appears more *ideologically focused* than the Malaysian peasants' practices. To be sure, there is an ideological dimension to the expressions of resentment or defiance that Scott discovers as he moves into private, "off-stage" sites of peasant life, and the coherence of this ideological dimension encourages Scott to speak of a larger, fuller "hidden transcript" on which these expressions draw. In Paul's letters, by contrast, we see exhortations to specific practices regularly joined with ideological justifications, allowing us a fuller glimpse into the "hidden transcript" in the Pauline communities.

AN INTERMEDIATE CASE: PEASANT COMMUNITIES IN MODERN HAITI

A brief examination of a third situation—that of contemporary peasant organizations in the Haitian countryside, on whose behalf I was privileged to work in 2000 and 2001—provides a "bridge" example that I believe justifies plotting Malaysian peasant resistance and Paul's advocacy of economic mutuality as points on a single continuum. Like the Malaysian society Scott studied, Haiti's economy is largely agricultural; like Paul's Roman context, however, the people have experienced centuries of violence and exploitation, continuing in the present under U.S. hegemony.

Some 80 percent of Haiti's productive economy is agricultural, though the state has historically relied on export tariffs and, covertly, on the drug trade, which is still reportedly a source of income for some elements of the police apparatus. Haiti is in this regard a good example of the pattern Scott identifies in other developing countries, in which the state is forced to rely on levies on imports and exports, a pattern "in no small measure a tribute to the tax resistance capacities of their subjects" (1985: 31.) In contrast to Malaysia, however, Haiti's experience as a former slave colony of the Spanish, then the French, then (after the tumultuous revolution of 1791–1804) a nation of freed slaves forced to return to fieldwork in virtual corvée labor, has decisively shaped Haitian history around the lethal interaction of a "predatory" state over against the nation. The predatory relationship was embodied in the sudden departure of President-for-Life Jean-Claude Duvalier in 1986, following mass demonstrations—organized by priests of the *ti legliz,* or liberation "little church"—that brought tens of thousands of Haitians into the streets of the capital. Duvalier fled the country aboard a U.S. military jet, carrying with him the entire national treasury, which he has since exhausted while living in France (Trouillot 1990; on the Haitian revolution, James 1963; on more recent developments, Dupuy 1997).

The popular democratic movement that swept Duvalier from power also gained tremendous strength in the countryside, where hundreds of thousands of cultivators were organized into regional peasant organizations, each based in dozens of local cells, or *gwoupman,* of eight to ten cultivating households each. This bottom-up organizational structure, and an insistence on democratic functioning at each level of representation up to the regional level, has given the peasant communities a powerful and flexible instrument for working for their own goals. For just this reason, the peasant organizations and affiliated workers' organizations in the cities were targeted in the late 1980s by a U.S. intelligence-gathering operation, run under the aegis of "in-country processing" for immigration applications, but modeled on the Vietnam-era "Operation Phoenix" (and reportedly run by several veterans of the Vietnam program). Violent suppression of the popular movement reached a climax during the brutal coup régime of Lt. Gen. Raoul Cedras and his colleagues (1991–94). Human rights reports speak of the "decapitation" of the democratic movement, a phrase not always metaphorical in its reference. Official estimates list five thousand men, women, and children murdered by the coup régime; the popular estimate is at least twice that. The Cedras régime has another notorious distinction: its systematic application of rape as a tactic of state terrorism was the first to be investigated under international law as a crime against humanity (Minnesota Advocates for Human Rights). The impunity enjoyed by most of the torturers and murderers from the Cedras régime, continuing violence by heavily armed gangs of "zenglendo," and repeated reports of coup attempts against the elected government by former military or police officers, have created a climate of political insecurity.

There is also economic insecurity, and a collapse of food security for the poor, leading to what the United Nations' Food and Agricultural Organization has described as the worst "depth of hunger" index in the Western hemisphere. (The 2001 report, available on the U.N. FAO Web site, describes "depth of hunger" as the ratio of per capita daily caloric intake to expenditure.) Since the return (effected by U.S. Marines) of elected President Jean-Bertrand Aristide in 1994, the United States has continued to withhold $50,000,000 in promised aid, while the Haitian government has been required to pay $5,000,000 as a "financing fee" for that aid. The elected governments of Aristide and his successor, Jean Preval, have been under pressure, from the U.S., the World Bank, and domestic opposition groups from the business sector (supported by U.S. government funds), to implement "structural adjustment" policies. These would convert the national economy from agricultural production to light assembly for export, along the lines of the "*maquiladora*" model imposed throughout much of Central America. The plan is known in the streets as "*Plan Grangou*," the "Starvation Plan."

In this hostile environment, peasant organizations in the countryside have tried since 1994 to regroup in order to secure basic survival, security, and human rights needs in their zones. The vast majority of Haitian cultivators are small farmers, facing tremendous challenges (Elliott et al. 2001):

- ✦ a rapacious market in which they must sell their crops at rock-bottom prices to brokers or middlemen, who transport the food to urban markets at a huge profit;
- ✦ consequent lack of food security in their own agricultural communities;
- ✦ constant lack of resources to buy basic goods and services (clothing, fuel), leaving them at the mercy of predatory lending agencies that normally charge 20 percent interest per month (a practice popularly known as *kout ponya*, "a dagger to the heart");
- ✦ competition from the state-subsidized sugar and rice production in the neighboring Dominican Republic;
- ✦ a general lack of even basic agricultural equipment, exacerbated by a 1993 campaign by the Haitian Army to confiscate iron tools in the countryside, including mattocks and machetes;
- ✦ the remnants of a corrupt and predatory civil service, generally beholden to large landholders, the *chef seksyon*;
- ✦ apparent state indifference (an admitted improvement over active repression); and

✦ constant attrition from peasant communities as members give up on a failing agricultural economy and move to the cities in search of assembly work.

One 2001 field report identified "demoralization" as the greatest obstacle faced by community organizers. To borrow a phrase from Scott, if one had to be a peasant somewhere in the Western Hemisphere, there is little doubt that Haiti would be the *last* choice by nearly every standard.

Nevertheless, hundreds of peasant organizations across the country have adopted consistent goals and a common survival strategy to address their situation. In several programmatic statements, these organizations have called for

✦ peasant control over the whole agricultural production process, and thus

✦ control over food stocks for their communities, and fair prices for their crops;

✦ participation by all cultivators in grassroots cooperatives, in order to consolidate power;

✦ the appropriation of all unused state-owned land for cultivation;

✦ full agricultural reform throughout agricultural zones;

✦ fuller peasant participation in the decision making processes that determine their living standards (including participation in state elections);

✦ ultimately, economic self-sufficiency within their communities.

The basic principles infusing these grassroots organizations include complete democratic functioning at every stage of organization; full community participation in all decisions affecting the life of the community, especially participation by women cultivators (who traditionally do more of the actual labor); complete transparency in all administrative processes affecting community life; and cross-fertilization with other peasant organizations, in order to share reflection and analysis on the most urgent needs in a zone, share successful strategies, and increase common morale—in Kreyol, *pou fe tet nou yo fò,* "to keep our heads strong."

Several aspects of the experience of these peasant organizations are instructive for my discussion of mutuality and resistance in the Pauline congregations. First, I notice that the Haitian organizations regularly open a social space within their communities, and in meetings with other organizations in their zones, to reflect on their most urgent political and economic needs. These meetings normally combine discussions of very practical group concerns—regarding a group's operating funds, interpersonal relationships, the maintenance of tools and equipment—with

penetrating socioeconomic analysis. At a conference for women cultivators in the summer of 2001, for example, thirty participants moved from a
vigorous and insightful analysis of World Bank structural adjustment
proposals to a discussion of how the participants could begin literacy
courses. These meetings regularly involve a ceremonial sharing of food,
singing (themes include invoking the Voudun *lwa*, and the importance of
"weaving strength" through united effort), and dancing. There is a clear
and consistent tone of commitment to the goals of the community: the
participants are aware they are building something new, and that they
need mutual support and encouragement to persist.

In addition, the reflections shared in the social space opened up
within these communities constitutes what Scott has called a hidden transcript, most dramatically patrolled and protected during the 1991–94
coup regime, when community members were stationed at roads enter-
ing their village to watch for agents of FRAPH or the repressive *chef
seksyon* apparatus.

Second, these organizations insist on full participation and complete
transparency in community decision-making so that the sanctions used
to enforce mutuality are clear and communally owned. This practice
minimizes the possibilities for mismanagement or misappropriation of
shared resources.

Third, these organizations are very clear about the social and economic practices they must *resist* in order to achieve a genuine mutuality.
Usually one of their first goals is a pooling of funds to establish a modest
micro-lending fund, a practice that community members quickly
acknowledge is intended to free them from dependence on extortionary
outside lenders. The model of grassroots agricultural development immediately and inseparably involves an explicit opposition to "structural
adjustment" plans and the neoliberal ideology that undergirds them.

Fourth: while peasant organizations are eager to participate in decision-making processes in their zone, they are normally very cautious
about the potential for partisan or electoral politics to fracture their communities. Some Haitians have described politics as their national sport;
and even with the very best intentions, the Haitian state is years away
from overcoming the patronage and nepotism that characterized Duvalierism. History has taught most peasant groups to be suspicious of state
institutions. There is often a strong ethos that political energy is to be
channeled into the *group's* activities; individual political aspirations are
actively discouraged.

With appropriate qualifications, we can find rough parallels for all
these practices in the Pauline *ekklesiai*. In particular, the combination of
ideological critique with *practices of economic mutuality* in the Haitian *gwoupman* provide a model for what I am proposing was the Pauline strategy of

resistance. The Haitian practice clearly illustrates Scott's point that "it is precisely the fusion of self-interest," in the peasant's pursuit of basic material survival needs, "and resistance that is the vital force animating the resistance of peasants and proletarians." It is impossible, Scott declares, "to divorce the material basis of the struggle from the struggle over values—the ideological struggle" (1985: 295–97).

Unfortunately, by failing to connect specific economic practices in the Pauline congregations (mutuality, the refusal of patronage, the collection for Jerusalem) with their ideological warrants, scholarship has too often presented just such a divorce. The mutuality that Paul sought to realize among the congregations he served involved the sharing of material resources and a conscious effort to avoid dependence on outsiders (1 Thess 4:11–12; Rom 13:8; see Elliott 1994: 189–204). It also involved disciplines of resistance to specific exploitative practices inherent in the "political capitalism" of the Roman economic system.

PAUL'S RHETORIC AND THE "VOICE UNDER DOMINATION"

As I mentioned above, one of the central insights of Scott's work is the observation that even in the absence of overt violence or rebellion, practices in Malaysian peasant society manifested aspects of a hidden transcript of defiance. That is, the resistance Scott observed was broad, systematic, and carefully managed to be largely invisible to "overseers." In barely detectable patterns of obstructive and resistant behavior Scott finds evidence of class struggle at both the ideological and material level.

This aspect of Scott's work may be particularly fruitful for our interpretation of Paul's rhetoric. The last twenty years have seen an explosion in studies of the rhetoric of Paul's letters. Most of this work examines Paul's letters in terms of the categories discussed in the classical rhetorical handbooks. But these handbooks were written to describe and to prescribe effective communication among the powerful. The law court, the legislative assembly, the civic ceremonial—these are the arenas where political power was constructed and choreographed; and these are the only arenas in which the handbooks describe meaningful discourse as taking place (Horsley 2000a; Elliott 2000: 27–33). We will look in vain in the handbooks for penetrating discussions of the rhetoric of the slave's groan, the prophet's denunciation, the apocalyptist's vision.

We may get further by using Scott's categories of "hidden" and "public transcripts" and the "voice under domination" (1990). Scott is interested precisely in the difference between the "public transcript," that is, "the open interaction between subordinates and those who dominate" (2), and the "hidden transcript," that is, "discourse that takes place 'off-stage,' beyond direct observation by powerholders" (4–5). The public transcript includes "the public performance required of those subject to elaborate and systematic forms of social subordination"; normally, for that reason, it will, "out of prudence, fear, and the desire to curry favor, be shaped to appeal to the expectations of the powerful." Where the public transcript "is not positively misleading," Scott declares, it is nevertheless "unlikely to tell the whole story about power relations," since it is "frequently in the interest of both parties"—the subordinate and the dominant alike—"to tacitly conspire in misrepresentation." Social pressure produces "a public transcript in close conformity with how the dominant group would wish to have things appear."

As a consequence, "any analysis based exclusively on the public transcript is likely to conclude that subordinate groups endorse the terms of their subordination and are willing, even enthusiastic, partners in that subordination" (2). But such a conclusion would be false. "Virtually all ordinarily observed relations between dominant and subordinate represent the encounter of the *public* transcript of the dominant with the *public* transcript of the subordinate.... Social science is in general, then, focused resolutely on the official or formal relations between the powerful and the weak" (13).

The hidden transcript, on the other hand, consists of "those offstage speeches, gestures, and practices that confirm, contradict, or inflect what appears in the public transcript." Scott is interested, not simply in identifying glimpses of hidden transcripts where they (occasionally) appear, but also in assessing the discrepancy *between* the hidden transcript and the public transcript as a way to measure "the impact of domination on public discourse" (4–5):

> The frontier between the public and the hidden transcripts is a zone of constant struggle between dominant and subordinate—not a solid wall. The capacity of dominant groups to prevail—though never totally—in defining and constituting what counts as the public transcript and what as offstage is, as we shall see, no small measure of their power. The unremitting struggle over such boundaries is perhaps the most vital arena for ordinary conflict, for everyday forms of class struggle. (14)

I find a striking illustration of what Scott describes as a partially "hidden transcript" in a speech given by the first democratically elected president of Haiti, Jean-Bertrand Aristide, on 27 September 1991. Aristide had just been informed of plans for a military coup against him, which would remove him from power in a matter of hours. He addressed a crowd of supporters:

> Now whenever you are hungry, turn your eyes in the direction of those people who aren't hungry.... Ask them why not? What are you waiting

for ... And if you catch a [thief], ... if you catch one who shouldn't be there, *don't hesitate to give him what he deserves* [staccato for effect, repeated twice.] Your tool in hand, your instrument in hand, your constitution in hand. *Don't hesitate to give him what he deserves.* Your equipment in hand, your trowel in hand, your pencil in hand, your constitution in hand, *Don't hesitate to give him what he deserves....* What a beautiful tool! What a beautiful instrument! What a beautiful device! It's beautiful, yes it's beautiful, it's cute, it's pretty, it has a good smell, wherever you go you want to inhale it. Since the law of the country says Macoute isn't in the game [the 1986 Constitution forbade the participation of the former Duvalierist security apparatus in electoral politics], whatever happens to him he deserves, he came looking for trouble. (trans. Dupuy 1998: 128–29)

The speech was widely condemned, especially by the U.S. government, as inflammatory, an incitement to mob violence. In particular, the comment that the "instrument" in the people's hands "has a good smell" was read by some observers as a veiled reference to "necklacing" (assassination by placing a burning tire around a political enemy's neck)—a suggestion that was quickly publicized as fact by the U.S. Embassy. Meanwhile supporters could accurately protest that the speech referred explicitly to the Constitution, and made no reference to violence. In Scott's terms, the "public transcript" allowed only a glimpse into an offstage transcript. In the fuller offstage transcript, the "tool in the people's hands" might have been a clear enough reference to the only means of resistance left at the disposal of the poor in the face of a military coup.

The key question, of course, is how the analyst who stands outside the social location of the hidden transcript may recognize its reiteration beyond that location. Scott observes that occasionally what had been a hidden transcript comes to be expressed beyond the boundaries of the subordinate group, in a breach of the etiquette of power relations that carries "the force of a symbolic declaration of war" (8)—surely an appropriate expression in the case of Aristide's speech on the eve of a murderous military coup! It is only when the analyst can detect a *discrepancy* between the values expressed in speech, gesture, and practice of a subordinate group and the values that dominate in the public transcript that the analyst may speak of an emergence or upsurge of a hidden transcript.

Scott speaks with optimism about the prospect thus opened up for the interpreter:

The analysis of the hidden transcripts of the powerful and of the subordinate offers us, I believe, one path to a social science that uncovers contradictions and possibilities, that looks well beneath the placid surface that the public accommodation to the existing distribution of power,

> wealth, and status often represents.... The analyst ... has a strategic
> advantage over even the most sensitive participants precisely because
> the hidden transcripts of dominant and subordinate are, in most circum-
> stances, never in direct contact.... For this reason, political analysis can
> be advanced by research that can compare the hidden transcript of sub-
> ordinate groups with the hidden transcript of the powerful and both
> hidden transcripts with the public transcript they share. (15)

On the other hand, Scott recognizes that his subject is "the often fugitive
political conduct of subordinate groups." He admits that the "immod-
esty" of his goal "all but ensures that it will not be achieved except in a
fragmentary and schematic form" (17). Nevertheless, any disguised or
"offstage" political acts or gestures that we can identify help us to "map a
realm of possible dissent":

> Here, I believe, we will typically find the social and normative basis for
> practical forms of resistance ... as well as the values that might, if condi-
> tions permitted, sustain more dramatic forms of rebellion. The point is
> that neither everyday forms of resistance nor the occasional insurrection
> can be understood without reference to the sequestered social sites at
> which such resistance can be nurtured and given meaning. Done in
> more detail than can be attempted here, such an analysis would outline
> a technology and practice of resistance analogous to Michel Foucault's
> analysis of the technology of domination. (20)

A Case Study in "Hidden Transcript": Philo of Alexandria's *On Dreams*

We may readily identify "hidden transcripts" in some Jewish writings from the Second Temple period. When the Habakkuk Pesher from
Qumran refers to the Romans as "Kittim" (1QpHab, passim) or when the
author of Mark's Gospel warns, "Let the reader understand" (13:14), we
know we are in contact with a more extensive transcript that is largely
hidden from view. We may never be able to recover these fuller transcripts, but we must recognize they are there. The situation is far more
complicated, of course, in other materials that do not obviously bear the
marks of a hidden transcript. But Scott urges us to imagine, not that the
public transcript is "all that there is" on the social landscape, but rather
that hidden transcripts are constantly "press[ing] against and test[ing] the
limits of what may be safely ventured in terms of a reply to the public
transcript of deference and conformity":

> Analytically, then, one can discern a dialogue with the dominant public
> culture in the public transcript as well as in the hidden transcript. Read-
> ing the dialogue from the hidden transcript [when this is available] is to

read a more or less *direct* reply, with no holds barred, to elite homilies.... Reading the dialogue from the *public* oral traditions of subordinate groups requires a more nuanced and literary reading simply because the hidden transcript has had to costume itself and speak more warily. It succeeds best—and, one imagines, is most appreciated, too—when it dares to preserve as much as possible of the rhetorical force of the hidden transcript while skirting danger. (164–65)

I find a useful example of such a hidden transcript—"costumed," so to speak, as allegorical biblical interpretation—in book 2 of Philo's *On Dreams,* to which E. R. Goodenough drew attention decades ago (Goodenough 1962). Philo's theme here is "caution" (*eulabeia*). Ostensibly treating Joseph's dream of sheaves of grain bowing down to him, Philo takes the occasion to describe the arrogant who "set themselves up above everything, above cities and laws and ancestral customs and the affairs of the several citizens," proceeding so far as to impose "dictatorship over the people," bringing "into subjection even souls whose spirit is naturally free and unenslaved" (*Somn.* 2.78–79, trans. Goodenough).

Note, first, that Philo's chosen medium, allegorical biblical interpretation, allows him a certain "deniability," a "disguise" for his political views (see Scott 1990: 136–82). And what are those views? Philo describes an unnatural imposition of dictatorship upon those who are naturally free. This theme, which has no basis in the text of Genesis, provides us a glimpse into a hidden transcript in which Philo participates. Immediately, however, he retreats (to protect the larger transcript from being divulged, or in Scott's terms, to avoid a "declaration of war"?). "Surely that is natural," Philo writes, for

> The man of worth who surveys, not only human life but all the phenomena of the world, knows how mightily blow the winds of necessity, fortune, opportunity, force, violence and princedom, and how many are the projects, how great the good fortunes which soar to heaven without pausing in their flight and then are shaken about and brought crashing to the ground by these blasts. And therefore he must needs take caution to shield him, ... for caution is to the individual man what a wall is to a city. (*Somn.* 2.81–82)

Abruptly conforming to the "public" transcript, Philo describes necessity, fortune, opportunity, force, violence, and princedom as natural "phenomena of the world." So they seemed, also, to Roman elite authors like Cicero or Tacitus or Plutarch. But Philo has already indicated that these are *not* equally "natural" forces, for some represent the application of force on the part of human beings.

Of tremendous importance to our subject, Philo makes a distinction similar to Scott's distinction of "public" and "hidden" transcripts. "Caution," warns Philo, must be exercised preeminently by avoiding "untimely frankness" (*parrhēsian akairon*). Philo knows there are "lunatics and madmen" who "dare to oppose kings and tyrants in words and deeds." Interestingly, Philo does not say they are "lunatics" because they fail to recognize the inherent benefit of accepting their subordination to the imperial order (as the official transcript would define lunacy). Rather, they are lunatics because they fail to recognize just how harmful that order is: they fail, that is, to see that

> not only like cattle are their necks under the yoke, but that the harness extends to their whole bodies and souls, their wives and children and parents, and the wide circle of friends and kinsfolk united to them by fellowship of feeling, and that the driver can with perfect ease spur, drive on or pull back, and mete out any treatment small or great just as he pleases. And therefore they are branded and scourged and mutilated and undergo a combination of all the sufferings which merciless cruelty can inflict short of death, and finally are led away to death itself. (*Somn.* 2.83–84)

Note that Philo's distinction of "caution" and "untimely frankness" closely resembles Scott's distinction of "hidden" and "public transcripts":

> Tactful prudence ensures that subordinate groups rarely blurt out their hidden transcript directly. But, taking advantage of the anonymity of a crowd or of an ambiguous accident, they manage in a thousand artful ways to imply that they are grudging conscripts to the performance. (Scott 1990: 15)

Scott recognizes (as does Philo) that it is the "frustration of reciprocal action" that informs the hidden transcript: "The cruelest result of human bondage is that it transforms the assertion of personal dignity into a mortal risk. Conformity in the face of domination is thus occasionally— and unforgettably—a question of suppressing a violent rage in the interest of oneself and loved ones" (37).

Philo reports elsewhere that Roman tax gatherers have conducted their work with particular savagery, especially against Jewish villages (*Spec.* 2.92–95; 3.159–163). Although he does not name Romans in *On Dreams*, his rhetoric is brazen enough: The speeches Philo puts into the mouths of the praiseworthy (2:93–95) are worthy of any Zealot call to arms. The political subordination Philo describes is tantamount to living as brute livestock, suffering torment and indignity until finally being butchered. No reason for honoring the rulers is expressed here. Indeed, Philo interprets the taunt of Joseph's brothers—"will you indeed reign over us? Not so!" (Gen 37:8)—as the appropriately defiant speech of the truly wise, *to be spoken under circumstances that allow it* (*Spec.* 2.93–94).

Philo provides yet another glimpse of an offstage transcript when he turns to an allegorical interpretation of Gen 23:7, describing Abraham's obedience to the sons of Heth. Although the text does not present these terms, Philo insists that Abraham's obedience was compelled by "fear," not "respect," playing on a well-known political topos (see Elliott 1997: 198–99):

> For it was not out of any feeling of respect for those who by nature and race and custom were the enemies of reason ... that he brought himself to do obeisance. Rather it was just because he feared their power at the time and their formidable strength and cared to give no provocation. (2.90)

"To give no provocation" is the mark of true caution, true prudence, under domination. Just as a wise pilot will "wait" until storms pass over before setting sail; just as a traveler encountering a bear or a lion or a wild boar on the road will seek to soothe and calm the beast, so the wise citizen will manifest patience and deference to rulers (2.86–87). All this is said obliquely, in the most general of terms, and while the comparisons are hardly flattering to rulers, neither are they specific or openly defiant enough to spark offense. (Josephus puts the same topos into the mouth of Agrippa, appealing to the rebels of Jerusalem to surrender [*War* 2.396].) At just one point does Philo allow the pretense that he is speaking in abstraction to slip:

> Again, do not we too, when we are spending time in the market-place, make a practice of standing out of the path of our rulers and also of beasts of carriage, though our motive in the two cases is entirely different? With the rulers it is done to show them honor, with the animals from fear and to save us from suffering serious injury from them. (*Spec.* 2.91)

Of course, these qualifications come a moment too late. The distinction between rulers and brute animals is explicit but is undermined by everything else Philo has said about the brutality of rulers. And his insistence that "honor" is shown to rulers is belied by his preceding comment that fear, not honor, compels the outward deference of the subordinate.

"The sarcasm at the end is obvious," Goodenough writes, though not obvious enough to resolve the careful ambiguity of the whole passage:

> Philo has compared harsh rulers to savage and deadly animals throughout. When he mentions how in the marketplace the Jews have to make place for their rulers and the pack animals alike, it is part of

the very caution he is counseling that he should distinguish between the two, once the rulers in Alexandria have been distinctly referred to, and say that one gives way out of honor to the rulers, but out of fear to the beasts.

Goodenough thus maintains the pretended deference to the legitimacy of Roman rule that is essential to the public transcript.

> But [Philo's] Jewish readers would quite well have understood that the reason Philo gave way to each was the same, because he knew that if he did not he would be crushed. (Goodenough 1962: 57)

That is, Jewish readers would have immediately picked up hints that seem merely incongruous in the treatise, but that make perfect sense within another, "offstage" transcript.

Here we see Philo explicitly distinguishing two transcripts: the "public" transcript of deference to the imperial order, and the "offstage" transcript of defiance, under the categories of "speaking most freely," or "boldness of speech" (*eleutherostomeito phaskein*), and speaking with "untimely frankness" (*parrhēsian akairon*). "When the times are right," when a social space is opened in which the "offstage" transcript can come onstage, the hidden transcript of defiance become public, then "it is good to set ourselves against the violence of our enemies and subdue it; but when the circumstances do not present themselves, the safe course is to stay quiet" (*Spec.* 2.92).

Paul's Participation in an Apocalyptic "Hidden Transcript"

Despite the significant differences between the theological, cultural, and political stances of Philo and Paul, we may readily recognize aspects in Paul's letters of a similar hidden transcript of defiance and resistance toward Roman overlords. For example, while he will not tell the Corinthians what "a man" saw in the third heaven (2 Cor 12), he clearly expects them to recognize his reticence as the proper discipline of a true visionary (Segal 1990: 34–71). Again, Paul can make oblique reference to "the time," "the hour," "the day" (Rom 13:11–13), obviously expecting these terse phrases to be meaningful to his hearers without elaborating the apocalyptic scenario to which they refer. Indeed, these apparently glancing references refer to a world of meaning that was obviously alive enough to his congregations.

Against a modern tendency to "demythologize" these apocalyptic elements and to insist that apocalyptic expectation had "lost its motive power" for Paul (Bultmann 1956: 184), J. Christiaan Beker insisted that apocalyptic expectation was "the central climate and focus of his thought" (1980: 144). Interestingly, Beker felt constrained to argue that case against the apparently disconfirming fact that Paul "uses little of the traditional apocalyptic terminology," and shows no interest in "apocalyptic timetables, descriptions of the architecture of heaven, or accounts of demons and angels. He does not relish the rewards of the blessed or delight in the torture of the wicked" (145). It is nevertheless evident that Paul is familiar with those aspects of apocalyptic thought, and expected his readers to recognize his references to them. That is, they constitute elements of a larger worldview, a transcript that is not fully evident in the text of his letters.

More to our purpose here, Horsley has rightly observed that the Judean apocalyptic tradition functioned as a symbolic repertoire by which the Judean communities preserved their own identities by covertly rehearsing defiance of imperial regimes. "The scribal circles that produced this literature were able, through their revelations, creatively to envision a future for their society in freedom and justice beyond their present oppression under imperial rulers and/or their local client rulers.... The fundamental message of most of this Judean apocalyptic literature ... focused on future deliverance from imperial domination" (2000a: 95). Paul shares fully in that tradition (96–98).

Using Scott's terminology, we might speak of a fully apocalyptic *off-stage* transcript to which Paul makes repeated references. Indeed, the very intentionality of apocalyptic or "revelatory" rhetoric is to refer to a reality that is not universally, or "publicly," evident—as Paul puts it, a reality that must be "revealed" as a "mystery" (Rom 11:25) but is otherwise "unsearchable" and "inscrutable" (Rom 11:33). These observations lead to the suggestion that *every performance of one of Paul's letters, before a group constituted as an "ekklesia," generated a social site for the rehearsal and reiteration of a hidden apocalyptic transcript.* This is, admittedly, a novel way to read Paul's rhetoric. Many scholars are more accustomed to taking the letters at face value, which explains the exertion with which Beker was compelled to argue his point, against a nonapocalyptic, "christocentric" interpretation of Paul. Interpreters easily gravitate to more self-evident language, and are tempted to minimize the importance of fragmentary glimpses into the fuller apocalyptic transcript; thus Dunn, for example, is forced in the face of Rom 13 to puzzle "why the apocalyptic character of the Thessalonian letters appears relatively isolated, and why Paul did not set out his theology on [apocalypticism] with greater coherence in the later letters, not least the more carefully laid-out Romans" (1998: 310).

The question is not whether, but where and how we may distinguish a hidden transcript in Paul's letters. One hermeneutical key is provided in the way Paul describes his own apostolic presence by reference to the cross of Jesus, which Paul understands in a distinctively apocalyptic context. Just as the cross is "foolishness to those who are perishing," but "the power of God" to those who understand the hidden Pauline transcript (1 Cor 1:18–25), a "secret and hidden wisdom of God," concealed from the "rulers of this age" (1 Cor 2:6–8), just so Paul's own apostolic presence represents "a fragrance from death to death"—we might say, the smell of "dead meat"—among those who are perishing, but "the aroma of Christ to God," a "fragrance from life to life," among those being saved (2 Cor 2:15–16).

Here Paul makes use of a powerfully ironic metaphor, speaking of God in Christ "always leading us in triumph" (*thriambeuon*). The public transcript regards Paul as simply a humiliated captive (e.g., in his arrest in Ephesus, 2 Cor 1:8–9); the hidden transcript reveals that even in such distress Paul is "captive" to God, and thus a manifestation of God's power. That here and elsewhere Paul establishes a distinction between public and hidden transcripts in terms borrowed from the ceremonial of the imperial cult suggests that the larger transcript of Paul's gospel is powerfully ironic and subversive of the imperial order (see Duff 1991; Elliott 2004b). The same conclusion may be drawn from Paul's pointed inversion of a slogan of Augustan propaganda, "*Pax et securitas*," in 1 Thess 5:2–4 (Koester 1997).

GLIMPSES OF A HIDDEN TRANSCRIPT IN ROMANS 13:1–7

Another possible glimpse into the Pauline hidden transcript appears, surprisingly, in Rom 13:1–7. Here Paul's comments about the ruling authorities are far more reserved than that of other Jews under Roman rule (e.g., Josephus). As Meggitt observes, according to Paul, God "orders" the ruling authorities (*tetagmenai,* 13:1), "he does not ordain them" (1998: 186). There is no enthusiasm here for the divinely apportioned destiny of the Roman people, such as infects Josephus in *Jewish War* 2:350–358. Indeed, there is no recognition whatsoever of the commonplace—as old as Aristotle—that the world is "naturally" divided into rulers and ruled, masters and slaves. To the contrary, every soul is to be subject to "the authorities who are presently in charge" (*exousiais hyperechousais,* 13:1), a participial phrase remarkable for the modesty of its claim.

Paul's seemingly blithe expectation that the authority will reward good behavior and punish bad (13:3–4) and thus act as God's servant (*diakonos,* 13:4; *leitourgoi,* 13:6) is marred by two remarks: that the authority "does not bear the sword in vain" (13:4 NRSV) and that one therefore must "fear" the authority—not only in the instance that one does evil (13:4) but because fear is "owed" to the authority as such (13:7). These remarks are all the more startling in light of the commonplaces of Roman rhetoric. Propagandists such as Cicero consistently held that fear and the threat of force was necessary only for insubordinate and uncivilized peoples. Citizens would naturally yield their happy consent. (Thus the wise statesman would be qualified in rhetoric, to persuade his peers, and in military skills, to coerce his subordinates [*Resp.* 5.6, 3.41].) The historian Velleius Paterculus similarly recognized that persuasion and forceful coercion were the twin instruments of social order (*History of Rome* 2.126). Later, Plutarch would distinguish the Romans' reliance on Fortune, the god who had ensured their countless military triumphs, with the Greek predilection for Wisdom or Prudence, the virtues of rhetorical persuasion (*Fortune of the Romans* 318). Nero's propagandists relied on this common distinction of persuasion and force to argue that strategies of coercion belonged to a bygone era: The emperor had come to power without resort to violence, and had thus ushered in a golden age of "Clemency," which "has broken every maddened sword-blade," and "Peace ... knowing not the drawn sword" (Calpurnius Siculus, *Eclogue* 1.45–65; text in Duff and Duff 1954: 222–23). The weapons of earlier wars were mere historical curiosities (*Einsiedeln Eclogues,* lines 25–30). Seneca even had the emperor declare, "With me the sword is hidden, nay, is sheathed; I am sparing to the utmost of even the meanest blood; no man fails to find favor at my hands though he lack all else but the name of man." Seneca gushed that so noble a ruler need not fear for his own protection: "The arms he wears are for adornment only" (*Clem.* 1.3; 13.5; text in Basore: 356–59, 398–99).

Clearly Paul has a different view. The Roman sword is still wielded, provoking terror (*phobos,* 13:4). Thus one's posture must be one of "subjection" or "subordination" rather than revolt (13:2). Just here we may detect a glimpse of a "hidden transcript" in the Pauline *ekklesiai,* expressed in terms very similar to Philo's carefully calculated remarks in *De Somniis.* While Roman propaganda leads us to expect that a beneficiary of the Roman order would extol *consent* and *agreement* (cf. *syneidēsis,* 13:5), Paul speaks, with what would have sounded like the ingratitude of the uncivilized, of two alternatives: subjection (*hypotassesthai*) or revolt (*antitassesthai; anthistēmi*). His declaration that "rulers are *not* a fear [*phobos*] to the good work, but to the evil," is in line with Roman propaganda, as is the remark that the one working good will thus avoid having to "fear the authority" (13:3); only the evil doer has reason to fear (13:4). But then Paul exhorts his readers to return what they "owe" to others: to some, fear (*phobos*), to others, honor (*timē,* 13:7). And then he insists that his readers "owe no one anything except love" (*agapē,* 13:8)!

Given the exuberant currents of political rhetoric in the Neronian age, Paul's phrases encouraging submission are remarkably ambivalent. I suspect that in a Roman official's ear, Paul's language would have seemed to offer a peculiarly grudging compliance, rather than the grateful contentment of the properly civilized. Scott cites Zora Neale Hurston's observation that the verbal art of subordinate groups is often character-ized by "indirect, veiled, social comment and criticism" (1990: 153); note also his remarks on the rhetoric of "grumbling," which always "stops short of subordination—to which it is a prudent alternative" (155–56).

Despite the proximity of the "riots" that, in Suetonius's view, justi-fied police action against "the Jews" (Suetonius, *Tib.* 43), and of recent unrest over taxes in Rome and nearby Puteoli (Tacitus, *Ann.* 13.48), we cannot tell from this distance whether Paul in fact considered an attempted uprising to be an imminent danger. (His reference to paying taxes in 13:6–7 has been read this way.) Any reasonable Jew could have imagined what the probable imperial response would have been to even modest popular agitation, however.

Perhaps we should read Rom 13:1–7 as part of an ad hoc survival strategy in an impossible situation (see Meggitt 1998: 155–78); Dunn calls it the "realism of the little people who had the most to lose" in the event of civil unrest (1998: 679–80). Paul's "eschatological realism"—a realism determined by the unwavering conviction that God had raised the cruci-fied Jesus from the dead—was never an otherworldly realism. Paul was at least as adroitly political a creature as Philo, whose insistence on dis-cerning the political moment in his allegorical treatise *On Dreams* sounds surprisingly modern. "When the times are right," Philo wrote, "it is good to set ourselves against [*anthistanai*] the violence of our enemies and subdue it: But when the circumstances do not present themselves, the safe course is to stay quiet." Otherwise, one risks sharing the fate of those who have been "branded and beaten and mutilated and suffer before they die every savage and pitiless torture, and then are led away to exe-cution and killed" (*Somn.* 2.83–92).

The modest remarks in Rom 13:1–7, or in the second book of Philo's *On Dreams,* are hardly unusual. Indeed, such "realistic caution" was required of "all people of the Empire" (Goodenough 1963: 54–62). What is remarkable is how out of step this caution would have sounded to ears accustomed to the exultant themes of Roman eschatology. In effect, Paul declares: "The empire is as dangerous as it has ever been. Nothing has changed. Exercise caution."

Paul expresses no fantasy that the powers that be are about to vanish in a miraculous puff of smoke, but neither are they permanent (13:11–12). The Christian's arena of responsibility is much closer, in any event, for the Christian must be diligent for the common good (12:3–21) and fulfill the obligation of mutual love (13:8–10). The "hinge" between the "argu-ment" of the letter, Rom 1–11, and the exhortative material in Rom 12–15 is the broad exhortation to resist conformity to the world (12:2). This resistance clearly involved, for Paul, a defiance of the empire's ideological insolence, by which it sought to legitimize a brutal rapacity (i.e., to "suppress the truth," 1:18; Elliott 1994: 190–95).

Whether or not this last suggestion regarding Rom 13:1–7 prevails, it should be evident enough from the preceding that James Scott's work holds out tremendous promise for a new critical approach that will contextualize Paul within the dynamics and ideology of Roman imperialism. Perhaps the effort will also contribute to greater awareness of our own situation vis-à-vis the imperial cultures and ideological pressures that surround us today.

THE ROLE OF SYMBOLIC INVERSION IN UTOPIAN DISCOURSE: APOCALYPTIC REVERSAL IN PAUL AND IN THE FESTIVAL OF THE SATURNALIA/KRONIA

Erik M. Heen

[W]hen you were still lord [Kronos] ... the earth produced its good things for the folk without sowing and without ploughing, an ample meal ready to each person's hand; the rivers flowed some with wine, some with milk, and others again with honey. And, above all, they say the people themselves were gold and poverty was nowhere near.... We [the poor] should be less distressed about it, you may be sure, if we did not see the rich living in such bliss, who, though they have such gold, such silver in their safes, though they have all that clothing and own slaves and carriage-horses and tenements and farms, each and all in large numbers, not only have never shared them with us, but never deign even to notice ordinary people....

Tell, them ... to invite the poor to [the Saturnalian] dinner, taking in four or five, not as they do nowadays though, but in a more democratic fashion, all having an equal share, not one man stuffing himself with dainties with the servant standing waiting for him to eat himself to exhaustion, then when this servant comes to us he passes on.... And tell the wine-servers not to wait for each of us to ask seven times for a drink but on one request to pour it out and hand it to us at once, filling a great cup as they do for their master. And *let the wine be one and the same for all the guests*—where is it laid down that he should get drunk on wine with a fine bouquet while I must burst my belly on new stuff? If you correct and adjust this, [Kronos], you will have made living really living and your festival a real festival....

— Lucian, *Saturnalia* 20–23

In *Domination and the Arts of Resistance: Hidden Transcripts* (1990), James C. Scott investigated the interaction between elites and those whom they dominated in a manner that has caught the attention of scholars who, in different fields of study, are seeking to recover the social dynamics of subaltern formations. Scott's analysis—based on his distinction between the public transcript of a culture controlled by the elite and the respondent hidden transcripts of the subordinate—can help us understand the complex interaction of Paul's communities with the hegemonic urban culture of his day (Heen 1997, 2004). In particular, Scott's work can help identify a range of responses to the culture of the *polis* generated by Paul's communities that includes criticism and resistance as well as accommodation.

My contribution to this volume explores one aspect of the hidden transcripts of the underclass that has long fascinated anthropologists and historians of popular culture—symbolic inversion. In doing so the study brings together what appears, at first glance, to be two dissimilar things, Paul's preferred way of celebrating the Lord's Supper and the ancient festival referred to by the Romans as "the Saturnalia." There is, however, a similarity in the story-lines that run through both tradition clusters that justifies a comparison: (1) the enthronement of a deity (Saturn/Jesus) (2) marks the beginning of a utopian rule (3) characterized by both a reversal in the status of society's weak and strong (e.g., client/patron, slave/master) as well as an expression of an egalitarian ethic. The specific texts I explore in this article—Lucian's *Saturnalia* and Paul's 1 Corinthians—similarly criticize the introduction of inappropriate social practices (e.g., the "everyday" deference of clients to patrons) into ritual meals (the Saturnalian banquet and the Lord's supper) that assume both role reversal as well as the leveling of social distinctions. Paul could have exhorted the community in Corinth regarding the proper celebration of the eucharist in 1 Cor 11 with the very words of Lucian quoted above, "let the wine be the same for all!"

What emerges from this study is how the response to the public discourse of the cities of the East that emerged in the Pauline communities, while it shares a family resemblance to the reversals of the Saturnalia, contains a new twist. The "old" Saturnalia, by the first century, had become domesticated by the encroachment of timocratic values. In the assemblies guided by Paul, however, the ever-present threat of accommodation to the established patterns of domination and submission were addressed by means of what academic tradition has come to call a "theology of the cross." That is, within the *ekklēsiai* of the crucified Messiah, Paul taught that it was inappropriate to establish one's own esteem (honor) at others' expense (subordination/humiliation).

PUBLIC TRANSCRIPT: TIMOCRATIC CULTURE

Scott employs the term "public transcript" as a "shorthand way of describing the open interaction between subordinates and those who dominate" (Scott 1990: 2). Although the "transcript" of this interaction is objective, it is a living record that inevitably favors the elites. This bias of the public transcript results from the fact that elites control all aspects of its presentation (Scott 1990: 18). The public transcript is, then, the record of the social interactions of a culture as seen from the top down. In addition to being an inscription of an elitist reading of culture, it has a utilitarian function in that it provides a detailed map of the behavior required of subordinates when they encounter their superiors.

The range of the scale of the social interactions included in Scott's theoretical sweep is enormous. On one end of the scale it includes the face-to-face encounters between two individuals of disparate social positioning (e.g., master and slave). Yet, since the elite-controlled public discourse is designed to be impressive, it also involves moments of high drama that characteristically enfold ostentatious displays which make much use of court ritual, panegyrics, and triumphal progresses (Scott 1990: 12). Ramsey MacMullen has collected many different examples of these public displays of dominance/submission in antiquity (1974: 8–12; 1986: 512–24; 1988: 58–126). Such "full-dress" displays were well choreographed dramatizations of the basic script of Greco-Roman culture—the patron/client relationship.

It has long been recognized that ancient society was timocratic and that the elite, in particular, were obsessed by the love of honor. Paul Veyne, who made an extensive study of the public patronage in antiquity, concluded that it was *philotimia* (the desire for glory and honors) that provided the best explanation for the culture of benefaction (Veyne 1992: 10). This system was not generally philanthropic (Meggitt: 166). Little of the munificence given by the elite trickled down to those who, from a modern perspective, needed it most. Yet, even though it was *philotimia* and not a concern for the welfare of the city that motivated the largess of the elite, the picture of elite rule that the rhetoric of *euergetism* projected was that of a happy exchange—the enthusiastic awarding of honors by loyal and grateful citizens for the benevolence of the elite.

A lopsided division into two classes lay behind *euergetism's* language of "mutual benefit" in the city. These classes exhibited an inverse ratio of power to size. Although the high elite controlled most of the property and hence the power in antiquity, it has been estimated that they represented less than one percent of the total population (Holmberg: 22; Meggitt: 50). One of the more important functions of the culture of *euergetism* in antiquity, therefore, was that it provided a rationale (i.e., the two-class system functioned to mutual benefit) that justified the domination of the elite. "The notables were not magistrates and *euergetai* in order to defend their landed property, but because the status of notable separated them from the people" (Veyne 1992: 153).

One repercussion of this bifurcation of the city's populace into two unequal classes was that it provided an odd kind of communality for the ninety-nine percent of the population who were not of the elite. Whatever were the differences that existed in the vast majority of a city's population (i.e., between free and slave, citizen and noncitizen, man and woman, Jew and Gentile, etc.), these residents shared one thing in common: according to the public transcript they were subservient to the elite in whose cities they lived. As Peter Brown notes (240), "In every city a crushing sense of social distance between the notables, the 'wellborn,' and their inferiors was the basic fact of Roman Imperial society. The most marked evolution of the Roman period was the discreet mobilization of culture and of moral grooming to assert such distance."

The public honors awarded to the elite preserved in the epigraphic evidence (Danker) represent only the most concrete acknowledgement of the hierarchical relationship that existed between the city's elite benefactors and its other residents. These power relations were also displayed in many subtle and not so subtle ways in the daily life of the city. The elite were distinctly marked by differences in dress, education and speech, the means of their travel, and even their diet. The homes and public buildings they built in the city, and their villas in the countryside set them apart. So also did their aristocratic mores, which required a display of contempt for cultural entities construed to be below one's own station, such as labor, social inferiors, and low culture.

It was, however, not simply that the elites of antiquity exhibited markers of a high status and were confident of their own superiority. Their dominance also required the ritualized performance of others' submission on a day-to-day basis. This script was basic to the public discourse of antiquity and it did not have much room for critical revision. "Submission and dignity were, at every stage, the most important lessons to be learned" (Meeks 1993: 39). Real or imagined public slights to the dignity of a notable could bring violent retaliations (MacMullen 1988: 69–71; Apuleis: 47–48). For the subordinate—and again in antiquity this class could include almost everyone—it was wiser and safer to defer to the high elite according to the well-worn script rather than to risk the consequences of insubordination. Often such submission masked the true feelings of the subordinate. In the Latin context the word that best captures this kind of deference is *dissimulatio*—"the concealment of one's true feelings by a display of feigned sentiments" (Rudich: xii).

Although the highest honors of a city were reserved for the benefactions of notables, patronage was practiced on other levels of community life in antiquity as well. There were in addition to the elite themselves, individuals who did not meet the eligibility requirements for membership in the city council who became benefactors of *collegia/hetairiai* (voluntary associations and clubs). They gave support to those lesser institutions of the city and received honors in return. The governing structures of these associations often mimicked those of the larger city.

Speaking specifically of the associations of craft workers, MacMullen (1974: 76) notes:

> It followed that their internal organizations should ape the high-sounding terminology of larger, municipal bodies, the nomenclature of officialdom, and honors like *proedria* and the award of gold crowns in their meetings. At least the larger craft associations constituted in every detail miniature cities.

Within the confines of *collegia,* then, the values associated with *philotimia* could also be adopted by the nonelite (Pomeroy: 60, 74). Given the evidence of this social dynamic at the lower level of society, it is not surprising that some researchers have identified such patron/client dynamics at work within the house assemblies of the Pauline mission. "Prestige," Scott reminds us, wherever it might be found, "implies ranking and is therefore something of a zero-sum game ... the accumulation of prestige by some entails the loss of standing for others" (Scott 1989: 146).

HIDDEN TRANSCRIPTS AND SYMBOLIC INVERSION: STATUS REVERSAL AND EGALITARIANISM

In *Domination and the Arts of Resistance,* Scott notes that the public discourse is not the only transcript produced in a culture in which there is a strong bifurcation between those that have power and those who do not. There is another realm of discourse in addition to that of the public space, one which occurs "off stage" and is, in part, a response to the social dynamics as encoded in the public transcript. This discourse of the subordinate is "spoken behind the backs of the dominant" and is, predictably, highly critical of the public transcript. It is here that subordinates experience a "realm of relative discursive freedom, which ... is the privileged site for nonhegemonic, contrapuntal, dissident, subversive discourse (Scott 1990: 25)." If one had, in addition to the public discourse, access to a transcript of the discourses of the subordinated strata of society, a more complete picture of how nonelites construed the power dynamics at play in any culture would emerge. Written sources for such hidden discourses are, however, largely nonexistent. They have, on the whole, perished with the groups who produced them.

According to Scott, however, not all traces of these "off-stage" discourses have been lost to historical inquiry. Though disguised in order to survive, aspects of the transcripts of subordinates emerge onto the public stage (Scott 1990: 19). It is to this realm, somehow between public and private, that one is forced to attend in order to tease out a fuller picture of how subordinate groups viewed their relationship to those who dominated them. Scott lists rumor, gossip, folktales, jokes, and slave and trickster tales as mediums through which the contrapunctual discourse of subject peoples emerges into the public space. Other researchers have observed that subaltern religion provides a unique platform for such genres to appear (B. Lincoln; Clarke: 125). Although many promising fields of inquiry open up for exploration when the New Testament is approached as providing windows onto a particular set of hidden transcripts of the urban underclass of the first century C.E., "symbolic inversion" is arguably the most central and certainly one of the more colorful ploys of this discourse.

Symbolic inversion, simply defined, refers to the reversal of terms set in opposition, such as man/woman, rich/poor, master/slave, up/down, black/white. Such inversions function to turn the social ordering of the public discourse upside down (Scott 1990: 166–82). Their presence in primitive cultures has long been an interest of the anthropological discipline (Bateson; Babcock; B. Lincoln). Popular culture of all ages is full of such reversals that emerge in jokes, broadsheets, satires, comedy, carnivals and other popular festivals. In the field of literary criticism, the work of the Russian critic Mikhail Bakhtin (1895–1975) led to a renaissance of interest in the subject (Stallybass and White). Students of antique culture and literature have long been fascinated by the phenomenon (Luria; Versnel). A wide range of inversions in antiquity has been studied, from those that occur in apocalyptic and wisdom literature to those associated with the festivals of the Saturnalia/Kronia. The topic is no stranger to the New Testament discussion (Crossan 1973). Symbolic inversion, therefore, is a widely diffused and well-studied phenomenon of primitive, popular, religious, and literary culture.

Most scholars tend to agree that when inversion occurs within the discourse of subservient groups it represents a response that is critical of the public discourse. There has been much discussion, however, concerning how such a critical response actually functions within the dynamic of the wider culture. Does it, as seems logical, work to subvert the public discourse? Or could symbolic inversions—whatever their intentions—somehow work to reinforce the status quo? Different studies of symbolic inversions have suggested that they may fulfill any number of functions that range from open rebellion to a somewhat counter-intuitive legitimization of the dominant order. A deep understanding of context is necessary for an accurate reading of how a specific inversion might function in a particular culture. Symbolic inversion is, therefore, a perfect candidate for the rigor of what Clifford Geertz called the "thick description" of symbolic operations (9–10).

While generalities regarding the function of symbolic inversions within the systemics of an entire culture are to be avoided, I do accept

Scott's characterization of its role within the discourse of subordinate groups (Scott 1990: 168):

> Inversions ... play an important imaginative function ... they do, at least at the level of thought, create an imaginative breathing space in which the normal categories of order and hierarchy are less than completely inevitable ... When we manipulate any social classification imaginatively—turning it inside out and upside down—we are forcibly reminded that it is to some degree an arbitrary human creation.

In addition to its cultural-critical role, Scott here indicates another possible function of inversion in a hidden discourse. The fact that the terms of the public discourse can be so manipulated suggest that the hidden transcripts of the subordinate not only record negative responses to the public discourse, but also are the mediums through which alternative social structures can be imagined. Hidden discourses are not only products of culture, but also produce culture (Scott 1990: 27):

> the dialectical relationship between the public and hidden transcripts is obvious. By definition, the hidden transcript represents discourse—gesture, speech, practices—that is ordinarily excluded from the public transcript of subordinates by the exercise of power. The practice of domination, then, *creates* the hidden transcript. If the domination is particularly severe, it is likely to produce a hidden transcript of corresponding richness. The hidden transcript of subordinate groups, in turn, reacts back on the public transcript by engendering a subculture and by opposing its own variant form of social domination against that of the dominant elite. Both are realms of power and interests.

Symbolic inversions, then, in addition to contesting the hegemony of the public transcript may also leverage the construction of alternative social worlds within the hidden transcript of the subordinate. Since the visions of social justice that evolve in private subcultures are reactive to to the public discourse, they will vary to the extent the local public discourses do. The work of the anthropologist Victor Turner, however, suggests that the great variety in these alternative social visions generated "from below" may be reduced to two basic types (Turner: 94–130, 166–203).

Turner calls the first type of social experiment observed in worlds turned upside-down "status reversal." Turner noted, as had many anthropologists before him, that during times of liminal inversion an individual (or group/class) might simply exchange a traditionally held role for its opposite. In "status reversals," the low become high, slaves become masters, the first become the last. In the second type of social experiment, Turner discerned that the critical edge of inversion was directed against the hierarchical assumptions of the dominant culture itself, that is, against the cultural "given" of inequality. This second sort of inversion, then, operates on what might be called "higher order" oppositions (inequality/equality) rather than those that reverse traditional roles (man/woman, master/slave). In doing so, such inversions "level" rather than "reverse" the distinctions of a hierarchically structured society. The end result of such inversions is a kind of egalitarianism that Turner called *communitas*. In the New Testament this social ideal is classically expressed in Gal 3:27–28: "As many of you as were baptized into Christ have clothed yourselves with Christ. There is no longer Jew or Greek, there is no longer slave or free, there is no longer male and female; for all of you are one in Christ Jesus."

The first type of inversion, what Turner called "status reversal," may help explain the attraction the *euangelion* of Christ held for people living in the Greek cities of the East. Open resistance to the public discourse was not tolerated. Only in the relative safety of subaltern sites could one imagine—by means of symbolic inversion—something different. The "status reversals" that lie at the heart of the Jesus tradition (last/first) were, in fact, similar to those that are at the core of the Saturnalia (servant/master). As such they were potentially attractive to the large portion of the ancient city's population that had been scripted into various kinds of subordinate and humiliating roles in the public discourse on a daily basis. In the Greco-Roman cultural sphere, the Saturnalia had provided a period of ritualized release from the power dynamics that structured the patron/client dyad. The status reversals of the subaltern communities that formed under the authority of the enthroned Jesus may have functioned analogously to those of the Saturnalia.

Turner's two ideal types of inversion, taken together, may also help explain some of the social tensions that evolved in the Pauline communities. As noted above, "status reversal" and *communitas* represent inversions that cut against the dominant order in very different ways. "Status reversal" maintains the bifurcations of the larger culture but inverts them (first/last); "communitas" deconstructs the binary oppositions that underlie the public discourse itself (equality/inequality). The utopian ideals that result are uneasy bedfellows. Yet Paul can still evoke them both in close proximity to one another. When he does, at least in 1 Cor 1:26–29, it appears that "status reversal" is enfolded into "egalitarianism":

[26] Consider your own call, brothers and sisters: not many of you were wise by human standards, not many were powerful, not many were of noble birth. [27] But God chose what is foolish in the world to shame the wise; God chose what is weak [*ta asthenē*] in the world to shame the strong [*ta ischyra*]; [28] God chose what is low and despised in the world,

things that are not, to reduce to nothing things that are, [29] so that no one might boast in the presence of God. (NRSV)

In 1:27 Paul notes the "status reversals" that come with inclusion into the community. The foolish and weak are chosen by God over the wise and strong. In these role reversals, the strong are dishonored (*kataischynō*) while, one assumes, the weak are raised up. In 1:28, however, a subtle shift takes place. Paul introduces a "higher order inversion" into his rhetoric to clarify the kind of community that is the result of such activity of God. He speaks of God's use of "low and despised things, *things that are not, to reduce to nothing things that are*." Here social distinctions are leveled rather than inverted. Having introduced the egalitarian perspective, Paul concludes with an ethical instruction: "no flesh should glory before God" (ASV).

According to 1 Cor 1:26–29, Paul's rhetoric could enfold "status reversals" into an egalitarian ethic. A similar pattern may be discerned in 12:22–26. What Paul's rhetoric deftly held together was, however, difficult for Paul's communities to live out in real human terms. Antionette Wire's analysis of the relationship between men and women in Paul's community in Corinth may be taken as illustrative of the problems that were encountered when members of Paul's assemblies tried to realize the egalitarian vision of Gal 3:28. Wire observed that any real moves toward egalitarianism in the *ekklēsiai* would have necessarily meant a *loss* in standing for men and a corresponding *rise* for women from what these groups experienced in relationship to each other in the wider culture (Wire: 62–71). The task of urging specific individuals to adopt what might be called an "elevated humility," especially among those who had anticipated a status reversal (from low to high) in joining the subaltern assembly, would not have been without its practical challenges.

THE CORINTHIAN SITUATION: EXALTATION VS. THE CROSS

In the Corinthian *ekklēsiai* social tensions resulted from the juxtaposition of the utopian ideal of egalitarianism with the expectation of at least some individuals of an inversion of status (low/high) upon joining the Pauline assemblies. The conflicts were complex involving various factions articulating differing interests. I will focus only on tensions between two groups that have been labeled, by some scholars, "the strong" and "the weak" (Martin: 69). Although these terms do appear in 1 Cor 1:27, whether or not such labels were used either by Paul or the Corinthians themselves to indicate specific groups in the Corinthian assemblies is a matter that is impossible to determine. I use them simply as heuristic categories to describe the social dynamic under review.

Gerd Theissen characterized "the strong" and "the weak" factions in Corinth as representing two different economic classes (Theissen 1982c, 1982d). His argument, followed by others (e.g., Gill) that "the strong" are members of the city's elite is not persuasive (Meggitt: 107). Indeed, although inequality in material culture may be somehow at play in the distinction between "the strong" and "the weak," one cannot reduce the membership of these two groups to economic factors alone. Such a reduction ignores the fact that the classification "the strong" may also have included individuals who experienced a new social freedom in Christ that was not tied to wealth (e.g., women, Wire 1990: 218). Turner's notion of status reversal should caution us that there is no inherent reason why those who were most marginalized by the public discourse of the city could not have made "elitist" claims for themselves in the church.

The classic analysis of the status reversal experienced by "the strong" in Corinth comes from before the time of social scientific criticism and is found in the second half of Ernst Käsemann's 1962 article "On the Subject of Primitive Christian Apocalyptic," under the rubric of "Hellenistic Enthusiasm and Paul." Käsemann, following William Bouset's *Kyrios Christos,* claims that the Christian communities in the cities of the East oriented their theological assertions around the *"theologoumenon* of the exalted Kyrios" (Käsemann 1969: 127). To discover the content of these assertions, Käsemann goes to the early christological hymns and recovers a pattern in which Christ, after dethroning the former "principalities and powers," becomes the new cosmocrator who enters into his sovereignty by means of elevation and enthronement. These events end the rule of fate and bring into being a kingdom marked by eternal peace and reconciliation. Käsemann thought that it was the enthronement of Jesus in particular that made possible the present realization of the benefits of salvation experienced as liberation from oppressive forces ("death and the powers") both human and divine.

Although Käsemann believed that all members of the Hellenistic mission communities benefited from Christ's exaltation, he also noted that this liberation brought with it different manifestations of "enthusiasm" as well as a reconfiguration of social roles in the community. This social reconfiguration led to various kinds of conflict in Corinth and, presumably, elsewhere in the early assemblies. One of the specific social problems Käsemann identifies is "the want of consideration for the weaker brother at the Lord's Supper and in daily life" by the dominant group (1969: 126). Those who styled themselves the spiritual elite of the congregation in Corinth were boasting of their own achievements and, in the process, denigrating others (1 Cor 11:17–22). Käsemann's insights here can be strengthen by references to the culture of *euergetism.* According to the rule of *philotimia,* the elite in Greco-Roman society were due deference and honor from the weaker members in the dyadic relationship. That "the strong" would imitate, within the *ekklēsia*, the hubris of the elite of the city is, from this perspective, understandable (cf. Pomeroy: 60, 74). Specifically, Paul found the behavior of those who ate and drank (and allowed others to go hungry) as reinforcing the factions that already existed in the assemblies (1 Cor 11:19). That is, Paul saw the way the Corinthians were celebrating the Lord's supper as encouraging a social stratification that mirrored that of the broader society. Such stratification blocked the subaltern community's movement toward *communitas*.

Käsemann also suggested that once Paul perceived that the status reversals that flowed from this exaltation Christology could be the basis of problematic divisions, he attempted to mitigate their negative effects by promoting a "theology of the cross" (Cousar). In a classic formulation of the *raison d'être* for both "poles" (i.e. exaltation/cross) in Paul's theology, Käsemann notes (1971: 57):

> Before Paul, the cross of Jesus formed the question that was answered by the message of the resurrection. The apostle decisively reversed this way of looking at things. In his controversy with the enthusiasts it was precisely the interpretation of the resurrection which turned out to be a problem, a problem which could only be answered in the light of the cross.

The challenge in Corinth was to discover a way to live out both the status reversals won in Christ and the egalitarian vision of a society without discriminations. This was, obviously, no easy task. When it was clear that the egalitarian ethos that Paul valued was under attack by the social dynamics of *philotimia*, Paul wrote to remind the church's own spiritual elite of the way of the cross (1 Cor 1:18–24). Paul's use of the symbol of the cross to level the claims of the community's spiritual elite represents a bold move. One might wonder, however, to what extent "the strong" found the logic of Paul's rhetoric compelling—that it was only through their deference to "the weak" (a group into which Paul placed himself, 1 Cor 4:9–13), that they might expect an increase in status in the *ekklēsia* of Christ. Even if one brackets the question of how persuasive such rhetoric was, simply to follow Paul conceptually here is not an easy task. Paul is, after all, presenting an inversion of a reversal. Or as Dale Martin put it (67):

> [Paul] uses assumptions about hierarchy and status to overturn the status expectations of Greco-Roman culture. And, ultimately, he claims the highest status for himself in order to convince those of high status in the Corinthian church to imitate him in accepting a position of low status.

The Saturnalia

In the study of the origins of Christianity, the subject of the Roman Saturnalia and its Greek counterpart, the Kronia, traditionally surfaces in discussions of: (1) the background to the pericope of the mock enthronement of Jesus (Mark 15:16–20 and parallels); (2) the mythological roots of Greco-Roman "political" eschatology (e.g., Aune: 599); and (3) the origins of the festival of Christmas. In addition to these traditional points of comparison, the Saturnalia may also provide analogies to the exaltation Christology of the Pauline (and pre-Pauline) assemblies as well as the utopian ideals leveraged by it.

"The Saturnalia" is a term that is used very loosely among scholars to describe various ancient festivals that celebrated an inversion of the social roles individuals held in everyday life. Given this broad definition, historians often see a continuity between the Greco-Roman festivals of inversion and those of the medieval, reformation, and renaissance folk culture. Following the lead of Mikhail Bakhtin, literary critics also have had a tendency to perceive in the ancient festivals the archetypal expression of "the second life of the people" (Bakhtin: 10–11) that emerged in the carnival culture of premodern Europe. Used more specifically, the term "Saturnalia" refers to the best known of these ancient festivals, the Roman variety that occurred in the middle of December. I shall use the term "the Saturnalia" to refer to both the Greek festival (the Kronia) and its Roman counterpart. Even though the ancient witnesses reveal more about the Roman festival than the Greek variety, no ancient author describes either festival in detail. References to the festivals often appear, for example, in the context of satire. Available information, therefore, is sparse and does not lend itself to easy interpretation.

The basic mythological structure that stands behind the festival of the Saturnalia concerns the old high god (Kronos/Saturn) who, having abdicated his throne long ago to his son (Zeus/Jupiter), regains it for the duration of the Saturnalia. As Kronos/Saturn is connected in Greco-Roman mythology with the golden age, his re-enthronement during the festival marks the momentary return of those halcyon days. Signifying this change is the inversion of roles between master/slave, feasts of eating and drinking, and games of chance. Of the many themes connected to the Saturnalia, that of masters waiting on their servants at table stands out most clearly, from the early tradition on.

The festival's basic story line may be clearly discerned in Lucian's (b. 120 CE) *Saturnalia*. In this satirical piece, Lucian creates the character of an impoverished priest of Kronos (*Kronosolōn*) who complains to the god that his Saturnalia is not being celebrated as it was meant to be. Rather than being a true festival of inversion, the rich have shut out the poor in order to celebrate the festival among themselves in their own homes. The satire begins with a dialogue between the priest and Kronos. At one point in this dialogue, the priest asks the god why he ever abdicated his throne in the first place. Kronos answers (Lucian, *Saturnalia*, 7):

> I will tell you. In brief it was because I was old and gouty owing to my years.... I hadn't the strength to deal with all the injustice of the present generation.... So I abdicated, thank goodness, in favor of Zeus.... nevertheless I thought it best to filch these few days ... and take over the sovereignty again to remind humankind what life was like under me, when everything grew for them without sowing and without ploughing.... Wine flowed like a river, and there were springs of honey and milk; for everyone was good, pure gold. This is the reason for my short-lived dominion, and why everywhere there is clapping and singing and playing games, and everyone, slave and free man, is held as good as his neighbor. There was no slavery, you see, in my time.

Following his dialogue with the priest, Kronos lays down a series of laws for the proper observance of the household banquet that, in Lucian, is the centerpiece of the god's festival. Of those laws, two in particular point to the egalitarian intent of the festival as well as the characteristic role inversion of master/slave within the banquet context "Each man shall take the couch where he happens to be. Rank, family, or wealth shall have little influence on privilege.... When a rich man gives a banquet to his servants, his friends shall aid him in waiting on them" (17–18).

While the Saturnalian festival may have involved the temporary reversal of social roles during the archaic and classical periods, by the early empire the Saturnalia had experienced a severe domestication. In the early empire the locus of the "festival" is not the public space of the city but the confines of the household, however extended that household might be by the social networks of clientage. R. Nauta notes, "As far as our evidence goes, the unit of celebration was not the community at large, but the household or circle of friends, gathered for a banquet" (85). In Seneca's *Apocolocyntosis*, the work that is the specific focus of Nauta's study, the revelers are a particularly privileged "circle of friends." The satire was probably performed for the emperor Nero and his associates during the Saturnalia of 54 C.E.

Lucian's *Saturnalia* also assumes that the festival takes place in the homes of the wealthy. The final portion of the Lucian's satire consists of a series of "letters." One epistle in this series is written by "Kronos" and is addressed to "the rich." The picture of the Saturnalia one gets from this letter is, in fact, the opposite of its usual characterization as a festival of carnivalesque inversion where slaves get the upper hand. In this letter, Kronos informs the rich that "the poor" have complained to him that they have been excluded from the celebration of the Saturnalia (32–35):

Greetings! The poor have recently written me complaining that you don't let them share what you have, and, to be brief, they asked me to make the good things common to all and let everyone have his bit....

Oh yes, the dinners and their dining with you—they asked me to add this to my letter, that at present you gorge alone behind locked doors, and, if ever at long intervals you are willing to entertain any of them, there is more annoyance than good cheer in the dinner, and most of what happens is done to hurt them—that business of not drinking the same wine as you, for instance—goodness! How ungenerous that is.... See to it then that they don't accuse you any more, but respect and like you for their share in these few things; the expense is nothing to you, but they will never forget that you gave in time of need. Besides, you could not even live in your cities if the poor were not your fellow-citizens and did not contribute in thousands of ways to your happiness; and you would have no one to admire your wealth if you were rich in isolation, privately, and in obscurity.... In the first place they will not allow your banquet to be deaf and dumb. No, their company means convivial stories, harmless jests, and all sorts of expressions of friendship.... They will talk to everyone next day of your sociability and get you liked. And this is rightly worth a great deal.

I will ask you something. Let us suppose the poor went about with their eyes shut; wouldn't you be cross when you had no one to show your purple clothes, your thronging attendants, the size of your rings? I leave aside the plots, the hatred you must stir up in the poor against you if you choose to enjoy your luxury alone. Terrible are the curses they threaten to utter against you.

This passage indicates, first of all, that the Saturnalian feast occurred within the confines of the household and had a tendency to be celebrated by the wealthy for the wealthy. The poor, if they participated, were allowed in at appointed times and were given limited quantities of inferior food and drink. It also reveals the kinds of complaints about the high elite that actually circulated among the lower class of the cities. Lucian's rhetorical stance in itself also is interesting. He draws out the practical consequences that will result if the rich treat the poor with more care during the Saturnalia (e.g., a lessening of tension between the classes) while he plays to their obvious love of honor.

It is worthwhile to compare this letter of Kronos to "the rich" to Paul's comments to "the strong" in his first letter to the Corinthians. These documents are quite different in both genre and tone. Still, in both letters, the authors are disturbed by the ostentatious and exclusionary behavior of the "elite." What was particularly troublesome to both Lucian and Paul is that the elites expected deferential treatment in ritual meals the intent of which was, as Lucian put it, that "all have an equal share." The Lord's Supper (says Paul in 1 Cor 11:17–34) and the Saturnalia (says

Lucian) were ritual banquets in which, by design, those of lesser rank were to be treated with elevated respect. Both Paul and Lucian complained that the insensitive behavior of the "strong" contributed to the polarization between social groupings. The intent of the meals was to underscore the mutuality that existed among the groups. The dismissive behavior of those adopting elitist behavior had led to the opposite result.

Lucian and Paul address the problematic behavior of the "elite" in very different ways. There is nothing in Lucian's rhetoric that approximates Paul's request that "the strong" in Corinth respect "the weak" in the household assembly (1 Cor 4:8–16, 12:22–24). Lucian does not advise the rich that they should undergo any form of "humiliation" at the hands of the poor in their own homes. Specifically, Lucian does not suggest that the masters need become the servants of the poor in the festive banquet. This is noteworthy since a "law" of Kronos (given in *Saturnalia*, 18) is for masters (and their friends) to wait on their servants. Lucian rather points out the various gains the rich shall reap if they are more hospitable during the Saturnalia. The most notable gain is that they will receive the honor due to them as patrons of the household festival. An interesting second benefit, Lucian points out, is that the rich might even enjoy themselves more at their banquets if they invite the poor into their homes this one day of the year. The nonelites, it seems, were better storytellers than the rich.

Rhetorical Use of the Saturnalian Metaphor

Lucian's *Saturnalia* indicates that the Saturnalia had become, by the early empire, a rather tame, in-house affair. If this satire is a witness to wider social behavior, the Saturnalia had—ironically—become a festival that the elites enjoyed more than did the more marginalized groups of the city. One might ask, therefore, how it is that the Saturnalia has come to be understood as the archetypical expression of the topsy-turvy world of carnival?

Michael Bernstein, I believe, has correctly discerned why the Roman and Greek "Saturnalia" is generally thought of as a riotous festival of inversion. Bernstein points out that in the academic reconstructions of the Saturnalia: "Habitually ... ethnographic data is introduced in a more or less random manner, without attention to the basic distinction between a textual representation of carnival and the actual festival rituals" (Bernstein: 37). Many of the ancient references to the Saturnalia do not refer to actual festivals but are part of a *literary* tradition that freely uses utopian imagery. The separate details spread throughout a variety of ancient texts, then, represent a world of "intertextuality" rather than a "historical" pattern of folk culture.

By the early empire, the Saturnalian motifs had floated free from the actual ritualized celebrations of the festivals. Ancient authors impressed these utopian motifs for quite different rhetorical purposes. Philo, for instance, uses tropes associated with the Saturnalia to make the point that the first seven months of Gaius's rule seemed particularly auspicious (Philo, *Legat.* 11–14):

> At ... this the Roman people, the whole of Italy, and the nations of both Asia and Europe rejoiced. For they were all delighted with him [i.e., Gaius] as they had been with no previous Emperor, not because they were looking forward to obtaining and enjoying benefits as individuals or communities, but because they believed that they now possessed a consummation of good fortune, with happiness attending it. At any rate, there was nothing to be seen throughout the cities but altars, victims, sacrifices, people in white clothes, garlanded and cheerful, showing their goodwill by their happy faces, banquets, religious assemblies, musical competitions, horseraces, revels, night-celebrations to the music of flutes and the lyre, enjoyment, recreation, holidays, and every kind of pleasure appealing to every sense. At that time the rich had no advantage over the poor, nor the nobility over the common people, nor creditors over their debtors, and masters were no better off than their slaves; for this period gave people political equality, *so that the "age of Kronos"* [*kronikon bion*] *described by the poets ceased to be regarded as a poetic fiction* [*plasma mythou*], because of the prosperity and plenty, the freedom from grief and fear, and the festivities which went on by day and night, in private houses and in public places alike, and continued without a break for the first seven months.

Many of the "details" often compiled by historians to describe the Saturnalia festival, including the leveling of hierarchical differences, appear in this passage from Philo as utopian tropes. His disclaimer to the contrary, Philo regards such stock references to "the age of Kronos" (*kronikon bion*) as a poetic fiction (*plasma mythou*). Philo's usage of these tropes is highly ironic. As the rest of *Legatio ad Gaium* indicates, Philo's depiction of the incarnation of the golden age that occurred with the accession of Gaius was exactly what the text's narrator claimed it was not—a poetic creation.

If one observes the distinction urged by M. Bernstein between the literary traditions which employ the Saturnalia and the ethnography of the festive rituals, one is struck by the fact that the Saturnalia of ancient literature approximated the "age of Kronos" more than the festival itself did. While the "real" carnival, so to speak, occurred within textual representations, the festival itself had a tendency to fall prey to the power dynamics that controlled everyday life. In Scott's terms, the festival of the Saturnalia was part of the "public transcript" of the Greek city. Since the textual representations of the festival (e.g., Lucian, Philo) were, on the whole, not subject to the same sort of social pressures as were the ritualized celebrations, the cultural-critical edge of the Saturnalia could reemerge in them (Bernstein: 38). Lucian's *Saturnalia,* for example, although it did satirize the taste and manners of the poor (36–39), was largely directed against the hubris of the elite. In the *Saturnalia,* Lucian reminds the elite that the patronage system, as inscribed in the public transcript, is a reciprocal arrangement of mutual benefit. He urges the elite to pay at least lip-service to the values of that transcript by accepting a toned-down version of the roles assigned to them in this festival of inversion. Philo's employment of the Saturnalian imagery, on the other hand, builds up the early days of Gaius's reign in order to make the emperor's fall from grace all the more dramatic.

In addition to "critical" applications by the nonelites the motif-complex of the Saturnalia could also be used by the elite to mock one of their own. The most famous example from antiquity of this usage is found in Seneca's *Apocolocyntosis,* a satire written during the early days of Nero's reign. Among the ploys the satire uses to discredit the reign of Claudius, is the lampooning of his apotheosis and the labeling of him as a *Saturnalicius princeps* (*Apocolocyntosis* 8.2). The intent of the latter analogy is clear. Seneca means to imply that Claudius ruled the empire as the *Saturnalicius rex* reigned over the festive household banquet. That is, Claudius' reign was one of misrule characterized by acts that were arbitrary, capricious, and foolish. In particular, it was a reign in which the emperor obeyed slaves and women. The ultimate humiliation of Claudius comes at the end of Seneca's satire when slaves are made the masters of the emperor. Note, however, that in this elitist critique, the Saturnalia is no longer associated with the return of the golden age but rather, ironically, with its disappearance. As R. Nauta observes (89):

> From the viewpoint of the *Apocolocyntosis,* the return of Saturnian times had taken place under the *Saturnalicius princeps* Claudius and had not been a Golden Age. On the contrary: it had been an inversion of the preceding Golden Age under Augustus, and it had given way to the subsequent Golden Age under Nero when the inversion had again been inverted and the period of license had come to a close.

In Seneca's *Apocolocyntosis,* in other words, the status-reversals (from low to high) that characterized the Saturnalia were seen by the aristocracy (from the top down), as representing a state of anarchy rather than pointing towards a social utopia.

Augustus and the *Regnum Saturni*

The literary trope of Saturn's return was a double-edged metaphor. It contained a critical subtext that could be directed against a social ethic or mode of governance that was construed by nonelites to be unjust (e.g., Lucian, Philo). In the case of Seneca's *Apocolocyntosis,* the critical edge could also be employed by the elite to discredit a rule thought ineffective or simply disruptive of the status quo. In addition to such critical applications, however, the elites of antiquity could also selectively appropriate Saturnalian motifs in order to *legitimate* hegemonic rule. In the *Apocolocyntosis,* the notion of a "golden age" that characterized the imperial regimes on either side of Claudius's reign, as Nauta observed, was also based on a Saturnian metaphor.

The positive linkage of the rule of Rome with the *regnum Saturni* is often seen to be epitomized in Virgil's Fourth Eclogue. While the protagonist is rather vague in this piece, later in the *Aeneid* (6.791–794) Virgil explicitly identified Augustus as the one to inaugurate the golden age: "the man whom you have often heard promised to you, Augustus Caesar, the offspring of a god ... once more shall establish the golden age in Latium, through those lands where Saturn reigned of old." The similarly famous decree of the assembly of the province of Asia in 9 B.C.E. (i.e., the Priene inscription) also functioned within this tradition of panegyric that relied on Saturnian imagery. The assembly of Asia desired to award honors to Augustus because his birth was an evangelical event (*euangelion*)—it represented the inbreaking of the reign of a god which put an end to strife and established all good things. As the decree itself says, "the birthday of the god marked for the world the beginning of tidings of joy through his coming." Philo's ironical application of the Saturnalian metaphor to Gaius's reign quoted above, therefore, was simply relying upon a rhetorical tradition of imperial panegyrics which began with (the Roman) Virgil and would extend to (the Greek) Aelius Aristides (ca. 117–180 C.E.) and beyond.

If one were to press further this identification of the advent of imperial government with the return of the golden age, then the emperor may also be seen as assuming the role of the king (i.e., the *basileus* Saturn/Kronos) in the story line of the myth. His enthronement as king has ushered in a time of peace and prosperity (the *pax Romana*). H. S. Versnel, after discussing various texts that specifically link the emperor with the Saturnian imagery, claims (201):

> Taken together, these passages sufficiently illustrate the firm connections between the idealization of the ruler and the Saturnian expectations cherished by his subjects. There can be no doubt: it was the new monarchical ideology that fostered the promulgation of this

imagery and stimulated its projection onto contemporary society. In other words: *Saturnia regna* presuppose a (Saturnian) prince (king, monarch, emperor).

Since the most common identification of the emperor in the iconography of the period is with that of Zeus/Jupiter, Versnel's confidence in the "firm connections" of the emperor with the Saturnalian king pushes the evidence a bit. Yet Versnel makes his point. The use of the Saturnian metaphor of the golden age in imperial propaganda does indicate that the emperor could, at times, be linked not only to the divine rule of Zeus/Jupiter, but also to the return of his father, Kronos/Saturn.

Although there was a significant range of applications of the images which stemmed from the Saturnalia, the dominant mythological story-line lying behind the Saturnalia was quite simple: (1) Kronos/Saturn regains his throne, an activity that (2) ushers in the golden age (3) which is marked by status reversals and/or egalitarianism. The exception to this pattern is found in the Roman imperial version (e.g., in the panegyrical tradition of Virgil and the Priene inscription). Here a critical social indicator of the age of Kronos (status reversal) is missing. Since the Saturnian imagery was being used in the imperial cult to legitimate hegemonic rule, it is understandable that the characteristic motif of role reversal (master/slave) would be absent in this application.

It is, however, this highly edited imperial appropriation of the Saturnian motif-complex that has most often caught the eye of New Testament scholarship. At the turn of the twentieth century, for example, Adolf Deissmann, among others, suggested that as early Christianity moved into the Greek cities of the Eastern Empire it entered into a dialectical relationship with the myth and ritual of the imperial cult. In the decades that followed, some exegetes continued to argue for the value of interpreting the *regnum Christi* against the background of a "realized" eschatology used to promote the emperor in imperial panegyrics (Beskow: 62). Although certain passages in the New Testament were often read in these terms (e.g., Luke 2:11, 14; Titus 2:13), some exegetes such as Dieter Georgi cast the comparative net wider (86–88):

Is Paul using the traditional formula [i.e., Rom 1:3–4] in order to support an alternative theory concerning true rulership and the legitimate *princeps*? Is he offering an alternative to the social utopia of Caesarism, with its promise of universal reconciliation and peace as the prerequisite for undreamed of achievements resulting in unimagined prosperity? ... If the terms chosen by Paul for his Roman readers have associations with the slogans of Caesar religion, then Paul's gospel must be understood as competing with the gospel of the Caesars. Paul's gospel enters into critical dialogue with the good news that universal peace has been achieved by the miracle of Actium.... The *sōtēria* represented by Caesar and his empire is challenged by the *sōtēria* brought about by Jesus.

For Georgi, Jesus—the "king" acknowledged in the subaltern discourse of his early followers—is being compared to the emperor, the "king" who ushers in the golden age of the "social utopia of Caesarism." When early followers of Christ viewed the *regnum Christi* from this perspective, it is the distinctive identity of their *basileus,* as one crucified by the Romans, that signals, in Georgi's words, an "alternative to the social utopia of Caesarism." Other Pauline texts have also been read as similarly resisting the ideology of the imperial cult. The liturgical fragment found at Phil 2:6–11 has become the focus of one such academic discussion (Seeley 1994; Vollenweider 1999; Heen 2004).

The inversions and motifs associated with the Saturnalia could be put to various uses in antiquity depending on who used them and to what end. The range of applications of the Saturnian metaphor (from resisting the public discourse "from below" to legitimating the public discourse "from above") indicates the importance of analyzing the ancient uses of utopian constructs in terms of a "thick description." One must carefully rebuild the syntax of the literary or social discourse in which such motifs appear in order to understand their cultural significance. The subject is a complex one and is deserving of more careful study. Enough has been said, however, to make some claims as to the value of this line of investigation for understanding Pauline social formations.

Conclusion: Status Reversal Seen "From Above" and "From Below"

In this article I have noted similarities between the cultural-critical inversions that flow from Jesus' enthronement in the Pauline assemblies with those that are associated with the enthronement of Saturn/Kronos in Saturnalian literary texts. The parallels drawn between the *regnum Saturni* and the *regnum Christi,* upon closer inspection, will break down at points. There are differences in the story lines of the two traditions. In the Saturnalia, for instance, it is the *re*-enthronement of a god who long ago abdicated his throne that ushers in the golden age. In those subaltern communities that worshipped Christ, it is Jesus—a Jew crucified by the Romans—whose enthronement leverages a new kingdom of God (1 Cor 2:7; 15:24b–27). I do not mean to minimize differences of this sort. Yet a more important difference between the two traditions exists, I would argue, than that identified by variations in their narrative structure.

The most significant difference between the two traditions appears only when one puts to the Saturnalian material what might be called the phenomenological questions of experience and belief. That is, to what extent did the people of antiquity, from the lower socioeconomic strata, actually *experience* the yearly Saturnalian festival as a liminal return of the golden age? Or, similarly, how many ancients *believed* the accession of Augustus or Gaius or Nero actually inaugurated the *regnum Saturni?* I believe the evidence from antiquity suggests the answers, "Not much, not many." As Lucian's Saturnalia indicates, by early imperial times the domesticated festivals of the Saturnalia themselves were not experienced by the underclass of antiquity as a return of the halcyon days of old, but as another arena for potential humiliation by the wealthy. In Lucian's satire, the poor were even shut out of the feast that was to be held in their honor. I suspect, also, that the selective application of the Saturnian myth to legitimate the emperor in imperial panegyrics was not particularly per-suasive to many in the empire. Philo's insight—that the Saturnalian myth was a poetic fiction that could be impressed into different kinds of serv-ice—was not unique. In contrast, we know from Paul's correspondence that at least some of the early Christians believed that the enthronement of Jesus actually did inaugurate a *regnum Christi* in which a certain free-dom from the hierarchical stratification of everyday life could be experienced in Jesus' *ekklēsiai.* Paul's correspondence to Corinth suggests that a kind of carnivalesque atmosphere did pervade some of those assemblies (1 Cor 4:8). Indeed, Paul himself thought the exuberance with which some in Corinth took to status reversals threatened the egalitarian ideal of the church as he interpreted it.

In his study of ancient utopian literature, Robert Elliot noted that: "The portrayal of an ideal commonwealth has a double function: it established a standard, a goal; and by virtue of its existence alone it casts a critical light on society as currently constituted" (Elliot: 30). The Pauline vision of the heavenly *politeuma* (i.e., commonwealth, Phil 3:21) follows the pattern discerned by Elliot. Paul's vision of a utopian *poli-teuma* not only represented a critique of the "society as currently constituted," but also established a standard for the sort of transforma-tion of human society that Paul imagined was possible for those who had been incorporated into the ideal commonwealth of Christ. Although the egalitarian vision expressed at Gal 3:28 may not adequately describe the actual social world of the Pauline communities, such utopian visions of equality provided the *ekklēsiai,* as Elliot would say, with "standards" or "goals." This ideal (egalitarianism), in turn, came to inspire very human attempts to incarnate the heavenly *politeuma* in actual assemblies of the enthroned Christ. At least they did as far as Paul was involved. Yet, again, such an ideal was always enfolded into the complex social dynamics that ensued in the wake of peoples' actual experience of status reversals (low/high).

The similarities in the narrative structures of the myth of Kronos/ Saturn's return and that of Paul's communities are such that Saturnalian myth and ritual may have functioned as a kind of *praeparatio evangelica* for the exaltation Christology of the Hellenistic assemblies. That is, the way of the exalted *kyrios* of Paul's communities was prepared by the Saturnian archetype of a *basileus* who ruled over a golden age. If such a relationship of promise and fulfillment did exist, however, it did not evolve by means of the simple borrowing of a mythological story line or individual motifs. It was, rather, the disjunction between the radical subtext of the Saturnalia and the lack of the carnivalesque in its "festivals" that constituted the more important "preparation" for the social experiments of the people who clustered below the symbol of the enthroned Christ. Again, the cultural-critical subtext of the yearly festival of the *regnum Saturni* had long been contained by the need of the city's elite to maintain their prestige in all public encounters with the subordinate of the city. Even during the carnival, masters remained masters and slaves remained slaves. The Saturnalia had, in fact, by the early empire, become as much a part of the public discourse of the city and empire as it represented a festive or ritualized interruption of it.

One needed to look elsewhere than the Saturnalia to experience the world upside-down. What the earliest household *ekklēsiai* offered to the lower class of the city, then, in addition to a certain imaginative freedom that flowed from God's inversion of the public discourse in Christ, was a liminal space in which the social structures of the everyday world could be reversed and, to some extent, leveled. The Pauline assemblies, at least, extended the promise that "real" symbolic inversions, so to speak, could be lived out behind the backs of the dominant, within the terms of its own hidden transcript.

The early message about the enthroned Christ was the cause of excitement among some segments of the large underclass of the cities of the East. I believe this excitement was due, in part, to the fact that the social experiments of the early assemblies, even if they neither extended beyond the liminality of the subaltern formations nor were immune from encroachment from the timocratic values of the dominant culture, incarnated the utopian ideals of the wider Greco-Roman culture in a way the festival of the Saturnalia no longer could. From this perspective, then, early Pauline communities may be perceived not only as presenting an "alternative utopia" (Georgi: 33–75) to the public discourse of the city, but also as offering the city an "alternative carnival" to that of the Saturnalia.

RECONSTRUCTING "RESISTANCE" OR READING TO RESIST: JAMES C. SCOTT AND THE POLITICS OF INTERPRETATION

Cynthia Briggs Kittredge

Political scientist James C. Scott's work on "hidden transcripts" of resistance to domination has been suggestive to those scholars of early Christianity who want to analyze the communities represented in the New Testament as communities of resistance in the face of a dominant Greco-Roman imperial system (Horsley 1987; Herzog 1999; Crossan 1991). Scott's category of the "hidden transcript" allows investigators to see a complex relationship between superiors and subordinates within a system of domination. Arguing against those theorists who see dominant ideologies as completely hegemonic and those social scientists who attend only to the formal exchanges between slaves and masters, Scott asserts that submerged forms of resistance operate outside the public transcript. His book, *Domination and the Arts of Resistance,* analyzes accounts of resistance from many historical periods to find common features of these hidden transcripts. In its emphasis on "hidden" expressions of resistance, Scott's approach has resembled important feminist scholarship that has attempted to recover the voices and struggles of women from early Christian texts (Schüssler Fiorenza 1983; Wire 1990; Kittredge). The feminist strategy of reading texts "against the grain" and Scott's "hidden transcript" both question the surface constructions of the text and claim that the relationship between superiors and subordinates within a system of domination is usually more complex than it appears. Because Scott's interpretive model allows one to see resistance to domination even when there is no direct threat to the political status quo, it might be attractive to feminist historians who reconstruct Christian history as a struggle between kyriarchal domination and egalitarian visions. Unlike those sociological models that see religion as serving the status quo, Scott's model envisions religious imagination/expression as one of the forms of the hidden transcript that resists domination (Wimbush: 6). Both the emphasis on resisting activity that is hidden as well as the emphasis on the role of religion in resistance suggest a possible alliance between the work of Scott and efforts of feminist interpreters to interrogate the rhetoric of texts, particularly those, such as Ephesians, that explicitly prescribe subordination for wives, slaves, and children, and thus seem to be the expression of one kind of system of domination.

In beginning to investigate the promise of Scott's work for thinking about texts like Ephesians and for the larger project of reconstructing Christian history, I want to raise several cautions about the promise of direct "application" of Scott to reading biblical texts. These problems are the relationship between the rhetoric of texts and historical reconstruction, the rhetorical context of biblical scholarship, and where and how we locate "resistance." My introduction to the work of James C. Scott raises the possibility that his thinking may be used more profitably to analyze how historical communities read the Bible. The experiment of trying to utilize Scott in our New Testament work quickly leads to the larger question, however, about how and why we scholars working on "Paul and Politics" go about putting Paul in the context of the Roman Empire. These questions present a challenge to our project in the Paul and Politics Group.

The Rhetoric of Texts and Historical Reconstruction

In trying to employ Scott's categories to interpret a New Testament text such as Ephesians, one immediately encounters the complex relationship between texts, their reconstructed histories, and the world "behind the text." The process of reconstructing history on the basis of texts and then reading the texts in light of that reconstructed history is stubbornly circular. Acknowledging that circularity focuses attention on the hermeneutical and political choices made by the interpreter in the process of reconstruction, that is, the "politics of interpretation."

Before one uses theoretical models from social or political science to interpret the New Testament, it is necessary to highlight differences between Scott's project and that of interpreters of the New Testament. Scott analyzes the activity of social groups for which he has evidence such as oral histories, diaries, historical accounts, anthropological material, and literary depictions of social interactions such as novels. The historical contexts in which these are written are recognizable, identifiable situations of domination—for example, the antebellum south or tenant farming in the nineteenth century. From these sources Scott interprets practices that he characterizes as "hidden transcripts" of resistance. He includes here elementary forms of disguise, such as the use of anonymity through gossip, rumor, euphemism, and grumbling, as well as more complex forms of popular and folk culture such as rituals of symbolic reversal. In contrast, interpreters of the New Testament have a

prescriptive text or texts which cannot be directly analyzed as an historical situation. Although some social activity certainly lies somewhere
behind the text, the text cannot be analyzed the way an anthropologist or
social scientist would describe and explain a modern situation or an historical situation for which there is ample evidence. New Testament
scholars have a text, in the case of the epistles, a letter with an author and
an audience whose identity and profile is constructed by the letter's
author. The only way to gain access to "the world behind the text" is
through historical reconstruction. Then, within this reconstructed historical situation, one can look for evidence of a hidden transcript in response
to a situation of domination. How one reconstructs the situation behind
the letter—how one defines the conflict and the positions involved—has
an enormous impact on how the letter is read. How one defines the domination and the resistance is dependent upon this intermediate step of
reconstruction. To a greater extent than the data that Scott analyzes, the
New Testament texts are only very indirect evidence of social practices.

Feminist historians have attended to the methodological problems of
reconstructing history and the critical role played by the sociological and
historical models employed by the interpreter. A model that assumes
women's roles to be peripheral will be unable to redescribe history
wherein women figure at the center (Schüssler Fiorenza 1983: 68–95; Tolbert 1993: 264–270). Employing a sociological model of integration makes
the first century appear different than when one chooses a crisis model to
understand the relationship of early Christian communities with Roman
imperialism (Schüssler Fiorenza 2000: 102). For example, a model of early
Christianity as a conflict between orthodoxy and heresy creates a reconstruction in which Paul's positions represent orthodoxy and the positions
of his "opponents" as they are characterized in his letters are understood
to be those who deviate from a position that is already established as
authoritative. In this traditional model, the categories of "domination"
and "resistance" do not neatly cohere. On the other hand, a model that
conceives of early Christianity as a struggle between different articula-
tions of the gospel in a pluralistic culture envisions orthodoxy and heresy
as anachronistic categories. If Paul is seen as upholding traditional
gender roles within marriage against those who revise them, then Paul
might represent the domination system and other positions "resistance."
Models and theories make some explanations possible and others impossible. Acknowledging the way models shape interpretation, feminist
historians such as Elisabeth Schüssler Fiorenza have made their interests
explicit, claimed a model for early Christian history that sees women as
historical actors and reread the New Testament "evidence" in that light.
That effort has recovered Christian positions that had been made invisible in other models (Schüssler Fiorenza 1983; Wire 1990; Kittredge). In the

work of reconstruction historians of women's history have called for a renewed self-consciousness about the use of models and impact of historical reconstruction on interpretation.

THE RHETORICAL CONTEXT OF BIBLICAL SCHOLARSHIP

In addition to the difference in the kinds of sources Scott and New Testament scholars study, a second key difference between Scott's work and that of New Testament interpreters is the way those sources are valued. In interpreting Paul, scholars are not dealing with historical artifacts preserved and valued only by a specialized guild, but with texts that are, for many people, scripture that continues to have a formative effect and an authoritative role for religious institutions and for society. The historical situation that historians of early Christianity reconstruct is not nineteenth century France, but an historical time that for many Christians is a privileged period for forming and setting the pattern for Christian history (although the privilege given to "original meaning" of the text has been critically questioned by Tolbert 1995). The readings of Paul generated by alternate reconstructions of Paul's context are highly disputed because Paul's letters, pseudonymous or not, continue to matter deeply to people, and it is in this social context that New Testament scholars do their work. The limited, perspectival nature of the texts and the fact of their enormous authority and effect upon people's behavior are key elements to take into account in the adoption of Scott's theory of domination and resistance.

One of the primary aims of the Paul and Politics Group has been to understand the letters of Paul within a reconstructed historical world that takes seriously the reality of the Roman imperial system. Unlike other perspectives on Paul that read him in a more spiritualized or theological manner, the contributors to the discussion of Paul and Politics have used the work of Simon Price and Paul Zanker on the Roman imperial cult and of Richard Saller and Peter Garnsey on Roman patronage to better understand how the Roman imperial context shapes Paul's rhetoric and the early communities (Horsley 1997: 72–86, 96–103). James C. Scott's analysis of resistance appears to be ideally suited to interpret the early Christian assemblies in the Roman Empire as assemblies that resist the dominant Roman imperial order. Eric Heen has compared the "symbolic inversion" in the Roman Saturnalia with the ritual meal of the Lord's supper in the *ekklēsia* (Heen, above). Neil Elliott has analyzed the practices of mutualism in the Pauline communities as resistance to the Roman economic order (Elliott, above). Both have used Scott's categories in productive and insightful ways in this volume. By placing Paul into this Roman imperial context, the contributors to the Paul and Politics Group have tried to move away from a confessional reading of Paul to one that sees his politics—his relationship with structures of power in the ancient world—as most significant. By relying on the scholars of the Roman world and on Scott, a social scientist who describes and interprets hidden transcripts of resistance, many of the essays have sought to describe a more fully fleshed out picture of the Roman imperial situation and to view Paul within it. However, these valuable contributions have been, for the most part, focused on placing Paul in his (reconstructed) political context rather than in explicitly locating ourselves. Neil Elliott's use of the analogy of contemporary Haiti in his analysis of Pauline communities is an important attempt to be more explicit about the contemporary political context of interpretation (Elliott, above). Both the methodological problem of reconstructing history and the theologically charged nature of the sources that scholars of Paul interpret make it absolutely vital that they be as attentive to analysis of the way their own political context shapes their readings as they are to the imperial context of Paul.

Interpretation of the letter to the Ephesians exemplifies the difficulty of employing Scott's categories of public and hidden transcript to the interpretation of a New Testament text. Claiming the authority of Paul, the letter counsels subordination for wives, slaves and children. Both the problem of reconstructing historical behavior and the problem of the experienced authority of the biblical text arise clearly in the study of Ephesians.

Scholars who try to reconstruct the historical situation of Ephesians have little to go on from specific references in the letter to its audience or setting. The lack of specificity has led some scholars to see the letter arising out of a need to reinforce common values (A. Lincoln: lxxviii) in a later generation of Christians. Despite the generality of the letter, some have postulated a crisis that leads to the writing of the letter—a conflict between Jewish and Gentile Christians (Käsemann: 291) or persecution under Domitian (Lindemann: 14–15). These reconstructed situations help interpreters to understand what gives rise to the specific content of the exhortation. Information about Christianity in Asia Minor (if Asia Minor is believed to be the setting for the letter) or problems of diffusion of identity of Pauline communities are proposed to aid in understanding the context and the content of the letter.

Of most interest to many commentators is the attempt to explain the background and context of the exhortations to submission in Eph 5:21–6:8. Often referred to as the "household code," these exhortations to wives, slaves, and children to be obedient appear to resemble so closely other passages in Greco-Roman morality that commentators endeavor to explain the reasons for its incorporation into the letter and emphasize its Christian distinctiveness. Often the reconstructed situation provides the justification for the exhortation to submission. Sometimes the reasons are found in behavior within the community, sometimes from pressures from "outside," and in some cases both: "It may well have been external factors, the need to respond to accusations from outsiders and to set standards in line with common notions of propriety, as much as internal ones, the need to respond to enthusiastic demands for freedom on the part of believers, that led Christians to take up the household code" (A. Lincoln: 358). Since exhortations to submission of inferior to superior are characteristic of the domination system, many commentaries on Eph 5:21–6:8 stress either that the passage is an accommodation to the conventional and dominant morality because of external pressure or that it resists dominant morality by Christian modifications to "mutual" submission or submission modified by love (O'Brien: 406).

In my work on Ephesians I have looked at the same evidence in the letter noted by all commentators: its generality, the character of Paul claimed by the letter's author, and its culminating exhortations to submission in the final part of the letter. After observing the rhetorical features of the letter, I proposed a different historical situation to explain the rhetoric of Ephesians including the climax in 5:21–6:8. I analyzed the rhetoric of Ephesians as a tension between two competing views of unity: one view that understood unity akin the Gal 3:28 baptismal formula, exemplified and expressed in Eph 2:1–11, and a hierarchical view in which unity is expressed in analogy with the marriage relationship. Without directly contradicting the value the audience places on unity or denying the role of baptism in accomplishing that unity, the author attempts to persuade the audience to modify their view of *ekklēsia* in favor of another view built upon the model of the kyriarchal family (146). In my reconstruction of the historical situation, I attributed the view of unity as "two becoming one" to women leaders in the *ekklēsia* who understand baptism as abolishing the privilege of husbands over wives in patriarchal marriage. This stood in contrast with the view of the author for whom the marriage metaphor formed the foundation for the reality of Christ and the Church. Observations about the way the author of Ephesians reworks Colossians gives further insight into the possible historical situation of Ephesians. The author of Ephesians repeats much of the language of Colossians, emphasizes baptism while omitting the baptismal formula and the Christ hymn in Col 1:15–20, and expands and integrates the exhortation to submission more thoroughly into the letter as a whole. These revisions suggest that the author of Ephesians was writing to address the ongoing dispute over the interpretation of oneness of Christian baptism, especially as it affected gender roles. This summary of my study of Ephesians shows how the very different historical situation I reconstruct shapes my interpretation of the rhetoric of the letter. Like other commentators, I "explain" the exhortations to submission. Unlike other commentators, my primary goal is not to justify the presence of the "household code," but to read the rhetoric of the author in light of other theological positions in the assemblies. In this case, those who hold the position of baptismal unity as "oneness" "resist" the kyriarchal system, the system of domination, while the author of Ephesians reasserts a key aspect of the domination system with the use of the metaphor of marriage. In this analysis then, to use Scott's categories, the text of Ephesians is a "public transcript" of the author, the "hidden transcript" would be the baptismal unity position that my analysis has made accessible through historical reconstruction.

Commentators postulating a different historical situation might read Ephesians as a public transcript that is in itself "resistance" to the Greco-Roman household model by its Christological modification of the motifs of marital, parental, and slave subordination. For some commentators, "domination" is the pagan environment in which the Pauline communities work to survive and to allay their critics from "outside." It is clear from a brief review of approaches to Ephesians' interpretation that the way one reads domination and resistance or hidden and public transcripts in that letter is closely allied with the model of Christian history one uses, the way one evaluates the pagan context, how much power and autonomy Christian communities are thought to have in the empire, and what linguistic and symbolic options were available, among other questions. In order to evaluate and compare different historical reconstructions and the different readings they engender, one must clarify and make explicit the sociological, historical, and theological models used in their creation. Their historical adequacy can be evaluated by how well they give account of the evidence.

However, because the text of Ephesians is loaded with heavy theological freight and because the letter's prescriptions for submission of wives, slaves and children have so shaped society and the church, historical reconstructions that call into question a straightforward reading of the text as divine prescription will be highly disputed. On the basis of historical reconstructions, people who continue to read Ephesians as in some way authoritative will draw conclusions about contemporary interpretation and draw analogies between historical and modern context. Some interpreters argue that as Ephesians' emphasis on love and mutuality was distinctive from a purely patriarchal society, so Christian teaching about marriage should set itself apart as a counterculture to rampant sexual license in contemporary society. Others might argue that Ephesians' accommodation to the expectations of its pagan environment by adopting the household code can serve as a negative example for modern Christians who capitulate to the excesses of modern culture.

The powerful role that scholarly historical reconstruction plays in the interpretation of Ephesians and the ongoing importance of the first century letter to the Ephesians for contemporary understandings of church organization, marriage, and gender roles point to the way that biblical studies may be best conceptualized as a rhetorical-political activity. As Elisabeth Schüssler Fiorenza has argued, the political context of biblical interpretation means that scholarly reconstructions have a rhetorical character—they are persuasive proposals in a context of competing discourses (Schüssler Fiorenza 1999: 44–55).

Where and How We Locate Resistance

Given the caution about the circularity inherent in the reconstruction of "the world behind the text" from texts and becoming aware of the role of the scholar in constructing alternate histories and readings of texts, I think a natural next step is to think about using Scott's categories to analyze the human social activity for which we do have evidence—that is the reading/interpretation of texts in the present. James C. Scott's categories may be profitably allied with feminist criticism in thinking about the activity of reading texts in the present. Gerald West has used Scott's notion of domination and resistance to understand the role of socially engaged biblical scholars who read with "ordinary readers" among the poor and marginalized in his South African context (West 1999a). He depends upon the work of socially engaged feminist biblical scholars who state their advocacy stance, identify the ideology of a biblical text, foreground their reading method, and then read "behind" the text to recover resources and models in historical biblical sources (75). West describes how in the contextual bible study process ordinary readers are in constant dialogue and argument with the dominant discourse (136). Against this dominant discourse, the participants in these conversations use the resources that critical biblical scholarship offers them to "remember" the dominant discourse and enact ideological resistance (137). From his experience with Bible study, West claims only to offer "glimpses of readings that are to be found offstage among the poor and marginalized who call us to share their struggle with the God of life against the forces of death" (142). In West's context, the dynamics of domination and resistance do not have to be imaginatively reconstructed from texts but are the lived reality of the participants.

Resistance to dominant discourse happens even within social groups that are very different from both the academic guild and from West's Institute for the Study of the Bible group. A kind of resistance occurs even within communities where the view of biblical authority is inviolate and where the discourses of subordination are unquestioned. In her work on the Women's Aglow Fellowship, R. Marie Griffith analyzes the narratives of evangelical women and their interpretations and enactments of the teaching of submission, particularly as it is expressed in Eph 5:21–6:4 (Griffith 1997). Through careful reading of the first person reports of these women over a span of years, Griffith observes that the stories reveal "multiple possibilities for reinterpreting and even subverting the doctrine of submission to women's own ends" (163). Even with a very strict view of biblical authority and an extremely conservative model of gender roles, the women's testimonies show, Griffith notes, that "personal power may be encoded in the doctrine of submission" (166). "Surrendering one's will to an authority is a vital meaning of submission, but this is not its sole meaning for evangelical women" (172). In a situation where open resistance to a dominant discourse is theologically ruled out, even the stance of "surrender" can become a doctrine that leads to freedom and transformation. Griffith shows how the cultural factors such as the twelve-step movement and other movements of personal liberation have shaped the self-understanding of evangelical women and marked their testimonies. Over the course of the period in which she studied these narratives, Griffith notes how gender elements of submission have been perceptibly de-emphasized (177).

Griffith further discovers that the notion of spiritual warfare, referred to in Eph 6:10–17 "provide the means by which female submission may be subverted and transformed into a tool of authority" (186). Although direct exegesis of Eph 5 and 6 is not part of these testimonies, Griffith's work shows an example of how women resist with a tradition of spiritual warfare deeply shaped by the Ephesians imagery. In a situation where direct opposition to submission teaching is impossible, by emphasizing other features of the text, such as engagement in spiritual warfare, women still reread and "re-member," in Gerald West's phrase, the biblical tradition within which they live.

The example of the arts of resistance that West describes in the South African context and that Griffith explores among the evangelical Women's Aglow Fellowship directs our attention to the practices of reading authoritative texts that have been complicit in undergirding the social system of domination and subordination in which individuals live. Reading authoritative texts such as these is what we as biblical scholars do. We have been projecting the model of resistance and domination into the past. But what we do when we redescribe Paul's imperial context, the inextricability of "politics" and "religion," or the economic dimension of the practices of the *ekklēsia*, is itself a kind of "resisting" reading. However, we have not explicitly named it as such. In the conflict between those scholars who do New Testament interpretation claiming historical objectivity and theological neutrality and those who name their theological commitments at the outset and admit, as Gerald West does, to being socially engaged, we remain in the dominant discourse of scientific objectivity when we use Scott's model only to analyze the reconstructed "world behind the text."

Although I understand the pressure to take on the dominant discourse about Paul in an indirect manner by keeping our social engagement and theological commitments "hidden," I think that we would be more effective if we named our strategy and subjected it to critical questions. If we took seriously the character of our readings as rhetorical and if we situated our reading within our own political commitments, we would explain why we choose the model of power relations of James C. Scott over another. We would heed the warnings of feminist scholars against uncritical use of theoretical models from sociology and anthropology for historical Jesus research (Schüssler Fiorenza 2000: 84; Tolbert: 264–66). Heuristic models used to explain the world also shape that world and the possibilities within it. We would explore what this particular model can and cannot recognize and what it can and cannot explain. We might ask whether the model understands gender to be part of the domination system or whether gender is considered as a separate category. We might question how much the model of domination and resistance, although now nuanced with the category of hidden transcript, remains a simple oppositional construction. According to it domination can only be resisted in disguised form until it breaks out in open rebellion. On the basis of the questions we want to ask and the data we observe, we might want to modify the model itself.

I suggest that the essential political and theological problem for feminist historians, and perhaps also for some who want to read Paul in the politics of empire is this: because of the commitment to liberation and life as the overall thrust of the gospel proclaimed by these texts, these socially engaged biblical scholars seek resources for that movement from texts that are in many respects, conservative, apologetic, and elite. In androcentric texts from a patriarchal society, women seek resources for emancipation. From texts from a slave-owning society, those committed to the abolition of slavery have sought good news. In texts from communities that had to survive within the Roman Empire and drew on categories from a kyriarchal system and patronage, interpreters read resistance to empire. To read only the public transcript or the surface of the text would result in failure. So because of the authority of these texts and the privileged nature of this historical period, these readers go beneath the surface, behind the text, to the hidden transcript. I think that shifting the focus from the texts and the reconstructed world behind the text to the activity of reading offers more promise for us.

If we focus on using Scott's categories only for our reconstructive efforts and do not recognize our own readings as acts of resistance coming out of our own political commitments, then we will remain in a standoff between our reconstructions and those of others who do not take into account factors such as empire the same way we do. But if we brought the hidden into the open, then we would not claim to have "found" authoritative prototypes of resistance to empire or to patriarchal models of marriage. We would say that as readers in the present, our concern about global capitalism and our commitment to communities of equal discipleship have shaped the questions we ask of the text and the models with which we reconstruct the past.

Hidden Transcripts and Arts of Resistance in Paul's Letters: A Response

Susan M. (Elli) Elliott

It would not be surprising for a biblical scholar confronted with applications of James C. Scott's work to New Testament texts to wonder aloud, "What? Something else to remind us how little we can say for certain? 'Splain me how we needed this?" Scott's work might seem at first glance to shine a shadow, as it were, rather than a light, on the texts of the early Christian communities. The very concept of the hidden transcript tells us that a world of discourse lies in obscurity. These essays, however, show us that the realization that a hidden transcript exists can, indeed, help to reveal it.

In his introduction to this volume Richard Horsley suggests that Paul's letters provide us with glimpses into the development of the hidden transcripts in the early Christian communities, and the authors in this section demonstrate that in many instances the hidden transcripts lurk just below the surface. Neil Elliott and Erik Heen tease out the hidden transcript of a horizontally oriented project of community formation in Paul's own letters while Cynthia Kittredge indicates that we should look for layers of hidden transcript especially in gender-based intracommunity power relations. She illustrates this in her analysis of the letter to the Ephesians. Kittredge also introduces a larger question in her attention to the politics of interpretation by suggesting that Scott's work be used to understand scripture as part of the present-day public transcript and "creatively resistant" interpretation by members of subordinate groups as an example of hidden transcripts.

A common assumption prevails among all three writers, however, that Scott's work is useful for interpretation in our present-day context because the notion of the hidden transcript is applicable and relevant, even in societies that do not precisely fit the extreme forms of domination he surveys (Scott 1990: x, 20). Scott offers a valuable heuristic tool, and it may be helpful to understand that hidden transcripts are being written wherever there are unequal power relationships and social space for the hidden transcript to emerge. The question of public and hidden depends in some sense on our delineation of the arena of power, from family units to the global economy. As Scott remarks, "power relations are ubiquitous" (Scott 1990: 26), and these essays indicate that several arenas of power are in view that could be delineated more carefully.

First, however, I can think of no better description of the hidden transcript in our present context than a telling comment made by a Mexican immigrant student in one of the English and citizenship classes I taught in a church basement in Chicago. In a discussion of the Bill of Rights in the U.S. Constitution and the meaning of freedom of speech, students who knew refugees from Guatemala, El Salvador, and Cuba were affirming how different it is in the United States where you can say what you believe without fear of being tortured or killed. This young man interjected, "Yes, Teacher, we can say whatever we want, but nobody is listening." As we unpacked what he meant, students gave many examples of their voicelessness in the workplace, the unresponsiveness of police, and especially the complete inaccessibility of the media to them, Spanish and English media alike.

"We can say whatever we want, but nobody is listening" means "We have no access to the public transcript." It speaks to the nature of the hidden transcript in an increasingly globalized arena of power in which the social space where the hidden transcript may emerge appears to be relatively large, and the transcript is often hidden more by lack of attention to it than by any apparent suppression. The "writers" of the public transcript may even be faceless to the broad mass of the population and the element of personal terror may be remote. The notion of the hidden transcript is nevertheless useful for understanding the dynamics of an increasingly globalized network of unequal power.

The contemporary process of global consolidation bears some similarities to the process at work in the early Roman Empire, the context of the New Testament texts. These points of contact give special significance to the work represented here. The articles in this section make an effort to listen to the hidden transcript both in the New Testament texts and in this new globalizing context. Even if such listening does not reach the globalizing public transcript to rewrite it, the activity is part of defending the social space for transcripts of resistance.

My own response will begin with attention to what Cynthia Kittredge refers to as "reconstructing resistance," the activity of reconstruction of the New Testament context, where I will comment primarily on the papers of Neil Elliott and Erik Heen. Then I will offer some thoughts in response to Kittredge's case for attention to the activity of interpretation as the development of the hidden transcript. This will include some thoughts on the interrelation of the two activities and the social location of New Testament scholars.

HIDDEN TRANSCRIPTS AND HYPOTHETICAL RECONSTRUCTIONS

The essays in this section offer a number of insights for the use of Scott's work on hidden transcripts to reconstruct the context of Paul's letters. They demonstrate that attention to the hidden transcript is indeed useful for "reconstructing resistance."

Neil Elliott is at careful pains to legitimate the application of Scott's work specifically in the urban context of Paul's community formations, characterizing Scott's analysis as specifically rooted in rural peasant formations. While this concern is appropriate given Scott's original work on forms of resistance among Malaysian peasant communities (Scott 1985), no apology is needed for application of the theoretical work which frames this Semeia Studies volume, *Domination and the Arts of Resistance* (Scott 1990).

In this more general theoretical work, Scott sets forth a description of the public and hidden transcripts as they operate in extreme forms of domination which bear what he calls a "family resemblance" to one another. These forms of domination, these "institutionalized means of extracting labor, goods, and services from a subject population," are characterized by (1) "formal assumptions about superiority and inferiority" supported by ideology and "a fair degree of ritual and 'etiquette'" regulating public conduct; (2) ascribed status; (3) minimal social mobility; (4) few political or civil rights for subordinate groups; (5) "a strong element of personal rule" with the infusion of "an element of personal terror"; and (6) social space in which "the subordinate group has a fairly extensive offstage social existence which, in principle, affords it the opportunity to develop a shared critique of power" (Scott 1990: 20).

Whether we look at exploitation in rural agrarian settings or in urban centers, the forms of domination that characterize the Roman Empire certainly fit this "family resemblance" in every aspect. The Roman system was a patchwork of forms of exploitation, including a massive slave system present on the *latifundia* and a pastiche of other forms of agricultural exploitation tied together by onerous taxation as well as the interrelated slave-family and patron-client systems present in the urban areas. Nevertheless, all of the forms of domination share a family resemblance to the forms Scott describes. No defense of the use of Scott's work in relation to Paul's urban community formations is really necessary other than noting this "family resemblance."

Elliott also takes care to clarify briefly why the so-called "new consensus" about the "social status" of the early Christian communities must be deemed suspect at least. Care on this note proves especially useful in light of Cynthia Kittredge's notes on the politics of interpretation. While it is certainly important to acknowledge that one's standpoint influences interpretation and there is no omniscient standpoint, we do not need to concede that all reconstruction is completely circular (even if it tends to be "stubbornly" so, as she says). Interpretation, at least in the reconstructive activity, need not be reduced entirely to relative free choice. Historical evidence offers some restrictions, even though we must attentively deconstruct literary sources given the bias of their standpoint—and their general inclusion in the "public transcript." If the reconstruction of the so-called "new consensus" about the social status of early Christian communities is based on an anachronistic and inaccurate interpolation of a "middle class" into Greco-Roman society, then a reconstruction based on a more accurate description of social relations in the New Testament context has arguably greater validity. That "more accurate description" emerges, of course, from analysis of the evidence from a variety of standpoints.

While all such descriptions are laden with bias and the limitations of the observer's viewpoint, the reconstructive project logically suggests that we seek enlightenment from social conditions and locations in the present that are similar to the context of the early Christian communities. The emergence of Christian community formations as a new social-religious movement in the context of a newly consolidating empire argues for the priority of comparison to similar social locations in the present for our reconstructions. For example, Elliott's experience of Haitian peasant organizations forming in the context of a repressive local system in a newly consolidating global economy offers insights for reconstruction that are arguably more valid than experience from social locations with less similarity to the early Christian communities. This does not make such reconstructions factual or true, simply more useful and more probable.

Elliott introduces experience from Haiti ostensibly to solve the problem of applying Scott's analysis from a rural peasant setting to urban community formations, a nonexistent problem as we have seen. We may also legitimately wonder how the move to modern peasant organizations gets us to the urban poor of the Roman Empire and exactly how Elliott's example relates to his subsequent exposition. While this experience may not be absolutely necessary for his stated purpose, Elliott's apparent "detour" into Haiti nevertheless aims us toward several other, and perhaps more important, worthy purposes.

There is, of course, the importance of social experience beyond literate middle class academia as a vital lens for understanding the dynamics of the early Christian communities. We can see in Elliott's exposition a move toward economic analysis that allows a systemic alignment for interpretation. Such an alignment recognizes the similarities of the present-day globalizing economy and the consolidation of the Roman Empire during the first century C.E. Elliott's description of the Haitian context points us toward a need to devote further attention to the application of Scott's criteria for the "family resemblance" among forms of domination to an analysis of power in the present global economic system. Elliott's assertion of the need for Pauline studies to move beyond the "divorce" between the "material basis of the struggle" and "the struggle over values—the ideological struggle" is also vitally important.

Further attention is also warranted to the specific characteristics of forms of domination in economic empires as they are in the process of consolidation. An important aspect of the context of the early Christian communities, both urban and rural, is the very newness of the empire. The combination of changing alignments of power and social dislocation that happen during such periods of consolidation have aspects of "family resemblance" well worth examination for an understanding of the social context of the early Christians. In such changing conditions, social experimentation, such as the experimentation Elliott describes in Haiti and the experimental community formations of the early Christians, becomes more possible. This aspect of experimentation is what creates the bridge that Elliott perceives as necessary to link Scott's work on "Malaysian peasant society" and "intentional communities of mutuality among the poor in Roman cities." Elliott's use of this bridge points us toward the usefulness of investigation of other such "bridges" in contemporary experience as well. We would also do well to seek out experiments in urban conditions where social dislocation is a major factor that poses different challenges for the formation of intentional communities of mutuality than the challenges for peasants in the countryside where the same extended families and support networks have often been rooted for generations.

Elliott's choice of the experience of peasants' organizations is nevertheless helpful for the reconstructive activity, especially by comparison to merely personalized readings from individuals in social locations outside the traditional social contexts of biblical scholarship. The choice to introduce knowledge gained in observant participation in the social project of Haitian peasants specifically helps us to uncover the notion of the social project present in Paul's letters. This is especially important since, as Elliott points out, Scott's primary Malaysian experience "does not offer examples of formally organized peasant movements." This can open a much richer field of investigation for future work.[1]

---

1. I know that some of my own experiences (living in a village in Mexico with leaders who formed both the Arizona Farmworkers Union and a peach-growers cooperative, and organizational work with the urban poor in Chicago) have offered many rich insights for understanding the dynamics behind a number of New Testament texts. Such insights have

In offering the experience of the Haitian peasant organizations, Elliott offers an outline of a "family resemblance" of social projects of resistance that might emerge in similar contexts. Dissident subcultures might take a variety of forms, not necessarily democratic or egalitarian ones, as Scott points out (Scott 1990: 26). Even in a mutualistic subculture, Scott cautions that the "hidden transcript that develops in this case may be experienced as no less tyrannical despite the fact that all have a hand in shaping it," and the mutualism relies on coercive pressure to maintain "conformity to standards that violate dominant norms" (Scott 1990: 26–27, 129).

Elliott and Heen both assess Paul's strategy more positively as a social project of egalitarian community formation characterized by horizontal relationships of mutual dependency counterposed to the vertical relationships of dependency in the patronage system. Elliott terms this "mutualism," Heen, *communitas.*

While such a social project requires strategies of enforcement (with varying degrees of success as both Elliott and Heen indicate), it is an intentional and profoundly creative activity. Elliott describes Haitian peasant organizations based on goals and survival strategies that respond to basic aspects of the "hostile environment" created by the form of domination in which they live. The organizational principles and the aspects of their experience he enumerates, however, clearly draw creatively on a variety of sources in their generation of a hidden transcript and are not simply reactive to the public one.

Heen similarly indicates this creative aspect in his analysis of symbolic inversion. He portrays symbolic inversion as a liminal activity. Seen this way, whether in ritual or in utopian tropes of literary imagination, symbolic inversion cannot be precisely pigeonholed as "radical social critique" or "letting off steam to maintain the social order." As a liminal-creative activity it has what Scott calls an "imaginative function" (Scott 1990: 169). We should understand the role of symbolic inversion, as Heen does, in an interstitial social space which functions not only as a place where the hidden transcript can emerge as a negative response but also where alternative cultures can be imagined. This creative-generative aspect is important to remember as a caution against too reductionist a reading of Scott, an issue I will revisit below.

---

frequently been unwelcome or simply unintelligible in academic circles specifically because the "hidden transcript" is often remote from the experience acknowledged in academia. Scott's work offers a welcome tool to make such insights useful and intelligible in academic work.

An additional characteristic of the Haitian social project that Elliott describes goes unnoticed in his description and is relevant for a social description of the early Christian communities and for our reading of Paul as engaged in an analogous "mutualistic" social project. This is Elliott's own participation in the project and the "benefaction" of the Lambi Fund. While the members of the Board of Directors listed on the Fund's Web site (www.lambifund.org) can hardly be described as members of the international ruling elite, they are relatively privileged in comparison to the peasants who have formed the organizations Elliott describes. What is significant, however, is that such supportive individuals and organizations have chosen to participate in a mutualist social project not as "patrons" but as project companions. If experience from similar projects is any indication, even with the best of intentions and good will, constant vigilance is necessary to maintain the mutual relationship in the context of disproportionate resources and privileges. Paul's letters reflect that struggle, not so much of the "status ambivalence" of the "new consensus" but the defense and promulgation of a social project not fully owned by all the members of the communities he formed. We need not assume the absence of relatively privileged individuals from those communities in order to understand their social project as one rooted in the subordinate groups.

Before we become too enthused about the distinctiveness of the early Christian communities on this point, however, we need to examine a complex web of mutual support in other community formations in the early Roman Empire. These include popular religious formations such as the various organizational forms connected to the mystery cults as well as the example mentioned in Erik Heen's paper: the *collegia*. Heen's work provides a helpful summary. He describes the *collegia* as a form of "lesser euergetism" formed to allow the honor of benefaction and an elite standing within the group to those unable to participate in positions in the *polis* reserved for the ruling elite. Heen's comments appear to assume that because of the presence of patronage and benefaction, the *collegia* mimicked upper-class values and presumably the vertical relationships of the patronage system. As Heen indicates, this interpretation of the *collegia* has been used to characterize the house churches. As he points out, however, "[t]he governing structures of these associations often mimicked those of the larger city." This mimickry included monthly business meetings modeled after the city council and a monthly social gathering for a meal and some form of *symposium*.

We need to consider these meetings not only as mirror reflections of the vertical relations of the patronage system, however, but also as social space for the generation of the hidden transcript among socially dislocated members of the vast class of subordinate groups in the Roman

Empire. We should also not discount the mirroring of the lateral social bonding among members of the elite and the ideology of equality among them. Viewed this way, we can see that the form of organization we have in the written record may well reflect not their actual organization but the "cover" under which they met to make social space for the hidden transcript, even while making their organizations appear nonthreatening to the elites. We know that the elites perceived such gatherings and associations with some level of threat. A frequently cited example of this perception of threat is the Emperor Trajan's prohibition of the formation of a fire brigade in Nicomedia in Bithynia (Pliny, *Epistle* 10.33–34). It is unlikely that they were just paranoid given the catalog of popular disturbances Elliott offers.

Overlaying the two examples of community formation in view in light of Scott's notion of the hidden transcript allows us to consider a deeper and more complex set of relationships being formed in the early Christian community formations addressed in Paul's letters. Paul defined the social project as one of *mutualism/communitas*, yet the pesky human beings who participated, drawn primarily from the urban slums, required constant coaching to learn new habits and patterns of relationship, different from what Heen terms "timocratic culture." Participants with some relative privilege could prove especially irksome on this point, and certainly all the members of the communities came with mixed motivations. The internal power relations were, of course, as complex as they are in any human grouping.

Paul's social project thus required strategies of enforcement. One of these, as Elliott indicates, was the collection Paul took for the "poor" at Jerusalem (see 101–102, above). His analysis on this point, and the overall argument that hidden transcripts of resistance to the patronage system may be found in Paul's letters, is supported also by John K. Chow's work on the Corinthian correspondence. On the collection described in 1 Cor 16:1–4, for example, Chow indicates that the call for every member of the community to take part on a voluntary basis, saving up bit by bit, was a way of disempowering the patrons by making the source of benefaction community-wide (Chow 1992: 185–86). This aspect of Paul's strategy in the collection bears even more directly on the formation of mutual and horizontal relations within the *ekklēsia* than the establishment of equal relations among communities on which Elliott focuses. While the intercommunity mutuality is an important aspect of the strategy, it is this intracommunal aspect that would enforce the ethos of mutuality in an especially effective and enduring way, precisely because it would allow the poor to engender and know their own collective power and honor even as it diminished the power and honor of the would-be benefactor-patrons. This only strengthens

Elliott's argument about the considerable internal disciplines required to maintain mutualism.

Heen analyzes a second element in a strategy of enforcement of mutualism: Paul's use of the symbol of the cross. He emphasizes the intracommunity dynamics and returns profitably to Ernst Käsemann's use of William Bousset's work to show that Paul "lifts" the cross to counter the "'misuse' of exaltation Christology at Corinth." Heen indicates that, because of the status reversal in baptism, status within the *ekklēsia* may have been based on different criteria than those of the polis at large, a "spiritual status" that may not necessarily have corresponded to deference to wealth and privilege. We would do well not to leap too quickly to discount the assumption of superior status by those who held relative privileged status in the *polis,* namely, those who aspired to function as the community's patrons and had some wherewithal to do so. Nevertheless, Paul's rhetoric of the cross counters those who would perpetuate any pattern of vertical relationship in imitation of the prevailing "timocratic culture" and seek the upper position for themselves. Paul presents the cross as a humbling symbol for all. Paul's rhetoric of the cross has, however, something of a somersaulting effect as an "inversion of a reversal," as Heen indicates.

Heen's analysis of symbolic inversion incorporates the two types of alternatives envisioned in symbolic inversion as analyzed by Victor Turner and shows the role of the rhetoric of the cross in both. One alternative is the reversal or interchange of the upper and lower roles for which the rhetoric of the cross brings a critique of imperial cult and ideology. I will return to this below. The other alternative is the deconstruction of the inequality itself, what we have already been discussing as *communitas* or mutualism. In this we have the stream of egalitarian community formation in early Christianity that both Elliott and Heen (as well as many other New Testament scholars) perceive as the major thrust of Paul's social project.

We should, however, maintain caution before we trumpet unrestrained enthusiasm for the idyllic egalitarianism of the early communities or the purity of Paul's frustrated intentions for them. Power relations are indeed ubiquitous, and almost always complex, and no one, Paul included, comes into the mix with pure motivations. Heen and Kittredge both contribute important cautions on this point, pointing toward the layers of power relations and the patterns of relations in the mix. On this point we might well take note of a comment Scott makes in a footnote that there may be "domination within domination" that engenders a "hidden transcript within the hidden transcript" (Scott 1990: 27 n. 13). Kittredge's work on Ephesians seeks just such a definition of layers of hidden transcripts with particular attention to the complexity of the relation of gender domination to other forms.

As a second large topic in the reconstructive activity, both Elliott and Heen offer insightful analyses of the ways that a hidden transcript derived from the Roman imperial context can be discerned in Paul's letters. Elliott offers a glimpse of a hidden transcript in Philo that bolsters his reading of Rom 13 as an exceedingly reserved "affirmation" of Roman power, reflecting a hidden transcript of begrudging acceptance of the Empire's superior capacity for physical terror. Elliott also offers Paul's rhetoric of the cross as a counter to the public transcript of the imperial ideology and cult.

We have already seen that both Heen and Elliott perceive Paul's use of the cross as a symbol of enforcement of mutualism as a resistance strategy. Heen provides an ampler discussion of the cross as a central symbol counterposed to the imperial cult in the context of a symbolic inversion with utopian tropes similar to the narrative structure of the Saturnalia. In this analysis of Paul's use of the cross, Heen takes us into a more detailed interaction with Scott's theoretical work in an analysis of symbolic inversion and into a more detailed look at the ceremonial aspect of the imperial public transcript.

A few additional elements of his analysis are particularly noteworthy. Heen makes an especially careful analysis of the discrepancy between the literary tradition of the Saturnalia and the evidence of its actual practice in the early imperial period. It would appear that, far from being a festival of rowdy reversal reconstructed in the scholarly imagination, the actual practice occurred in a domesticated form within the home and in many instances actually excluded the poor. The utopian vision, however, is preserved in the literary record. Here the literary record conveys the hidden transcript, perhaps as the memory of a previous era when the subordinate groups had claimed more social space for a ritual of reversal, a space reclaimed in the eras studied by Bakhtin and Scott (1990: 172–82). Perhaps by the early Roman imperial era, the "hidden" transcript in the Saturnalia had become apparent to the elites and the ritual observance had been claimed for the public transcript. Yet the Saturnalian literary motifs floating free of the ritual apparently provided utopian tropes for the creative imagination generating the hidden transcripts—even as they were used in reverse in the public transcript to ridicule the Emperor Claudius.

Heen shows that this same hidden transcript lurks beneath Lucian's letter from Kronos about the distortion of the festival. The letter itself is an example of the first form of political discourse among subordinate groups that Scott describes, an appeal to the elite based on their own own self-flattering rhetoric asking that they mitigate the conditions of their subordinates (1990: 18). This is an especially useful text for comparison to

Paul's Corinthian correspondence, and Heen uses it well to show that Paul's appeal to the relative elite in the *ekklēsia* is based not on their own rhetoric but Paul's own definition of a different social project.

We have seen then, that these three articles illustrate how useful Scott's work can be for the reconstruction of the context of the Pauline correspondence, especially Paul's own letters.

SCRIPTURE AS PUBLIC TRANSCRIPT AND HIDDEN TRANSCRIPTS OF INTERPRETATION

Cynthia Kittredge's article for this volume provides a brief but incisive presentation of a larger question for the use of Scott's work and for the project of the Paul and Politics Group. She brings us to the present in a different manner than Neil Elliott does and asks us to apply the notion of the hidden transcript to the interpretation of scripture. She correctly diagnoses the appropriation of scripture as public transcript in a manner not so dissimilar, perhaps, from the appropriation of the ritual of the Saturnalia by Roman elites. Inasmuch as the hidden transcript is also visible in the text of scripture, we can look for its revelation also in the manner of the literary use of the utopian tropes of the Saturnalia. It is there to be found, whether by reconstruction in the academy or by reinterpretation by members of subordinate groups in their own generation of the hidden transcript.

Kittredge also argues for making explicit what sociological models we are choosing and for openness in our politics of interpretation. Making our choice of model explicit is especially warranted in our use of Scott's work. While Scott himself indicates awareness of the multiplicity of hidden transcripts as specific to given social sites and consisting not only of speech but also of practices (Scott 1990: 14), his work could be read simplistically to imply that subordinate groups think universally in terms of conflict. Use of his work is also susceptible to a simplistic reduction of the hidden transcript to a unified version beneath the surface hypothetically reconstructed to fit a single model, a politics of interpretation of the hidden transcript, if you will. Nothing could be further from the actual situation.

Just as different sociological models undergird assumptions in today's public transcript, a panoply of views exists offstage as well. To lay out a method of approach to draw lines of correspondence between sociological models defined in the academic arena and the worldviews discerned in offstage conversations of subordinated groups is a large task that merits further attention and discussion. A few initial observations may advance the discussion, however. While I have no direct experience of the absolutely extreme forms of domination that Scott studies, my own overhearing of "offstage" conversation (in Mexican villages that send large numbers of men to the groves of Arizona, among the urban poor in Chicago, and among farmers and workers in the economically depressed U.S. heartland) indicates to me that just as great a variety of models and worldviews exist in the hidden transcripts. In this we might assume that the hidden transcripts are derived from the public transcripts of their contexts, that the modern contexts of public transcripts defined in allegedly democratically ruled centers of power yield a variety of points of view and the hidden transcripts reflect that multiplicity. Yet the context of the Roman Empire also yields abundant evidence of such multiplicity as well and has certain structural similarities in this aspect. An array of philosophies is present in the literary record and there is abundant indication of the participation of more than dominant classes in a wide variety of philosophical and popular religious persuasions. These various worldviews are not all founded in the assumption of conflict.

We must account, for example, for the theme of forgiveness evident at times in the hidden transcript as it emerges into confrontation with the public transcript in forms of active nonviolent resistance in the present day, forms which often draw heavily on Christian theology and scripture. While one interpretation of such movements is surely a conflict model, there is also a symbolic universe envisioned that encompasses the dominating forces and even identifies with them as fellow victims. There are worldviews rooted also in a unified perception of the natural world that absorbs and ultimately heals all. The recognition of and alignment with a power larger than the current transitory power allows members of subordinated groups a means to recognize the weakness and humanity of the dominating group and even to forgive them. Certainly the role model of Jesus on the cross saying, "Father, forgive them, they don't know what they're doing," can be read as the voice of the hidden transcript of such a spiritual perception by victims seeking transcendence rather than conflict. For example, participants in antiwar movements often experience this tension. Some resisters seek a victory of the forces of peace over the forces of war-making in accordance with a symbolic universe of conflict that requires victory over the destructive forces. Others oppose the same war from a symbolic universe of transcendent unity that avoids combative language in a transformative model. More than one symbolic universe may be at work even among members of the same movement, perhaps even within the same person.

Scott's analysis of the hidden transcript of resistance lets us see that a variety of symbolic universes can be constructed to allow the "inward" noncompliance of the mind-soul-spirit while complying physically. In this aspect we can see evidence of a hidden transcript of resistance in the profound body-denial and search for "peace of mind" present in many of the philosophical movements of the Greco-Roman era and in many currents of thought in the early Christian communities, including Paul's thought. We can perceive a hidden transcript of resistance to a condition of general social dislocation and disturbing violence. Especially when we consider a culture based on a family system that included slaves (children as well as adults) as objects of sanctioned sexual exploitation, we can understand that the people so used had to have found ways to distance themselves as persons from their abused bodies. Even some of the more privileged members of such households, those who only witnessed or were aware of such exploitation and the violence of beatings and the gruesome entertainments enjoyed especially by the Romans, needed the psychological distance provided by the bifurcation of mind and body. Similar lines of thought suggest numerous questions for exploration of present-day hidden transcripts of interpretation of the mind-body split that has justifiably formed a pivotal element for feminist reflection on Christian theology. This is to suggest that the notion of the hidden transcript opens worlds within worlds for interpretation. We have only begun to scratch the surface of the implications of Scott's work for the interpretation of scripture.

In our enthusiasm for Scott's work, we should exercise caution in other areas, however. Allen Callahan's cautionary comments should help us to distinguish actual resistance from mere anger and resentment. That is, what we seek as a transcript of resistance is an alternative set of relationships that stimulates opposition to and contravention of the public transcript. We must likewise acknowledge that Scott's theoretical work (*Domination*) is admittedly preliminary in many areas and does not claim to provide all that we need to understand the functioning of subordinated peoples. We might do well to nuance Scott's analysis with a notion of an array of forms of nonacquiescence, not all of which can be named "resistance."

We must also acknowledge, for example, that while there are hidden transcripts of resistance, there are also hidden "transcripts" of outright self-destruction in the widespread patterns of addictive behaviors among subordinated groups pushed into varying states of despair. At one level, such forms of slow suicide may express a refusal to submit willingly to the humiliations of subordination, but on another level they enact the personal destruction of the subordinated people scripted by the ideological stereotyping characteristic of the public transcript. We should acknowledge, too, that such self-destruction also forms part of the hidden transcript of the powerful. Release from addictive and personal self-destructive behaviors can be a major factor in transgression and resistance, one also worth exploring in the themes of Paul's letters and in present-day hidden transcripts.

A major contribution of Scott's work, however, is the recognition of the creative and generative potential in the hidden transcript. In this we err if we reduce Scott's work too narrowly to a conflict model. We make a serious error if we believe that the generation of the hidden transcript is only a reactive activity and not an immensely creative one, the "seed growing secretly" in the fiercely defended social spaces of those denied a voice in the generation of the public transcript. We also make a serious error if we believe that the hidden transcripts must fit our definitions of what they should say in response to our analysis of the world.

This is the essential insight of Scott in response to the problem of "ideological hegemony" (Scott 1990: 70–109): rather than try to explain why "the people" do not do what we (intellectual observers in whatever form) think they should according to our analysis of the world, we should instead "listen louder" to the voiceless and try to understand their perspective and the creative power at work in their struggle for existence. This listening is required both in the reconstructive activity of the Paul and Politics Group within the academy and in the activity of attentiveness to the generation of the hidden transcript in the interpretation of scripture by those whose social location most closely approximates the context of the early Christian communities.

This brings us to further implications of Kittredge's larger question of the politics of interpretation. Her observations point us toward an even more basic question for examination and discussion—the question of our social location and social project as New Testament scholars. If we seriously probe the issues Kittredge raises of the politics of interpretation in the hidden transcript of interpretation of scripture-as-public-transcript, and if we also take seriously the need for participant observation in social locations similar to the location of the early Christian communities in order to reconstruct the New Testament context more plausibly, this question is unavoidable. The question is less a matter of reading *or* reconstruction, as a superficial reading of Kittredge might indicate, but a question of which social spaces we choose to share and defend, with whom we participate and how we share in the generation of the transcript. With whom do we work and what is our social project?

The purpose of historical reconstructive activity (i.e., historical criticism) need not be divorced from the social project of interpretation, at least insofar as biblical scholarship relates to the formation of community leadership, particularly religious leadership. The reconstructive activity is related to the development of leaders who are able to engage scriptural texts in their original historical contexts in order to understand how to read those texts in the context of history "then and now," in the past historical contexts of the texts and in the present historical context. The question is our integrity in the formation of leadership who can read both the contexts critically, hear the hidden transcripts, and participate effectively in shaping the social project of communities of resistance. For this, the Paul and Politics Group may be understood as a social space for the generation of transcripts of resistance, whether hidden or public, in which our intellectual work is understood to serve a larger social project. Sometimes we may feel that "We can say whatever we want, but nobody is listening," but the first task is to sustain and expand the social space for the discussion that generates the transcript.

EXPLICATING DOMINATION AND RESISTANCE: A DIALOGUE BETWEEN JAMES C. SCOTT AND BIBLICAL SCHOLARS

Gerald West

INTRODUCTION

I first came across James C. Scott's work while staying with a South African friend, Paul Germond, in New York in 1993. I had recently completed my Ph.D. on the use of the Bible in liberation struggles, focusing on the struggle for liberation from apartheid in South Africa, during the course of which I had become increasing frustrated concerning a tension between the recurring claim of liberation theologies that the poor have an epistemological privilege and the paucity of the voices of the poor in liberation theologies. Like many activist intellectuals (Haddad) of the 1980s I had imbibed the writings of Karl Marx and Paulo Freire and saw my role as one of conscientizing the masses, albeit, in my case, cautiously and indirectly because of my ambiguous identity as a white, male South African. However, in my attempt to serve our struggle for liberation with the resources I had and within the constraints of my identity (West 2003: 15–18), I became increasingly uneasy about the apparent absence of any real presence of ordinary "readers" of the Bible, whether literate or not, in our biblical interpretation in contexts of liberation. My visit to Brazil in 1990 did little to dispel my worry, impressed though I was by the committed efforts of the Bible movement coordinated by the Centro de Estudos Bíblicos (CEBI) (West 1995: 216–19). The emergence of our own "Bible movement," initiated by the formation of the Institute for the Study of the Bible (ISB) in 1990 and modeled on CEBI, increased my disease. Somehow the theory we had inherited from the struggle was no longer adequate to account for what we were experiencing within the struggle as we tried to interpret the Bible—a profoundly important text in South Africa—for liberation.

Working with groups of organized poor, working-class, and marginalized black South Africans we were encountering a more complex context than the theory we had inherited allowed for. We were not able to put our fingers exactly on what was bothering us about this theory, yet it felt inadequate to our reality. In the heat of the struggle, with death and destruction proliferating in our region of KwaZulu-Natal as the apartheid regime with its regional accomplices entered its death throes, there was little time for reflection on our evolving Bible-reading practice. A term's sabbatical leave in 1993 provided an opportunity to reflect more fully, particularly as I was able to probe colleagues who shared similar commitments, especially Daniel Patte, Gary Phillips, Cain Hope Felder, Phyllis Trible, Vincent Wimbush, and Norman Gottwald. Their conversation provided the nourishing environment, but the meat (as we would say in South Africa) came from James C. Scott.

During my month in Paul Germond's apartment in New York I shared my frustrations, fears, and visions with him. One day he returned to the apartment with a smile on his face and a gleam in his eye and gave me a book. I hardly looked up from that book over the next day or so as I devoured Scott's *Domination and the Arts of Resistance* (Scott 1990). Here was an articulation of what was incipient and inchoate in our ISB experience. Here was another vocabulary with which to supplement what we already had. Here was an explanation of our reality.

Though this sounds rather gushy, it does capture my "aha" experience as I read, page after page. The power of Scott's analytical categories and the careful and detailed case studies that undergird them provided a vocabulary and so helped to articulate much of what we had been groping for.

THE INTELLECTUAL AND THE COMMUNITY

As I have indicated, the first substantial contribution of Scott's work was to provide a language to talk about our emerging dis-ease with the categories and analysis of traditional Marxist-oriented liberation theology. As I have argued (West 2003), at the heart of liberation hermeneutics is the relationship between the biblical scholar (or theologian) and the ordinary Christian "reader" from a poor and marginalized community.

In a seminal article from that period, Juan Luis Segundo describes two competing lines of analysis of the relationship between the intellectual and the masses. The one line of analysis emphasizes the categories and contribution of the intellectual, while the other foregrounds the categories and contribution of "the common people."

Segundo looks at the history, aims, methods, and results of these two coexisting lines of analysis in Latin America. The first line of analysis has three characteristics: the solidarity of biblical scholars and theologians with the poor and marginalized; a methodological suspicion that Christian faith at all levels of society is ideologically distorted and thus serves the status quo; and, finally, a commitment to provide "the pastoral activities of the Church with a new and de-ideologized theology capable of speaking about the common themes of Christian faith" (Segundo: 22). Because it is the social sciences that "provide the theologian who wants to carry out a de-ideologizing task with valuable cognitive tools," and because these are "tools which ... are beyond the grasp of the majority of people" (28), the role of the theologian or biblical scholar is emphasized. An option is made for the poor, but the categories and contribution of their experience is subordinated to or translated into the terms of the intellectual trained in the social sciences.

However, Segundo shows that the rise of popular movements either outside or inside the church "had shown that common people had neither understood nor welcomed anything from the first theology of liberation, and had actually reacted against its criticism of the supposed oppressive elements of popular religion." It became clear, therefore, that "if theologians were still to be the 'organic intellectuals' of the common people, that is to say useful as intellectuals charged with the understanding of popular faith, they were obliged to learn how oppressed people lived their faith." So theologians wanting to be in religious matters the organic intellectuals of poor and marginalized people "began then to understand their function as one of unifying and structuring people's understanding of their faith, as well as grounding and defending the practices coming from this faith" (Segundo: 23–24). Here the categories and concepts of the poor and marginalized are foregrounded.

The tension between these two positions can be found in every context in which there is a struggle for survival, liberation, and life, and at the center of the tension, as I have already suggested, are the different understandings of the relationship between the socially engaged biblical scholar or theologian and the ordinary poor and marginalized believer. The emphasis tends to be either on the critical contribution of the trained reader or on the reading resources of the ordinary "reader." Although Segundo, like many other liberation theologians, empathizes with much in this latter line of analysis, he is reluctant to give up the *critical* function inherent in the first line of analysis. The reason for his reluctance lies in his understanding of the dynamics of oppression and domination and in the role of the (organic) intellectual in resisting oppression and domination.

Informed by forms of Marxist analysis and aspects of our experience, many of us, including Segundo, believed that forms of critical consciousness are necessary so that the poor and marginalized can "create their own language" (Frostin 1988: 10). Forms of critical consciousness, we argued, break "the culture of silence" created by the accommodation of the poor and marginalized to the logic of domination. This was certainly my own understanding in the early days of my work with local communities of the poor and marginalized in South Africa. But as I have said, now I am not so sure that this understanding is the whole story, and this is where Scott's work was so helpful.

When it comes to understanding the alleged silence of the poor and marginalized we find thick and thin accounts of ideological hegemony. The thick version emphasizes the role of ideological state apparatuses, such as education systems, the church, and government structures, in controlling the symbolic means of production, just as factory owners monopolize the material means of production. "Their ideological work secures the active consent of subordinate groups to the social arrangements that reproduce their subordination" (Scott 1990: 73). The thin theory of hegemony makes less-grand claims for the ideological control of the ruling class. What ideological domination does accomplish, according to this version,

> is to define for subordinate groups what is realistic and what is not realistic and to drive certain aspirations and grievances into the realm of the impossible, of idle dreams. By persuading underclasses that their position, their life-chances, their tribulations are unalterable and inevitable, such a limited hegemony can produce the behavioral results of consent without necessarily changing people's values. Convinced that nothing can possibly be done to improve their situation and that it will always remain so, it is even conceivable that idle criticisms and hopeless aspirations would be eventually extinguished. (Scott 1990: 74)

But because "the logic of domination represents a combination of historical and contemporary ideological and material practices that are never completely successful, always embody contradictions, and are constantly being fought over within asymmetrical relations of power" (Giroux: xii), organic intellectuals, who are able to learn from the poor and marginalized while simultaneously helping them to foster modes of self-education and struggle against various forms of oppression, are able to point to the spaces, contradictions, and forms of resistance that raise the possibility for social struggle. However, and this is a key element of this analysis, oppressed peoples' accommodation to the logic of domination may mean that they actively resist emancipatory forms of knowledge offered by organic intellectuals (xviii–xxiii).

Such accounts of ideological hegemony argue that, "when oppressed people live in silence, they use the words of their oppressors to describe their experience of oppression." It is only within the praxis of liberation and in dialogue with organic intellectuals that it is possible for the poor and marginalized "to break this silence and create their own language" (Frostin 1988: 10). So within liberation theologies, whether they be Latin American, black, womanist, or feminist, the role of the intellectual is crucial in breaking "the culture of silence"—in enabling a language and a speaking.

Emerging at about the same time as Scott's work, the work of Jean and John Comaroff provided a more nuanced analysis of hegemony, what we might call a thin-ish version of hegemony. Their work emphasized the instability and vulnerability of hegemony (Comaroff and Comaroff: 19–32). Drawing substantially on Antonio Gramsci, the Comaroffs pose a triangular relationship between culture, ideology, and hegemony. Culture, they suggest, can be viewed as the shared repertoire of practices, symbols, and meanings in which and with which the dialetics of domination and resistance operate. Hegemony and ideology are the two dominant forms in which power is entailed in culture. Placing power at the center of their analysis of hegemony and ideology, the Comaroffs characterize hegemony and ideology as the two faces of power.

Hegemony is the nonagentive face of power that hides itself in the forms of everyday life; it is a form of power that is not always overtly felt in that "it may not be experienced as power at all, since its effects are rarely wrought by overt compulsion."

> They are internalized, in their negative guise, as constraints; in their neutral guise, as conventions; and, in their positive guise, as values. Yet the silent power of the sign, the unspoken authority of habit, may be as effective as the most violent coercion in shaping, directing, even dominating social thought and action. (Comaroff and Comaroff: 22)

"Hegemony is that order of signs and practices, relations and distinctions, images and epistemologies—drawn from a historically situated cultural field—that come to be taken-for-granted as the natural and received shape of the world and everything that inhabits it" (22). Its power lies in what it silences—what it prevents people from thinking and saying .

Ideology is the agentive face of power that refers to the (relative) capacity of human beings to command and exercise control over the production, circulation, and consumption of signs and objects in specific historical contexts. Ideology articulates and owns systems of meanings, values, and beliefs for any group with a communal identity, whether dominant or subordinate, within a historically situated cultural field. While hegemony homogenizes, ideology articulates (22).

The particularly creative and insightful contribution of the Comaroffs' analysis is their suggestion that hegemony exists in reciprocal interdependence with ideology in that "it is that part of a dominant worldview which has been naturalized" (25). According to this account, hegemony and ideology are related along a continuum,

with the hegemonic proportion of any dominant ideology being greater
or lesser depending on the context and the control of the dominant. Typically, the making of hegemony requires the exercise of control over
various modes of symbolic production, including educational and ritual
processes, patterns of socialization, political and legal procedures, canons
of style and self-representation, public policy and communication, health
and bodily discipline, and so on. Hegemony is made when control is so
sustained that it becomes deeply inscribed in the signs and practices of
everyday life, becoming, to all intents and purposes, invisible. However,
because the ideology of the dominant never occupies nonideological terrain, while it might establish itself at the expense of prior ideologies, it
seldom succeeds in totally subjecting what was there before. Hegemony
"is always threatened by the vitality that remains in the forms of life it
thwarts" (25). Consequently, along the hegemony/ideology continuum,
the hegemonic is constantly being made—and, by the same token, may
be unmade. Hegemony, then, "is always intrinsically unstable, always
vulnerable" (27).

There remains a final element in the Comaroffs' construction. What
differentiates one face of power from the other (hegemony from ideology)
is the factor of human consciousness and the modes of representation
that bear it. Rejecting "the unspecified Cartesian assumptions about per-
sonhood, cognition, and social being that persist in mainstream Western
thought, both orthodox and critical" (28), the Comaroffs suggest that it is
much more plausible to see social knowledge and experience as situated
along a chain of consciousness that is akin to the hegemony/ideology
continuum. Consciousness, therefore, is a continuum "whose two
extremes are the unseen and the seen, the submerged and the apprehended, the unrecognized and the cognized" (29). And so just as
hegemonies and ideologies shift in relation to one another, so too consciousness may shift between these poles.

> One the one hand, the submerged, the unseen, the unrecognized may
> under certain conditions be called to awareness; on the other, things
> once perceived and explicitly marked may slip below the level of dis-
> course into the unremarked recesses of the collective unconscious [that]
> is the implicit structure of shared meaning that human beings absorb as
> they learn to be members of a particular social world. (29)

Along the continuum between the conscious and the unconscious,
the Comaroffs argue, "lies the most critical domain of all" for the analysis
of domination and resistance.

> It is the realm of partial recognition, of inchoate awareness, of ambigu-
> ous perception, and, sometimes, of creative tension; that liminal space of

human experience in which people discern acts and facts but cannot or do not order them into narrative descriptions or even into articulate conceptions of the world; in which signs and events are observed, but in a hazy, translucent light; in which individuals or groups know that something is happening to them but find it difficult to put their fingers on quite what it is. It is from this realm ... that silent signifiers and unmarked practices may rise to the level of consciousness, of ideological assertion, and become the subject of overt political and social contestation—or from which they may recede into the hegemonic, to languish there unremarked for the time being. (29)

This is also the realm from which the poets and organic intellectuals draw the innovative impulses that give voice to the struggles of the people (29).

But what if this analysis is inadequate and the poor and marginalized have not accommodated themselves to the logic of domination? What if they already have a language and already speak? What if the hegemonic/ideological continuum is *always* contested? What if the hegemonic is constantly having to be be made *because* it is always being unmade? What if we take out the "but cannot" in the paragraph quoted just above? These are questions that reflection on the contextual Bible-study process in South Africa has begun to generate, and they are precisely the questions that Scott's work addresses.

Scott problematizes both thick and thin versions of ideological hegemony and so too the relationship between the socially engaged biblical scholar and ordinary "readers" of the Bible in poor and marginalized communities. In his detailed study of domination and resistance we find an even more nuanced analysis than that of the Comaroffs, in which he argues that theories of hegemony and false consciousness do not take account of what he calls "the hidden transcript." The hidden transcript is the discourse, including speech acts and a whole range of other practices,[1] that subordinate groups create in response to their ordeal of domination—a discourse "that represents a critique of power spoken behind the back of the dominant" (Scott 1990: xii). Behind the scenes, subordinate groups "create and defend a social space in which offstage dissent to the official transcript of power relations may be voiced" (xi). The practices and rituals of denigration and domination routinely generated by slavery, serfdom, the caste system, colonialism, patriarchy, and racism usually deny subordinates the ordinary response of asserting their dignity through negative reciprocity: a slap for a slap, an insult for an insult

---

1. Among these other practices are activities such as poaching, pilfering, clandestine tax evasion, intentionally shabby work, and so on (Scott 1990: 14, 118, 189–94).

(xi–xii). Instead, subordinates establish their dignity, register their resistance, and elaborate their hidden transcript in a restricted "public" or social circle that excludes—that is hidden from—certain specified others.[2] In this relatively safe space subordinates find a partial refuge from the humiliations of domination. Suffering from the same humiliations and subject to the same terms of domination, subordinates for whom survival is the primary objective "have a shared interest in jointly creating a discourse of dignity, of negation, and of justice. They have, in addition, a shared interest in concealing a social site apart from domination where such a hidden transcript can be elaborated in comparative safety" (114).

The hidden transcript represents the safe articulation and acting out of forms of resistance and defiance that is usually thwarted in contexts where the exercise of power is nearly constant. "Discretion in the face of power requires that a part of the 'self' that would reply or strike back must lie low. It is this self that finds expression in the safer realm of the hidden transcript" (114). The hidden transcript speaks what must normally be choked back and takes back the speech or behavior that seemed unavoidable and was required for survival in power-laden encounters with the dominant (18, 114–15).

The crucial point of Scott's detailed argument is that "the hidden transcript is a self-disclosure that power relations normally exclude from the official transcript" (115). The public transcript—the open interaction between subordinates and those who dominate—where it is not positively misleading, is unlikely to tell the whole story about power relations, because it is frequently in the interests of both parties to tacitly conspire in misrepresentation (2).

However, it would be a mistake, Scott argues, to see the discourse of deference and subordination merely as performances extracted by power; such discourse also serves as a barrier and a veil that the dominant find difficult or impossible to penetrate. The appearances that power requires are, to be sure, forcefully imposed, but this does not preclude "their active use as a means of resistance and evasion" (32). While evasion comes at the considerable cost of contributing to the production of a public transcript that *apparently* ratifies the social ideology of the dominant, where the script for survival is rigid and the consequences of a

---

2. In instances those excluded may include members of a subordinate community that have voluntarily embraced the dominant ideology in order to occupy positions of power (see Scott 1990: 82) or sectors of the community that dominate other sectors, such as men over women or the not-yet-disabled over the disabled. In other words, there are for any particular actor several public and hidden transcripts, depending on the context and the audience addressed (14 n. 24).

mistake severe, the appearance of conformity is a necessary tactic (32–33). Within the normal constraints of domination, subordinates have both "a vested interest in avoiding any *explicit* display of subordination" and "a practical interest in resistance." "The reconciliation of these two objectives that seem at cross-purposes is typically achieved by pursuing precisely those forms of resistance that avoid any open confrontation with the structures of authority being resisted." "The greater the power exerted over them and the closer the surveillance, the more incentive subordinates have to foster the impression of compliance, agreement, deference" (89–90). The goal of subordinate groups, as they conduct their ideological and material resistance, is precisely to escape detection, and to the extent that they achieve their goal such activities do not appear in the archives. "In this respect, subordinate groups are complicitous in contributing to a sanitized official transcript, for that is one way they cover their tracks" (87).

The dominant, for their part, also play a role in maintaining the appearance of a public transcript of deference and compliance. To call attention to detected forms of resistance and defiance might expose the fissures in their power and erode their authority and perhaps encourage other acts of insubordination. Elites, in other words, "have their own compelling reasons to preserve a public facade of unity, willing compliance, and respect" (90) and so to keep conflict out of the public record.

So "unless one can penetrate the official transcript of both subordinates and elites, a reading of the social evidence will almost always represent a confirmation of the status quo in hegemonic terms" (90). The strategic appearances that elites and subordinates alike ordinarily insert into the public transcript make it a very unreliable vehicle for social analysis. "The official transcript of power relations *is* a sphere in which power appears naturalized because that is what elites exert their influence to produce and because it ordinarily serves the immediate interests of subordinates to avoid discrediting these appearances" (87). You cannot believe all you read or hear in the public transcript! A comparison of the hidden transcript of the weak with that of the powerful, who also develop a hidden transcript representing the practices and claims of their rule that cannot be openly avowed, and of *both* hidden transcripts to the public transcript of power relations offers a substantially new way of understanding resistance to domination (xii).

But, coming back to where we began this discussion, is there still not a case for Gramsci's notion of the dominated consciousness of subordinate groups? For Gramsci hegemony works primarily at the level of thought, as distinct from the level of action (Gramsci: 333). Scott turns this around. He considers "subordinate classes less constrained at the level of thought and ideology, since they can in secluded settings speak with comparative safety, and *more* constrained at the level of political action and struggle, where the daily exercise of power sharply limits the options available to them" (Scott 1990: 91). So, Scott argues, subordinate groups have typically learned, in situations short of those rare all-or-nothing struggles, "to clothe their resistance and defiance in ritualisms of subordination that serve both to disguise their purposes and to provide them with a ready route of retreat that may soften the consequences of a possible failure" (96). This is because most protests and challenges—even quite violent ones—"are made in the realistic expectation that the central features of the form of domination will remain intact" (93). Consequently, "Most acts of power from below, even when they are protests—implicitly or explicitly—will largely observe the 'rules' even if their objective is to undermine them" (93).

Scott believes that "the historical evidence clearly shows that subordinate groups have been capable of revolutionary *thought* that repudiates existing forms of domination" (101). However, because the occasions on which subordinate groups have been able to act openly and fully on that thought are rare, the conflict will usually take "a dialogic form in which the language of the dialogue will invariably borrow heavily from the terms of the dominant ideology prevailing in the public transcript" (102). The dominant discourse becomes, then, "a plastic idiom or dialect that is capable of carrying an enormous variety of meanings, including those that are subversive of their use as intended by the dominant," for in most contexts of domination "the terrain of dominant discourse is the only plausible arena of struggle" (102–3). So by recognizing that adopting and adapting the dominant discourse is a guise induced by power relations that is necessary outside of the safety of the hidden transcript, and by learning to read the dialects and codes generated by the techniques and arts of resistance, we can discern a dialogue with power in the public transcript (101–5, 138).

So instead of focusing on the public transcript, which represents the formal relations between the powerful and weak, as most social analysis does, we should attempt to "read, interpret, and understand the often fugitive political conduct of subordinate groups" (Scott 1990: xii; see also Comaroff: 261; Cochrane). A focus on "a partly sanitized, ambiguous, and coded version of the hidden transcript" that is always present in the public discourse of subordinate groups in the form of rumors, gossip, folktales, songs, gestures, jokes, theater, and other forms of popular culture reveals forms of resistance, defiance, and critical consciousness (Scott 1990: 19). In the words of the Ethiopian proverb with which Scott opens his study, "When the great lord passes the wise peasant bows deeply and silently farts." Theories of ideological hegemony look at the stage—the public transcript of the bowing peasant. Scott draws our attention to what is hidden, offstage: the silent fart.

I have reiterated my own reading of Scott at length here for two reasons. First, any analysis of the relationship between the socially engaged biblical scholar and the ordinary poor and marginalized "reader" of the Bible is incomplete if it does not take into account a more nuanced understanding of domination and resistance. While the role of the intellectual, whether organic or other, seems fairly clear in analyses of domination and resistance that hold to strong notions of hegemony, the role of the intellectual is less clear given Scott's analysis. In this analysis subordinate groups are already engaged in forms of resistance and already have a language. The culture of silence is a strategy and not the whole story. What is hidden is hidden for good reason, so any attempt to penetrate the disguise is dangerous. And when dignity and autonomy demand an irruption or an articulation, this must be done in ways determined by the dominated. There does not appear to be a silence to break or a language to create. In my reading of Scott, we encounter a theoretical framework that forces us radically to rethink the liberation project. This is no small contribution!

My second reason for beginning my response in this way is to show how different my orientation is from the orientation of most of the essays in this volume. As yet I have said almost nothing about the essays in this volume. This is because my appropriation of Scott—my take on his contribution to biblical studies—has had to do, primarily, with how I work with local communities of the poor, the working-class, and the marginalized. What Scott's work means for the actual engagement of the socially engaged biblical scholar with such communities is not the central focus of any of the essays, though Cynthia Briggs Kittredge's essay comes closest to voicing this dimension of Scott's contribution. She rather helpfully identifies two levels at which Scott's analysis shows "promise" for (New Testament) biblical studies. The first level has to do with using Scott to understand the first century; the second has to do with how historical communities read the Bible, including the theological and political "commitments" of the New Testament scholar in her particular context.

Prompted by Kittredge's levels and her fine analysis, I turn now away from my primary appropriation of Scott's work to the form social engagement/activism takes in most of the essays in this volume.

LITERARY AND SOCIOHISTORICAL ANALYSIS

I am probably not offending any of the authors who have contributed to this volume by stating that I detect forms of social engagement or activism in their essays. This in itself is a cause of celebration. Though often implicit rather than explicit, each of the essays in this collection shows signs of a socially engaged biblical scholar. Their essays drip with implications for working with the Bible in the real world. While this would be my own focus, their contributions—in these essays—take a different form. They do the primary literary and sociohistorical analysis that socially engaged scholars such as I feed on. Put differently, in my use of Scott my scholarly energies are invested in making sense of the interface between the socially engaged biblical scholar and the poor, working-class, and marginalized "readers" of the Bible I work with. In their uses of Scott the scholarly energies of these essays are focused on the literary and sociohistorical analysis of the biblical text and the contexts that produced (and are reflected in) the biblical text.

Kittredge's essay examines the potential of Scott's work for analyzing the world behind Paul's letters, suggesting that Scott's work "appears to be ideally suited to interpret the early Christian assemblies in the Roman Empire as assemblies that resist the dominant Roman imperial order" (148). Neil Elliott also uses Scott's analysis to probe Paul's letters, concentrating on mutuality among the urban poor of Paul's world as a survival strategy. Erik M. Heen, like Elliott, uses comparative materials, together with Scott's categories, as heuristic devices to investigate Pauline social formations in general and to puzzle out the cultural-critical or resistance angles of Pauline and other New Testament texts in particular. William R. Herzog II appropriates Scott's categories of resistance to "catch a glimpse" of what the conflict reflected in Mark's Gospel between peasants and the ruling sectors "might have looked like in the context of first-century Palestine" (44). Similarly, though more generally, Richard A. Horsley finds much of Scott's work useful in delineating the political-economic conditions and the "usually unrecognized emotional-cultural dimension" (63) of the Jesus movement (and so the historical Jesus). Though expressing grave reservations about the analytical utility of Scott's distinction between the public and the hidden transcript for understanding resistance in Roman Palestine, in his rebuttal Allen Dwight Callahan provides a compelling sociohistorical account of the "recklessness" of resistance in the biblical tradition.

My task in this section of my response is not to engage with the sociohistorical location of these essays; they both speak for themselves and constitute a dialogue among themselves. However, I do want to comment on the hermeneutic orientation of these contributions. All of the essays (except perhaps Callahan's, though I will come back to this) implicitly or explicitly demonstrate the (heuristic) value of Scott's "theory" for moving from literary text to sociohistorical context. This is a hermeneutic move worth further reflection. Kittredge addresses this move directly, but the other essays do so only indirectly. What is the relationship between the literary dimensions and the sociohistorical dimensions of the text with respect to the presence/absence of domination and resistance?

All the essays take it for granted that the text bears signs of the hidden transcript of the dominated. The assumption that goes along with this recognition in all of the essays (except Callahan's) is that there is plenty of the public transcript of the dominant in the text. In fact, Horsley, Herzog, Heen, Elliott, and Kittredge take it for granted that most of what we find in the New Testament is the public transcript of the dominant. The significant contribution of Scott, they argue, is that his work facilitates their reading of the New Testament against this ideological grain. This is precisely why Callahan finds Scott's "theory" so unconvincing; he views the biblical text (both the Old and New Testaments) as predominantly the discourse of resistance to domination—there is nothing hidden about it! For Callahan the "voice" of the biblical text is the voice of "reckless resistance" to all forms of domination.

Though I think that Callahan overstates this position somewhat, it is refreshing because it does go against the stream of progressive socially engaged biblical scholarship. Those of us who work within a liberation paradigm, which grants an epistemological privilege to the discourses of the poor, the working-class, and the marginalized (Frostin 1988, 1985), refuse to accept the final form of the biblical text, the public transcript, as the last word. The text as we have it is an ideological product, usually, we suspect, of the ruling classes (Mosala 1989). The text has grain (West 2000).[3] While we accept that determining, or even talking about, the ideology of a text is problematic (Fowl), we refuse to accept the absence of the presence of the poor and marginalized in the formation of our faith tradition. We insist on reading against this grain. Difficult as it may be, given the hegemonic hold of the dominant groups in our contexts and in the text, we will not give up on the ancestors of struggle who have gone before us and who have forged our faith and sustained our present struggles. So we persist, using local knowledge and resources, together with the tools of biblical scholarship, to track and trace lines of connection between our present faith and struggles and the faith and struggles of communities similar to ours in the biblical tradition.

For those who stand in some form of continuity with the biblical traditions, it is important to believe that there are lines of connection between their particular stance and moments of the tradition. It matters

---

3. I discuss what follows in more detail in this essay and a companion piece (West 2002).

whether early Israel emerged from among the marginalized classes of Palestine; it matters whether women in early Israel were part of a non-hierarchical society; it matters whether Jesus was an organic intellectual working among the poor and marginalized; it matters whether women were an integral part of early Christianity. For the previously dispossessed it matters whether they too have a place in the founding moments of a tradition that is meaningful, powerful, and true for them, but who do not find themselves represented in its dominant discourse. Rosemary Radford Ruether says it well when she argues that to express contemporary experience in a cultural and historical vacuum is both "self-deluding and unsatisfying."

> It is self-deluding because to communicate at all to oneself and others, one makes use of patterns of thought, however transformed by new experience, that have a history. It is unsatisfactory because, however much one discards large historical periods of dominant traditions, one still seeks to encompass this "fallen history" within a larger context of authentic and truthful life. To look back to some original base of meaning and truth before corruption is to know that truth is more basic than falsehood and hence able, ultimately, to root out falsehood in a new future that is dawning in contemporary experience. To find glimmers of this truth in submerged and alternative traditions through history is to assure oneself that one is not mad or duped. Only by finding an alternative historical community and tradition more deeply rooted than those that have become corrupted can one feel sure that in criticizing the dominant tradition one is not just subjectively criticizing the dominant tradition but is, rather, touching a deeper bedrock of authentic Being upon which to ground the self. One cannot wield the lever of criticism without a place to stand. (Ruether: 18)

Thus, while Stephen Fowl is right to remind us that an interest in the origins of a text is just that—an interest—he perhaps underestimates the power of this particular interest in the struggle of various sectors of society for a place in the formative moments of their faith. What complicates this struggle for marginalized sectors of society, as Keith Whitelam's study, *The Invention of Ancient Israel: The Silencing of Palestinian History*, establishes, is not only that the dominant discourses have already co-opted moments of the biblical tradition—particularly originary moments—for their own ends but that the alleged objectivity of this "master" (*sic*) story masks the political subjectivity of the biblical narratives themselves and colludes with, for example, the literate elite of the Second Temple period to silence competing pasts (see Whitelam: 28, 232). Consequently, marginalized sectors of society have a legitimate interest in both the ideological uses to which a text is and has been put and the ideological aims of the text's author or of its production.[4] Those of us who work in solidarity and collaboration with the poor, the working-class, and the marginalzed cannot allow the dominant forces of today, whether they are reactionary and right-wing national governments/movements, military dictatorships, transnational corporations or more local forms of the forces of control (Welch), structure-legitimation (Brueggemann), and death (Hinkelammert) to plunder the Bible for their own (plundering) ends, even if much of the Bible leans in their direction.

For the experience of the poor and marginalized is that their presence cannot ever be fully absented; a trace of it always remains both in the formation of the biblical text and in its interpretation. As the Comaroffs and Scott argue, the ideology of the dominant never occupies nonideological terrain. While the dominant ideology might (by might) establish itself at the expense of other ideologies, it seldom succeeds in totally subjugating what was there before; subjects remain, never fully subjected. Hegemony "is always threatened by the vitality that remains in the forms of life it thwarts" (Comaroff and Comaroff: 25). This doubleness or "hybridity" of the final form(s) of the biblical text is not, Derek Petersen argues, only a function of native mimicry (Bhabha) or decoding (Hall). Drawing on the work of Mikhail M. Bakhtin and Hans-Georg Gadamer (Bakhtin; Gadamer), Petersen shows how hybridity is embedded within the final form(s) of colonial texts, such as the Bible, "precisely because they emerged out of a sustained dialogue with native others." Petersen suggests, therefore, following Bakhtin beyond Ferdinand de Saussure, that we take up an understanding of text as discourse pervaded by "a conflictual heteroglossia." Consequently, and his literary allusion resonates loudly with my own assessment of the matter, "'native' readings can therefore be recovered from a close reading of colonial texts" (Petersen: 36).

However, until relatively recently close literary readings of the Bible have not been the preferred mode of getting at this hidden transcript inscribed within the dominant discourse. In engaging in this dignifying and empowering task, liberation hermeneutics has generally taken up sociohistorical resources, beginning with historical-critical forms of analysis and then going on to sociological (including the socioanthropological, sociocultural, sociogeographical, socioarchaeological, etc.) tools and trajectories. The reason for this assumption, derived from adherence to "thick" notions of hegemony, is that the biblical text is perceived to be

---

4. These two senses of "the ideology of a text" are both acceptable senses in Fowl's analysis.

predominantly the discourse of the dominant. The tendency among those who have advocated sociohistorical modes of interpretation has been to view the biblical text in its final form as the product of the dominant sectors of society in any particular period. There has been general agreement that the biblical text exhibits a ruling-class and patriarchal "ideological unity" (Mosala 1989: 102; 1993: 265). Having said this, Mosala—and the authors of these essays would concur with him—recognizes that there are enough contradictions in this ideological unity to "enable eyes hermeneutically trained in the struggle for liberation today to observe the kindred struggles of the oppressed and exploited of the biblical communities in the very absence of those struggles in the text" (Mosala 1993: 269–70; 1989: 121).

In Mosala's analysis of Micah (Mosala 1989: 101–53; 1993), which draws on a similar analysis by Robert Coote of Amos (Coote), the voices of the marginalized do find some form of representation. While the text in its final form is cast in the dominant code of the priestly ruling elite, it contains traces of the social struggles that produced it, which can be detected by sociohistorical analysis in the hands of the socially committed biblical scholar (Mosala 1993: 265; 1989: 102). The ideologically astute and discerning reader can thus find (redactional) layers of representation, including some signs of the poor and marginalized. So, for example, in the book of Micah, the oppressed and exploited peasants, artisans, day laborers, and underclasses of Micah's Judah "are entirely absent in the signifying practice" of the ruling-class formulation that constitutes the final form of the text. However, "something of their project and voice has almost accidentally survived" in the respective representations of the scribal and/or prophetic sectors who have respectively negotiated and/or mediated the struggles of the poor and exploited peasants, but whose representations have in turn been co-opted and appropriated— re-represented—by the ruling classes (Mosala 1993: 291; 1989: 151).

The sociohistorical dimensions of this type of interpretation are well documented, and Mosala's sources and his own study of Micah provide examples of this type of interpretation in practice.[5] But it is his attempt to *theorize* the silences/absences of the text—"to explain the ideological necessity of those 'not-saids' which constitute the very principle of its [the text's] identity" (Eagleton 1978: 89, cited by Mosala 1993: 268; 1989: 119)—that particularly interests me in this essay. Here there appears to be something of a tension in Mosala's work (and those who share his assumptions). On the one hand, Mosala works with a strong notion of

---

5. Even if Mosala's own analysis is somewhat muddled at times.

ideological hegemony in which ideology is "a harmonization of contradictions in such a way that the class interests of one group are universalized and made acceptable to other classes" (Mosala 1993: 268; 1989: 119);[6] on the other hand, Mosala wants to foreground the struggles of the poor and marginalized and to give them some form of presence in the text. There is a tension here. If the class interests of the dominant group are universalized and "made acceptable" to other classes, then what does it mean to speak of "the struggles" of the poor and marginalized, and what type of presence do they have in texts? Is the resistance of the poor and oppressed, as Mosala asserts, "present only by its absence" (Mosala 1993: 283; 1989: 141)?

The problem with, and hence the tension within, Mosala's form of ideological analysis is that it does not allow for a sufficiently nuanced understanding of the relationship between domination and resistance. It is precisely here that Scott's work is so valuable. Scott's analysis not only recognizes that the poor and oppressed are already engaged in forms of resistance, but his analysis also accounts for the presence of their disguised discourses of resistance within the public transcript. The biblical text could, I think, be viewed as an example of infrapolitics, the zone of contestation between the hidden and public transcripts, in which is located "a politics of disguise and anonymity that takes place in public view but is designed to have a double meaning or to shield the identity of the actors" (Scott 1990: 19). No wonder, then, that its ideological grain can be read in opposing directions, depending on who is doing the reading! The text can be read both from below and from above.

Unfortunately, traditional "thick" understandings of ideological hegemony have prevented us from taking sufficient time with the text and so recognizing just how much of the resistance of subordinate groups is present in the public transcript. The tendency to emphasize just how much of the biblical text is the product of the ruling classes of any particular period is a common one among those who adopt sociohistorical forms of analysis and has a noble lineage in prophetic biblical scholarship (see Gottwald; Mosala 1989; Coote and Coote; Schüssler Fiorenza 1983). However, a consequence of too "thick" an understanding of ideological hegemony is that we have not paid enough attention to the need for, in the words of Scott, "a more nuanced and literary reading" of the public form that is the biblical text (Scott 1990: 165).

Scott reminds us of "the arts of resistance." By recognizing that adopting and adapting the dominant discourse is a guise induced by

---

6. See also Per Frostin's discussion of Mosala's use of "ideology" (Frostin 1988).

power relations, and by learning to read the dialects and codes generated by the techniques and arts of resistance, we can discern a dialogue with power in the public transcript—a task, Scott claims, requiring "a more nuanced and literary reading" of the public transcript than the social sciences have allowed for. So both Petersen and Scott call us to read ingrained texts in a close and careful, more nuanced manner.

This long discussion leads me to make three points in response to the essays in this volume. First, there are clear signs in these essays of a more careful and close reading of the text than is usual among those with an interest in sociohistorical forms of interpretation. I attribute this not only to the growing respect within the biblical studies establishment for literary modes of reading, and not only to postmodernism's destabilizing of the "vocabularies" of the natural and social sciences (West 1985: 270–71), but also to the impact of Scott's analysis on the authors of these essays. They have become, through his work, better equipped to engage in "a more nuanced and literary reading" of the biblical text.

Closely related to this first point is a second. For those of us working on the margins, in collaboration with poor and marginalized "readers" of the Bible, matters of survival, liberation, and life drive us to find resources that are useful and that work. So we are not perturbed about crossing disciplinary boundaries. We are prepared to take whatever tools are at hand to do the job. This is why most of the attempts at integrating literary and sociohistorical modes of criticism are to be found outside the mainstream of biblical studies, in the work of socially engaged biblical scholars (see, e.g., Myers; the various essays in Segovia and Tolbert 1995, 1998; Sugirtharajah). In the references cited there are plenty of models for a more integrated form of biblical scholarship. My purpose here is not to provide another model. My response is more modest: to encourage those whose interpretative interests are largely in the sphere of the social sciences to nuance, and so to enhance, their interpretative practices and products by finding a place for a more literary reading of biblical texts. I feel free to say this because there are clear signs in these essays of a more integrated reading practice.

Yet one thing remains, which brings me to my third point. If Mosala is right, and I think he is, that "eyes hermeneutically trained in the struggle for liberation today" are able "to observe the kindred struggles of the oppressed and exploited of the biblical communities in the very absence of those struggles in the text" (Mosala 1993: 269–70; 1989: 121), then we must provide a place in our scholarship for such eyes. We must begin, as Mosala does, with "eyes hermeneutically trained in the struggle for liberation today," but we must also give more weight than he does to their ability, disguised as it often is from the gaze of the dominant, "to observe the kindred struggles of the oppressed and exploited of the biblical communities in the very absence of those struggles *in the text.*" I place emphasis on this final phrase not because I want to privilege literary modes of reading above sociohistorical modes but because this is the mode of reading most accessible to ordinary poor and marginalized "readers" of the Bible. But of course none of this makes much sense if they—those with "eyes hermeneutically trained in the struggle for liberation today"—are absent from our scholarship! We need to be open to and provide ways for these hermeneutically struggle-trained eyes to come into forms of collaboration with the critical reading resources of the socially engaged biblical scholar, empowering them to locate for themselves signs of the hidden transcript in the infrapolitics of the biblical text. In the process we may discover—even those socially engaged biblical scholars whose eyes too have been trained by the struggle for survival, liberation, and life—that there are questions we have not asked and potential "realities" behind the text we have not explored. In the process of becoming biblical scholars we must, by definition, I would argue, become somewhat distanced from the realities of the poor, the working-class, and the marginalized; consequently, even those, unlike myself, who are organic intellectuals, once they become *biblical scholars,* even socially engaged ones, lose something of the sharpness of sight granted to those more deeply embedded in the struggle for survival, liberation, and life. As Renita Weems points out, the difference between "reading *on behalf of* previously unheard from communities of readers" and reading "*with* previously unheard from communities of readers ... is all the difference in the world" (Weems: 259). Speaking from her realities as an African American woman, Weems goes on to offer profound insights into what it means for those who are from among poor and marginalized classes to read with "one's own"—a commitment "fraught with ambivalence" (260). For, in reading with "one's own"

> [w]e see how much we remain indebted to members of our communities for our insights, our creativity, our subversive strategies, and for our passion for our work. More importantly, however, reading *with* them means for us who are both scholars and products of these communities to confront the ways in which we have been permanently changed by our academic training and new class privileges. Returning home and reading *with* our ancestors forces us to observe on a personal level the way education has altered our relationship to power in the society. We are forced to consider then that reading *with* poor and marginalized readers, or with any other ordinary reader for that matter, is potentially dangerous work. It is dangerous because it exposes scholars—and it exposes scholarship—to those elements of human interpretation that defy scholasticism and forces us to examine the concrete ways in which our scholarship and our privileges as scholars rely on the status quo. (260)

So our expertise must constantly be in the service of *their* sight, if the struggle for survival, liberation, and life is part of our purpose (and not just scholarship). They are better placed than us to detect the disguised forms of resistance that characterize the presence of the dignity and identity of subordinate groups in the "ritualisms of subordination" (Scott 1990: 96) they have found it necessary to perform (and this word is particularly apt) in the face of severe domination and surveillance.

As I have already said, the essays in this volume lend themselves to the kind of responses I have made, and I offer them by way of a collaborative dialogue. But I cannot end here, without briefly pointing to an important tension among the essays.

Explicating Domination and Resistance

Some years ago Elsa Tamez, a biblical scholar and social activist from Costa Rica, made the comment that Latin American biblical scholars would have to face up to the fact that there were biblical texts that resisted being read liberatively. One of the great contributions of Latin American biblical scholarship has been its resolute commitment to reading the Bible as a liberatory text (see Vaage; Hanks). While not questioning this contribution or orientation, Tamez was worried that she and her colleagues were sidestepping significant hermeneutical issues by not taking seriously those texts that seemed to have an antiliberation ideological agenda (or grain). Her comment arose from seeing my little book on *Contextual Bible Study* (West 1993), in which I try to come to grips with the text of 1 Timothy from a gendered perspective. She herself, she told me, was working on 1 Timothy for the very same reason. What do those of us who are committed to God's project of liberation for women do with texts such as 1 Tim 2:8–15, and what hermeneutical questions does this generate?

It seems to me that we have a similar tension in this volume, at the very least between the essay by Kittredge and the essay by Callahan. The other essays are not that explicit about to what extent the biblical text is a text of domination and to what extent it is a text of resistance. Callahan is clear. Callahan argues that the resistance we associate with the "little tradition" is in fact "canonical in Israel's 'great tradition'" (31), and as I read his essay I was reminded of Latin American readings of the Bible as God's project of liberation. Kittredge, however, echoes Tamez's concern and is deeply distrustful of "the surface constructions of the text" (145). Like Tamez, her experience is that gender is the litmus test of the text's ideological leanings.

In my own work on this tension (West forthcoming) I use Scott's work in dialogue with Fowl's analysis of textual ideology to probe how ideological grain might be detected in texts and why certain texts seem to have a more apparent grain than others. This collection of essays, particularly the juxtaposition of Callahan's and Kittredge's essays, both highlights and contributes to our attempts to come to grips with this important tension. Scott, it seems to me, provides rich resources for delving into what might be characterized as infrapolitical discourse, for a careful reading of the essays by Callahan and Kittredge reveals that they both recognize (though Callahan is reluctant to admit it) that there are contending voices in the biblical text.

Like Callahan I yearn to celebrate the voices of resistance and to privilege this trajectory, but like Kittredge I have seen too much damage wrought by this sacred text to leave it unproblematized. And Scott's work, in my opinion, is a significant resource with which to do both.

CONCLUSION

There is much more in each of the essays that warrants engagement, brimming as they are with useful insights and analysis, but that will have to wait for another occasion. My response here has been shaped by my context and the commitments and collaborations that my context has called forth from me. I have used this opportunity to place my use of Scott alongside that of the essays in this volume, joining in a discussion that I know will continue beyond this site.

But before I bring this response to an end, a final word on what it means to explicate resistance. For Callahan, we can only understand resistance in Roman Palestine by examining with great care those instances of open conflict. Why? Because

> The inner life of the subordinated, however violent its fantasies and however seething its outrage, by its very secrecy and subterfuge confirms the relations of domination and subordination. ... As long as flatulent subalterns bow downwind no one is the wiser, and both resentment and regime remain intact. In this way the hidden transcript tacitly reinscribes the public transcript. (39)

Who determines what constitutes resistance? From whose perspective do we decide what constitutes resistance? Who are the "we" that even asks these questions? Callahan raises an important point, and it is a fitting one with which to close. The short retort, of course, is that it is not at all clear that "no one is the wiser." The subordinated individual, his or her compatriots downwind, and perhaps even the lord passing by catch a whiff of what is to come. The individual survives—and mere survival in the face of severe domination and surveillance is resistance (Haddad); the group has the opportunity in a safe site—downwind—to discover that they share a similar ideology concerning the lord, and with this discovery the potential for an irruption into "reckless resistance" perhaps increases; and the lord himself, perhaps, walks on more worried than before encountering the bowing, perhaps (?) farting, peasant. Here is a rich discourse indeed, and it is Scott who provides tools, categories, and concepts with which to navigate this complex territory. Not that we should be complacent with what Scott has offered us; no, in trying to understand our realities we must continue to find and forge other tools, categories, and concepts that are useful.

WORKS CONSULTED

Abrahams, Israel. 1917. *Studies in Pharisaism and the Gospels.* Cambridge: Cambridge University Press.

Alcock, Susan E. 1993. *Graecia Capta: The Landscapes of Roman Greece.* Cambridge: University Press.

Apuleius. 1960. *The Golden Ass.* Translated by Jack Lindsay. Indiana University Greek and Latin Classics. Bloomington: Indiana University Press.

Aune, David E. 1992. Eschatology (Early Christian). *ABD* 2:594–609.

Babcock, Barbara A., ed. 1978. *The Reversible World: Symbolic Inversion in Art and Society.* Ithaca, N.Y.: Cornell University Press.

Bakhtin, Mikhail M. 1981. *The Dialogic Imagination: Four Essays.* Austin: University of Texas Press.

———. 1984. *Rabelais and His World.* Translated by Hélène Iswolsky. Bloomington: Indiana University Press.

Baltzer, Klaus. 1971. *The Covenant Formulary.* Philadelphia: Fortress.

Barnett, P. W. 1980–81. The Jewish Sign Prophets—A.D. 40–70: Their Intentions and Origins. *NTS* 27:679–97.

Basore, John W., trans. 1970. *Moral Essays.* Vol. 1 of *Seneca in Ten Volumes.* LCL. Cambridge: Harvard University Press.

Bateson, Gregory. 1958. *Naven: A Survey of the Problems Suggested by a Composite Picture of the Culture of a New Guinea Tribe Drawn from Three Points of View.* 2nd ed. Stanford, Calif: Stanford University Press.

Beker, J. Christiaan. 1980. *Paul the Apostle: The Triumph of God in Life and Thought.* Philadelphia: Fortress.

Belo, Fernando. 1981. *A Materialist Reading of the Gospel of Mark.* Translated by Matthew J. O'Donnell. Maryknoll, N.Y.: Orbis.

Bernstein, Michael Andre. 1992. O Totiens Servus: Horace, Juvenal, and the Classical Saturnalia. Pages 34–55 in Bernstein, *Bitter Carnival: Ressentiment and the Abject Hero.* Princeton: Princeton University Press.

Beskow, Per. 1962. *Rex Gloriae: The Kingship of Christ in the Early Church.* Stockholm: Almqvist & Wiksell.

Bhabha, Homi. 1985. "Signs Taken for Wonders": Questions of Ambivalence and Authority under a Tree outside Delhi, May 1817. *Critical Inquiry* 12:144–65.

Borg, Marcus. 1994. *Jesus in Contemporary Scholarship.* Valley Forge, Pa.: Trinity Press International.

———. 1998.*Conflict, Holiness and Politics in the Teachings of Jesus.* Harrisburg, Pa.: Trinity Press International.

Bradley, Keith R. 1983. The Slave Kingdoms and Slave Rebellions in Ancient Sicily. *Historical Reflections* 10/3: 445–46.

Brown, Peter. 1987. Late Antiquity. Pages 235–312 in *From Pagan Rome to Byzantium*. Edited by Paul Veyne and translated by Arthur Goldhammer. Vol. 1 of *A History of Private Life*. Edited by Philippe Ariès and Georges Duby. Cambridge: Harvard University Press.

Bruce, F. F. 1984. Render to Caesar. Pages 249–263 in *Jesus and the Politics of His Day*. Edited by E. Bammel and C. F. D. Moule. Cambridge: Cambridge University Press.

Brueggemann, Walter. 1992. A Shape for Old Testament Theology, I: Structure Legitimation. Pages 1–21 in Brueggemann, *Old Testament Theology: Essays on Structure, Theme, and Text*. Edited by Patrick D. Miller. Minneapolis: Fortress.

Bultmann, Rudolf. 1956. *Primitive Christianity in Its Contemporary Setting*. New York: Meridian Books.

———. 1963. *History of the Synoptic Tradition*. Translated by John Marsh. Oxford: Basil Blackwell.

Carter, Warren. 2000. *Matthew and the Margins: A Sociopolitical and Religious Reading*. Maryknoll, N.Y: Orbis.

———. 2001. *Matthew and Empire: Initial Explorations*. Harrisburg, Pa.: Trinity Press International.

———. 2003. *Pontius Pilate: Portraits of a Roman Governor*. Collegeville, Minn.: Liturgical Press.

———. Forthcoming. Going All the Way? Honoring the Emperor and Sacrificing Wives and Slaves in 1 Peter 2:13–3:6. In *A Feminist Companion to the Catholic Epistles and Hebrews*. Edited by Amy-Jill Levine, with Marianne Bleckenstaff. FCNTECW. Sheffield: Sheffield Academic Press.

Chow, John K. 1992. *Patronage and Power: A Study of Social Networks in Corinth*. JSNTSup 75. Sheffield: Sheffield Academic Press.

Clarke, Sathianathan. 1998. *Dalits and Christianity: Subaltern Religion and Liberation Theology in India*. Delhi: Oxford University Press.

Cochrane, James R. 1999. *Circles of Diginity: Community Wisdom and Theological Reflection*. Minneapolis: Fortress.

Cohen, Shaye. 1979. *Josephus in Galilee and Rome: His Vita and Development as a Historian*. Columbia Studies in the Classical Tradition 8. Leiden: Brill.

Comaroff, Jean. 1985. *Body of Power, Spirit of Resistance: The Culture and History of a South African People*. Chicago: University of Chicago Press.

Comaroff, Jean, and John L. Comaroff. 1991. *Of Revelation and Revolution: Christianity, Colonialism and Consciousness in South Africa*. Vol. 1. Chicago: University of Chicago Press.

Coote, Robert B. 1981. *Amos among the Prophets: Composition and Theology*. Philadelphia: Fortress.

Coote, Robert B., and Mary P. Coote. 1990. *Power, Politics, and the Making of the Bible: An Introduction*. Minneapolis: Fortress

Cousar, Charles B. A. 1990. *Theology of the Cross: The Death of Jesus in the Pauline Letters*. Minneapolis: Fortress.

Crossan, John Dominic. 1973. *In Parables: The Challenge of the Historical Jesus*. New York: Harper & Row.

———. 1991. *The Historical Jesus: The Life of a Mediterranean Jewish Peasant*. San Francisco: HarperSanFracisco.

————. 1998. *The Birth of Christianity*. San Francisco: HarperCollins

Danker, Frederick W. 1982. *Benefactor: Epigraphic Study of a Graeco-Roman and New Testament Semantic Field*. St. Louis: Clayton.

Deissmann, Adolf. 1927. *Light from the Ancient East: The New Testament Illustrated by Recently Discovered Texts of the Graeco-Roman World*. Translated by Lionel R. M. Strachan. 4th ed. London: Hodder & Stoughton.

Derrett, J. Duncan M. 1983. Luke's Perspective on Tribute to Caesar. Pages 38–48 in *Political Issues in Luke Acts*. Edited by Richard J. Cassidy and Philip J. Scharper. Maryknoll, N.Y.: Orbis.

De Ste. Croix, Geoffrey E. M. 1981. *The Class Struggle in the Ancient Greek World from the Archaic Age to the Arab Conquests*. Ithaca, N.Y.: Cornell University Press.

Donahue, John. 1971. Tax Collectors and Sinners: An Attempt at Identification. *CBQ* 33:39–61.

Duff, J. Wight, and Arnold M. Duff, trans. 1954. *Minor Latin Poets, with Introductions and English Translations*. LCL. Cambridge: Harvard University Press.

Duff, Paul Brooks. 1991. Metaphor, Motif, and Meaning: The Rhetorical Strategy Behind the Image "Led in Triumph" in 2 Corinthians 2:14. *CBQ* 53:79–92.

Dunn, J. D. G. 1998. *The Theology of Paul the Apostle*. Grand Rapids: Eerdmans.

Dupuy, Alex. 1997. *Haiti in the New World Order: The Limits of the Democratic Revolution*. Boulder, Colo.: Westview.

Dyson, Stephen. 1971. Native Revolts in the Roman Empire. *Historia* 20:239–74.

Eagleton, Terry. 1978. *Criticism and Ideology: A Study in Marxist Literary Theory*. London: Verso.

Eddy, Samuel K. 1961. *The King Is Dead: Studies in the Near Eastern Resistance to Hellenism 334–31 B.C.* Lincoln: University of Nebraska Press.

Elliott, Neil. 1994. *Liberating Paul: The Justice of God and the Politics of the Apostle*. Maryknoll, N.Y.: Orbis.

————. 1997. Romans 13:1–7 in the Context of Imperial Propaganda. Pages 184–204 in Horsley 1997.

————. 2000. "Paul and the Politics of Empire: Problems and Prospects." Pages 17–39 in Horsley 2000b.

————. 2002a. The Letters of Paul. Pages 122–47 in *The New Testament: Introducing the Way of Discipleship*. Edited by Wes Howard-Brook and Sharon Ringe. Maryknoll, N.Y.: Orbis.

————. 2002b. The "Patience of the Jews": Strategies of Accommodation and Resistance to Imperial Culture. Pages 32–41 in *Pauline Conversations in Context: Essays in Honor of Calvin J. Roetzel*. Edited by Janice Capel Anderson, Philip Sellew, and Claudia Setzer. JSNTSup 221. Sheffield: Sheffield Academic Press.

————. 2004. Apostolic Presence as Anti-Imperial Performance. Pages 67–88 in Horsley 2004.

Elliott, Neil, et al. (members of the Lambi Fund of Haiti). 2001. Successful Strategies among Peasant Organizations in Haiti. Position paper presented to the Annual Meeting of the Haitian Studies Association.

Elliott, Robert C. 1982. Saturnalia, Satire, and Utopia. Pages 17–32 in *Die englische Satire*. Edited by Wolfgang Weiss. Darmstadt: Wissenschaftliche Buchgesellschaft.

Farmer. W. R. 1952. The Patriarch Phinehas. *AThR* 34:26–30

Fiensy, David. 1991. *The Social History of Palestine in the Herodian Period: The Land Is Mine.* Lewiston, N.Y.: Mellen.

Finney, Paul C. 1993. The Rabbi and the Coin Portrait (Mark 12:15b, 16): Rigorism Manque. *JBL* 112:629–44.

Fitzmyer, Joseph, and Daniel Harrington. 1978. *A Manual of Palestinian Aramaic Texts (Second Century B.C.–Second Century A.D.).* BibOr 34. Rome: Biblical Institute Press.

Fowl, Stephen. 1995. Texts Don't Have Ideologies. *BibInt* 3:15–34.

Freyne, Sean. 1980. *Galilee from Alexander the Great to Hadrian.* Wilmington, Del.: Glazier.

———. 2001. The Geography of Restoration: Galilee-Jerusalem Relations in Early Jewish and Christian Experience. *NTS* 47:289–311.

Frostin, Per. 1985. The Hermeneutics of the Poor: The Epistemological "Break" in Third World Theologies. *Studia Theologica* 39:127–50.

———. 1988. *Liberation Theology in Tanzania and South Africa: A First World Interpretation.* Lund: Lund University Press.

Gadamer, Hans-Georg. 1975. *Truth and Method.* New York: Seabury.

Gager, John. 1985. *The Origins of Christian Antisemitism.* New York: Oxford University Press.

Garnsey, Peter. 1983. Grain for Rome. Pages 118–30 in *Trade in the Ancient Economy.* Edited by Peter Garnsey, Keith Hopkins, and C. R. Whittaker. London: Chatto & Windus.

———. 1988. *Famine and Food Supply in the Graeco-Roman World: Responses to Risk and Crisis.* Cambridge: Cambridge University Press.

———. 1991. Mass Diet and Nutrition in the City of Rome. Pages 67–102 in *Nourrir la plèbe: Actes du colloque tenu a Genève les 28 et 29. IX. 1989 en hommage à Denis van Berchem.* Edited by Adalberto Giovanni. Basel: Reinhardt.

Garnsey, Peter, and Richard Saller. 1987. *The Roman Empire: Society, Economics, Culture.* Berkeley and Los Angeles: University of California Press.

Geertz, Clifford. 1973. *The Interpretation of Cultures.* New York: Basic Books.

Georgi, Dieter. 1991. *Theocracy in Paul's Praxis and Theology.* Translated by David E. Green. Minneapolis: Fortress.

Gill, David W. J. 1993. In Search of the Social Élite in the Corinthian Church. *TynBul* 44:323–37.

Giroux, Henry A. 1985. Introduction. In Paulo Freire, *The Politics of Education: Culture, Power, and Liberation.* London: Macmillan.

Goldstein, Jonathan. 1976. *1 Maccabees.* AB 41. Garden City, N.Y.: Doubleday.

Goodenough, E. R. 1962. *An Introduction to Philo Judaeus.* 2nd ed. Oxford: Basil Blackwell.

Goodman, Martin. 1987. *The Ruling Class of Judaea: The Origins of the Jewish Revolt against Rome AD 66–70.* Cambridge: Cambridge University Press.

Gottwald, Norman K. 1979. *The Tribes of Yahweh: A Sociology of the Religion of Liberated Israel, 1250–1050 B.C.* Maryknoll, N.Y.: Orbis.

Gramsci, Antonio. 1971. *Selections from the Prison Notebooks.* London: Lawrence & Wishart.

Green, Joel. *The Gospel of Luke.* NICNT. Grand Rapids: Eerdmans, 1997.

Griffith, R. Marie. 1997. Submissive Wives, Wounded Daughters, and Female Soldiers: Prayer and Christian Womanhood in Women's Aglow Fellowship.
Pages 160–95 in *Lived Religion in America: Toward a History of Practice*. Edited
by David D. Hall. Princeton: Princeton University Press.

Guha, Ranajit. 1997. *A Subaltern Studies Reader 1986–1995*. Minneapolis: University
of Minnesota Press.

Haddad, Beverley G. 2000. Theologies of Survival: Intersecting Faith, Feminisms,
and Development. Ph.D. diss. University of Natal, Pietermaritzburg.

Hall, Stuart. 1980. Encoding/Decoding. Pages 128–38 in *Culture, Media, Language:
Working Papers in Cultural Studies, 1972–79*. Edited by Stuart Hall. London:
Routledge.

Halliday, Michael A. K. 1978. *Language as Social Semiotic*. Baltimore: University
Park Press.

Hanks, Tom. 2000. *The Subversive Gospel: A New Testament Commentary of Liberation*. Cleveland: Pilgrim.

Hanson, Kenneth C., and Douglas E. Oakman. 1998. *Palestine in the Time of Jesus:
Social Structures and Social Conflict*. Minneapolis: Fortress.

Hart, H. St. J. 1984.The Coin of "Render unto Caesar..." (A Note on Some
Aspects of Mark 12:13–17; Matt 22:15–22; Luke 20:20–26). Pages 241–48 in
Jesus and the Politics of His Day. Edited by Ernst Bammel and Charles F. D.
Moule. Cambridge: Cambridge University Press, .

Heen, Erik. 1997. Saturnalicius Princeps: The Enthronement of Jesus in Early
Christian Discourse. Ph.D. diss. Columbia University.

———. 2004. Phil 2:6–11 and Resistance to Local Timocratic Rule: *Isa theō* and the
Cult of the Emperor in the East. Pages 125–54 in Horsley 2004.

Hengel, Martin. 1974. *Judaism and Hellenism: Studies in Their Encounter in Palestine
during the Early Hellenistic Period*. Philadelphia: Fortress.

Herzog, William R., II. 2000. *Jesus, Justice and the Reign of God: A Ministry of Liberation*. Louisville: Westminster John Knox.

Hinkelammert, Franz J. 1986. *The Ideological Weapons of Death: A Theological Critique of Capitalism*. Maryknoll, N.Y.: Orbis.

Holmberg, Bengt. 1990. *Sociology and the New Testament: An Appraisal*. Minneapolis: Fortress.

Horsley, Richard A. 1984. Popular Messianic Movements around the Time of
Jesus. *CBQ* 46:471–95.

———. 1985. "Like One of the Prophets of Old": Two Types of Popular Prophets
at the Time of Jesus. *CBQ* 47:435–63.

———. 1986. The High Priests and Politics in Roman Palestine. *JSJ* 17:23–55.

———. 1986. Popular Prophetic Movements at the Time of Jesus, Their Principal
Features and Social Origins. *JSNT* 26:3–27.

———. 1987. *Jesus and the Spiral of Violence: Popular Jewish Resistance in Roman
Palestine*. San Francisco: Harper & Row.

———. 1989. *Sociology and the Jesus Movement*. New York: Crossroad.

———. 1991. Q and Jesus: Assumptions, Approaches, and Analyses. *Semeia*
55:175–209.

———. 1994. The Historical Jesus and Archaeology in Galilee: Questions from
Historical Jesus Research to Archaeologists. Pages 91–135 in *Society of Biblical*

Literature 1994 Seminar Papers. Edited by Eugene H. Lovering Jr. SBLSP 33.
Atlanta: Scholars Press.

———. 1995. *Galilee: History, Politics, People.* Valley Forge, Pa.: Trinity Press International

———. 1999. Jesus and Galilee: The Contingencies of a Renewal Movement. Pages 57–74 in *Galilee through the Centuries.* Edited by Eric M. Meyers. Winona Lake, Ind.: Eisenbrauns.

———. 2000a. "Rhetoric and Empire—and 1 Corinthians. Pages 72–202 in Horsley 2000b.

———. 2001. *Hearing the Whole Story: The Politics of Plot in Mark's Gospel.* Louisville: Westminster John Knox.

———. 2003a. *Jesus and Empire: The Kingdom of God and the New World Disorder.* Minneapolis: Fortress.

———. 2003b. Religion and Other Products of Empire. *JAAR* 71:13–44.

Horsley, Richard A., ed. 1997. *Paul and Empire: Religion and Power in Roman Imperial Society.* Harrisburg, Pa.: Trinity Press International.

———. 2000b. *Paul and Politics: Ekklesia, Israel, Imperium, Interpretation: Esssays in Honor of Krister Stendahl.* Harrisburg, Pa.: Trinity Press International.

———. 2004. *Paul and the Roman Imperial Order.* Harrisburg, Pa.: Trinity Press International.

Horsley, Richard A., with John S. Hanson. 1985. *Bandits, Prophets, and Messiahs: Popular Movements in the Time of Jesus.* San Francisco: Harper & Row.

Horsley, Richard A., and Jonathan A. Draper. 1999. *Whoever Hears You Hears Me: Prophets, Performance, and Tradition in Q.* Harrisburg, Pa.: Trinity Press International.

Howard-Brooks, Wes, and Anthony Gwyther. 1999. *Unveiling Empire: Reading Revelation Then and Now.* Maryknoll, N.Y.: Orbis.

James, Cyril L. R. 1963. *Black Jacobins: Toussaint L'Ouverture and the San Domingo Revolution.* New York: Vintage.

Judge, Edwin A. 1960. The Early Christians as a Scholastic Community. *JRH* 1:4–15, 125–37.

———. 1972. St. Paul and Classical Society. *JAC* 15:19–36.

———. 1980. The Social Identity of the First Christians. *JRH* 11:201–17.

Käsemann, Ernst. 1966. Ephesians and Acts. Pages 288–97 in *Studies in Luke-Acts: Essays Presented in Honor of Paul Schubert.* Edited by Leander E. Keck and J. Louis Martyn. Nashville: Abingdon.

———. 1969. On the Subject of Primitive Christian Apocalyptic. Pages 108–37 in Käsemann, *New Testament Questions of Today.* Translated by W. J. Montague. Philadelphia: Fortress.

———. 1971. The Saving Significance of the Death of Jesus in Paul. Pages 32–59 in *Perspectives on Paul.* Edited by Margaret Kohl. Philadelphia: Fortress.

Kelber, Werner. 1979. *Mark's Story of Jesus.* Philadelphia: Fortress.

———. 1983. *The Oral and Written Gospel.* Philadelphia: Fortress.

Kennard, J. Spencer. 1950. *Render to God: A Study of the Tribute Passage.* New York: Oxford University Press.

Kittredge, Cynthia Briggs. 1998. *Community and Authority: The Rhetoric of Obedience in the Pauline Tradition.* Harrisburg, Pa.: Trinity Press International.

Kloppenborg, John S. 1987. *The Formation of Q: Trajectories in Ancient Wisdom Col-
lections.* Studies in Antiquity and Christianity. Philadelphia: Fortress.
———. 2000. *Excavating Q: The History and Setting of the Sayings Gospel.* Minneapo-
lis: Fortress.
Koester, Helmut. 1997. Imperial Ideology and Paul's Eschatology in 1 Thessaloni-
ans. Pages 158–65 in Horsley 1997.
Lenski, Gerhard. 1984. *Power and Privilege: A Theory of Stratification.* 2nd ed.
Chapel Hill: University of North Carolina Press.
Lenski, Gerhard, and Jean Lenski. 1982. *Human Societies: An Introduction to
Macrosociology.* 4th ed. New York: McGraw-Hill.
Lincoln, Andrew T. 1990. *Ephesians.* WBC 42. Dallas: Word.
Lincoln, Bruce. 1985. Notes toward a Theory of Religion and Revolution. Pages
266–92 in *Religion, Rebellion, Revolution: An Interdisciplinary and Cross-Cultural
Collection of Essays.* Edited by Bruce Lincoln. Hampshire: MacMillan.
Lindemann, Andreas. 1975. *Die Aufhebung der Zeit: Geschichtverständnis und Escha-
tologie im Epheserbrief.* Gütersloh: Mohn.
Lucian. 1959. *Saturnalia.* Translated by K. Kilburn. LCL. Cambridge: Harvard Uni-
versity Press.
Luria, S. 1929. Die Ersten werden die Letzten sein: sur "sozialen Revolution" im
Altertum. *Klio* 22:405–31.
MacMullen, Ramsay. 1974. *Roman Social Relations: 50 B.C. to A.D. 284.* New
Haven: Yale University Press.
———. 1986. Personal Power in the Roman Empire. *AJP* 107:512–24.
———. 1988. *Corruption and the Decline of Rome.* New Haven: Yale University Press.
Malherbe, Abraham J. 1977. *Social Aspects of Early Christianity.* Baton Rouge:
Louisiana State University Press.
Malina, Bruce J., and Richard Rohrbaugh. 1992. *Social-Science Commentary on the
Synoptic Gospels.* Minneapolis: Fortress.
Marshall, Peter. 1987. *Enmity in Corinth: Social Conventions in Paul's Relations with
the Corinthians.* WUNT 2/23. Tübingen: Mohr Siebeck.
Martin, Dale B. 1995. *The Corinthian Body.* New Haven: Yale University Press.
Meeks, Wayne A. 1983. *The First Urban Christians.* New Haven: Yale University Press.
———. 1993. *The Origins of Christian Morality.* New Haven: Yale University Press.
Meggitt, Justin J. 1998. *Paul, Poverty, and Survival: Studies in the New Testament
World.* Edinburgh: T&T Clark.
Meier, John P. 1994. *Mentor, Message and Miracles.* Vol. 2 of *A Marginal Jew:
Rethinking the Historical Jesus.* New York: Doubleday.
Millar, Fergus. 1993. *The Roman Near East, 31 B.C.–A.D. 337.* Cambridge: Harvard
University Press.
Minnesota Advocates for Human Rights. 1995. *Another Violence against Women:
The Lack of Accountability in Haiti.* Minneapolis: Minnesota Advocates for
Human Rights.
Mosala, Itumeleng J. 1989. *Biblical Hermeneutics and Black Theology in South Africa.*
Grand Rapids: Eerdmans.
———. 1993. A Materialist Reading of Micah. Pages 264–95 in *The Bible and Liber-
ation: Political and Social Hermeneutics.* Edited by Norman K. Gottwald and
Richard A. Horsley. Markyknoll, N.Y.: Orbis.

Myers, Ched. 1988. *Binding the Strong Man: A Political Reading of Mark's Story of Jesus.* Maryknoll, N.Y.: Orbis.

Nauta, Ruurd R. 1987. Seneca's Apocolocyntosis as Saturnalian Literature. *Mnemosyne* 40:69–96.

Neusner, Jacob. 1979. *From Politics to Piety: The Emergence of Pharisaic Judaism.* New York: Ktav.

O'Brien, Peter T. 1999. *The Letter to the Ephesians.* Pillar New Testament Commentary. Grand Rapids: Eerdmanns.

Petersen, Derek. 1999. Translating the Word: Dialogism and Debate in Two Gikuyu Dictionaries. *JRH* 23:31–50.

Pomeroy, Arthur J. 1991. Status and Status-Concern in the Greco-Roman Dream-Books. *Ancient Society* 22:51–74.

Reasoner, Mark. 1999. *The Strong and the Weak: Romans 14:1–15:13 in Context.* SNTSMS 103. Cambridge: Cambridge University Press.

Redfield, Robert. *Peasant Society and Culture.* Chicago: University of Chicago Press. (orig. 1956)

Robinson, James M., Paul Hoffmann, and John S. Kloppenborg. 2000. *The Critical Edition of Q.* Minneapolis: Fortress.

Ruether, Rosemary Radford. 1983. *Sexism and God-Talk: Towards a Feminist Theology.* London: SCM.

Rudich, Vasily. 1993. *Political Dissidence under Nero: The Price of Dissimulation.* London: Routledge.

Saldarini, Anthony J. 1988. *Pharisees, Scribes and Sadducees in Palestinian Society: A Sociological Approach.* Wilmington, Del.: Glazier.

———. 2001. *Pharisees, Scribes and Sadduccees in Palestinian Society: A Sociological Approach.* Rev. ed. Grand Rapids: Eerdmans.

Sanders, E. P. 1992. *Judaism: Practice and Belief 63 B.C.E.–66 C.E..* Philadelphia: Trinity Press International.

Schäfer, Peter. 1997. *Judeophobia: Attitudes toward the Jews in the Ancient World.* Cambridge: Harvard University Press.

Schüssler Fiorenza, Elisabeth. 1983. *In Memory of Her: A Feminist Theological Reconstruction of Christian Origins.* London: SCM.

———. 1999. *Rhetoric and Ethic: The Politics of Biblical Studies.* Minneapolis: Fortress.

———. 2000. *Jesus and the Politics of Interpretation.* New York: Continuum.

Scott, James C. 1976. *The Moral Economy of the Peasant: Rebellion and Subsistence in Southeast Asia.* New Haven: Yale University Press.

———.1977. Protest and Profanation: Agrarian Revolt and the Little Tradition. *Theory and Society* 4:1–38, 211–46.

———. 1985. *Weapons of the Weak: Everyday Forms of Peasant Resistance.* New Haven: Yale University Press.

———. 1989. Prestige as the Public Discourse of Domination. *Cultural Critique* 12:145–66.

———. 1990. *Domination and the Arts of Resistance: Hidden Transcripts.* New Haven: Yale University Press.

Seeley, David. 1994. The Background of the Phillipian Hymn (2:6–11). *Journal of Higher Criticism* 1:49–72.

Segal, Alan. 1990. *Paul the Convert: The Apostolate and Apostasy of Paul the Pharisee*. New Haven: Yale University Press.

Segovia, Fernando F., and Mary Ann Tolbert, eds. 1995. *Reading from This Place*. 2 vols. Minneapolis: Fortress.

———. 1998. *Teaching the Bible: The Discourses and Politics of Biblical Pedagogy*. Maryknoll, N.Y.: Orbis.

Segundo, Juan Luis. 1985. The Shift within Latin American Theology. *JTSA* 52:17–29.

Skehan, Patrick, and Alexander Di Lella. 1987. *The Wisdom of Ben Sirh*. AB 39. New York: Doubleday.

Slingerland, H. Dixon. 1997. *Claudian Policymaking and the Early Imperial Repression of Judaism at Rome*. South Florida Studies in the History of Judaism 160. Atlanta: Scholars Press.

Smallwood, Mary E., ed. and trans. 1961. *Philonis Alexandrini: Legatio Ad Gaium*. Leiden: Brill.

Stallybass, Peter, and Allan White. 1986. *The Politics of Transgression*. London: Meuthen.

Stauffer, Ethelbert. 1955. *Christ and the Caesars*. Translated by K. and R. Gregor Smith. Philadelphia: Westminster Press.

Stegemann, Ekkehard W., and Wolfgang Stegemann. 1999. *The Jesus Movement: A Social History of Its First Century*. Minneapolis: Fortress.

Sugirtharajah, Rasiah S., ed. 1991. *Voices from the Margin: Interpreting the Bible in the Third World*. Maryknoll, N.Y.: Orbis.

Tannehill, Robert. 1975. *The Sword of His Mouth*. Philadelphia: Fortress.

Taylor, Vincent. 1966. *The Gospel according to Mark*. New York: Macmillan.

Theissen, Gerd. 1982a. Social Integration and Sacramental Activity: An Analysis of 1 Cor. 11:17–34. Pages 145–71 in Theissen 1982b.

———. 1982b.*The Social Setting of Pauline Christianity: Essays on Corinth*. Edited and translated by John H. Schütz. Philadelphia: Fortress.

———. 1982c. Social Stratification in the Corinthian Community: A Contribution to the Sociology of Early Hellenistic Christianity. Pages 69–119 in Theissen 1982b.

———. 1982d. The Strong and the Weak in Corinth: A Sociological Analysis of a Theological Quarrel. Pages 121–43 in Theissen 1982b.

Tolbert, Mary Ann. 1993. Social, Sociological, and Anthropological Models. Pages 255–71 in *A Feminist Introduction*. Vol. 1 of *Searching the Scriptures*. Edited by Elisabeth Schüssler Fiorenza. New York: Crossroad.

———. 1995. When Resistance Becomes Repression: Mark 13:9–27 and the Poetics of Location. Pages 331–46 in vol. 2 of Segovia and Tolbert 1995.

Trouillot, Michel-Rolph. 1990. *State against Nation: The Origins and Legacy of Duvalierism*. New York: Monthly Review Press.

Turner, Victor. 1969. *The Ritual Process: Structure and Anti-Structure*. Ithaca, N.Y.: Cornell University Press.

Vaage, Leif E., ed. 1997. *Subversive Scriptures: Revolutionary Readings of the Christian Bible in Latin America*. Valley Forge, Pa.: Trinity Press International.

Veyne, Paul. 1987. The Roman Empire. Pages 5–234 in *From Pagan Rome to Byzantium*. Edited by Paul Veyne. Translated by Arthur Goldhammer. Vol. 1 of *A*

History of Private Life. Edited by Philippe Ariès and Georges Duby. Cambridge: Harvard University Press.

———.1992. *Bread and Circuses: Historical Sociology and Political Pluralism.* Introduced and abridged by Oswyn Murray. Translated by Brian Pearce. London: Penguin.

Versnel, H. S. 1993. *Transition and Reversal in Myth and Ritual.* Vol. 2 of *Inconsistencies in Greek and Roman Religion.* Studies in Greek and Roman Religion 6. Leiden: Brill.

Vollenweider, Samuel. 1999. Der "Raub" der Gottgleichheit: Ein religionsgeschichtlicher Vorschlag zu Phil 2:6(–11). *NTS* 45:413–33.

Wan, Sze-kar. 1998. Collection for the Saints as Anticolonial Act: Implications of Paul's Ethnic Reconstruction. Pages 191–215 in Horsley 2000b.

Weems, Renita J. 1996. Response to "Reading with": An Exploration of the Interface between Critical and Ordinary Readings of the Bible. *Semeia* 73:257–61.

Welch, Sharon D. 1990. *A Feminist Ethic of Risk.* Minneapolis: Fortress.

West, Cornel. 1985. Afterword: The Politics of American Neo-pragmatism. Pages 259–75 in *Post-analytic Philosophy.* Edited by John Rajchman and Cornel West. New York: Columbia University Press.

West, Gerald O. 1993. *Contextual Bible Study.* Pietermaritzburg: Cluster.

———. 1995. *Biblical Hermeneutics of Liberation: Modes of Reading the Bible in the South African Context.* 2nd ed. Maryknoll, N.Y.: Orbis; Pietermaritzburg: Cluster.

———. 1999a. *The Academy of the Poor: Toward a Dialogical Reading of the Bible.* Interventions 2. Sheffield: Sheffield Academic Press.

———. 1999b. Disguising Defiance in Ritualisms of Subordination. Paper presented to the Biblical Criticism and Literary Criticism Section, Society of Biblical Literature Annual Meeting, Boston.

———. 2000. Gauging the Grain in a More Nuanced and Literary Manner: A Cautionary Tale concerning the Contribution of the Social Sciences to Biblical Interpretation. Pages 75–105 in *Rethinking Context, Rereading Texts: Contributions from the Social Sciences to Biblical Interpretation.* Edited by M. Daniel Carroll R. JSOTSup 299. Sheffield: Sheffield Academic Press.

———. 2002. Disguising Defiance in Ritualisms of Subordination: Literary and Community-Based Resources for Recovering Resistance Discourse within the Dominant Discourses of the Bible. Pages 194–217 in *Reading Communities Reading Scripture.* Edited by Gary A. Phillips and Nicole W. Duran. Lewisburg, Pa.: Trinity Press International.

———. 2003. *The Academy of the Poor: Toward a Dialogical Reading of the Bible.* Pietermaritzburg: Cluster. (orig. 1999a)

———. Forthcoming. Taming Texts of Terror: Reading (with or against) the Gender Grain of Biblical Texts. *Scriptura.*

Whitelam, Keith W. 1996. *The Invention of Ancient Israel: The Silencing of Palestinian History.* London: Routledge.

Wimbush, Vincent L., ed. 1997. *Rhetorics of Resistance: A Colloquy on Early Christianity as Rhetorical Formation. Semeia* 79.

Wink, Walter. 1992. Neither Passivity Nor Violence: Jesus' Third Way (Matt 5:38–42 par.). Pages 102–25 in *The Love of Enemy and Nonretaliation in the New*

Testament. Edited by Willard M. Swartley. Louisville: Westminster John Knox.

Wire, Antoinette Clark. 1990. *The Corinthian Women Prophets: A Reconstruction through Paul's Rhetoric.* Minneapolis: Fortress.

———. 2000. The Politics of the Assembly in Corinth. Pages 124–29 in Horsley 2000b.

Wolf, Eric R. *Anthropology.* New York: Norton, 1974.

Worsley, Peter. 1956. *The Trumpet Shall Sound.* New York: Schocken.

Wright, N. T. 1996. *Jesus and the Victory of God.* Minneapolis: Fortress.

CONTRIBUTORS

Allen Callahan, Visiting Professor of Religion at the University of Massachusetts and Harvard Divinity School, is author of the volume on the book of Philemon in the Trinity Social Commentaries series and of a forthcoming book on the Gospel of John, co-editor of and contributor to the volume of *Semeia* on *Paul and Slavery in Text and History,* and author of many articles on the Gospel of John, Paul, and the book of Revelation. He can be reached at Allen_Callahan@hotmail.com.

Warren Carter is Plierigo Professor of New Testament at Saint Paul School of Theology in Kansas City, Missouri. His recent publications include *Matthew and the Margins: A Sociopolitical and Religious Reading* (Orbis/Sheffield, 2000), *Matthew and the Empire: Initial Explorations* (Trinity Press International, 2001), and *Pontius Pilate: Portraits of a Roman Governor* (Liturgical, 2003). He has been co-chair of the Society of Biblical Literature's Matthew section and is the founding co-chair of the consultation on Jesus Traditions, Gospels, and the Roman Empire. He can be reached at wcarter@spst.edu.

Neil Elliott, Episcopal chaplain at the University Episcopal Center at the University of Minnesota, teaches New Testament studies at United Theological Seminary in New Brighton, Minnesota. He is the author of *The Rhetoric of Romans; Liberating Paul: The Justice of God and the Politics of the Apostle*; and numerous articles exploring a political reading of the apostle Paul. He can be reached at NeilElliott@msn.com.

Susan M. (Elli) Elliott, Minister for Faith and Learning at Plymouth Congregational Church in Minneapolis, Minnesota, is author of *Cutting Too Close for Comfort: Paul's Letter to the Galatians in Its Anatolian Cultic Context* (Sheffield, 2003) and scholarly articles in *Journal of Biblical Literature, Biblical Research, Listening,* and *Eerdmans Dictionary of the Bible.* She can be reached at elli@visi.com.

Erik M. Heen is Associate Professor of New Testament and Greek at the Lutheran Theological Seminary at Philadelphia. His contribution in this volume is a refinement of a chapter in "Saturnalicius Princeps: The Enthronement of Jesus in Early Christian Discourse" (Ph.D. diss., Columbia University, 1997). He has just completed co-editing (with Philip Krey) the Hebrews volume in the Ancient Christian Commentary on Scripture series (InterVarsity Press) and is currently engaged in writing a history of Lutheran biblical hermeneutics in the North American context in the twentieth century. He can be reached at Heen@ltsp.edu.

William R. Herzog II, Professor of New Testament Interpretation at Colgate Rochester Divinity School/Crozier Theological Seminary, is author of *Parables as Subversive Speech: Jesus as Pedagogue of the Oppressed; Jesus, Justice and the Reign of God: A Ministry of Liberation* and many articles on interpretation of Jesus and the Gospels. He is founding co-chair of the new Society of Biblical Literature Consultation on Jesus Traditions, Gospels, and the Roman Empire. He can be reached at bherzog@crcds.edu.

Richard A. Horsley, Professor of Religion at the University of Massachusetts Boston, is author of many books, including *Jesus and Empire; Hearing the Whole Story: The Politics of Plot in Mark's Gospel; Whoever Hears You Hears Me: Prophets, Performance, and Tradition in Q* (with Jonathan Draper); *Galilee: History, Politics, People;* and editor of *Paul and Empire* and the forthcoming *People's History of Christianity,* vol. 1. He can be reached at richard.horsley@umb.edu.

Cynthia Briggs Kittredge is Professor of New Testament at Episcopal Theological School of the Southwest and author of *Community and Authority: The Rhetoric of Obedience in the Pauline Tradition* (Trinity Press International, 1998), the article on Hebrews in *Searching the Scriptures,* and several recent articles on the politics of Pauline interpretation. She can be reached at CKittredge@etss.edu.

Gerald West is Professor of Hebrew Bible and African Biblical Hermeneutics in the School of Theology and Religion, University of KwaZulu-Natal, and Director of the Institute for the Study of the Bible and Worker Ministry Project. Among his recent publications are *The Academy of the Poor: Towards a Dialogical Reading of the Bible* (Sheffield, 1999; repr., Cluster, 2003) and editor (with Musa Dube) of *The Bible in Africa: Transactions, Trajectories and Trends* (2000), and many articles on biblical interpretation and on the interaction of ordinary readers and biblical scholars. He can be reached at West@ukzn.ac.za.

.

CPSIA information can be obtained at www.ICGtesting.com
Printed in the USA
BVOW061503080412

287105BV00001B/21/A

9 781589 831346